RÉSUMÉ POWER
Selling Yourself on Paper

Tom Washington

Mount Vernon Press
Bellevue, Washington

Cover design: Charles Fuhrman, Forest Knolls, California
Typesetting: Steve Wozenski, Novato, California
Editing/Writing: Fran Mason, Seattle, Washington

ISBN 0-931213-16-9

Library of Congress Cataloging in Publication Data:
Washington, Tom, 1949-
Resume power.
Bibliography: p.
1. Resumes (Employment) I.Title.
HF5383.W316 2003   650.14   84-20779

Acknowledgments

To my parents I owe more than words can state. Their love and support, demonstrated in so many ways at so many times, made this book possible.

Advice for improving the book came from many sources. Each person who reviewed the manuscript not only provided ideas for improving it, but also a dose of encouragement. The rough edges were knocked off and many significant improvements resulted. For their advice, encouragement, and friendship, I thank Michael Badger, Jody Burns, Diane DeWitt, Richard French, Michael Grubiak, Roxanne Legatz, Ivan Settles, and Nat Washington, Sr., my advisor and confidant. Jody Burn, Charles Clock, and Jack Porter were particularly helpful with the resume research.

While obtaining a master's degree in counseling at Northeastern Illinois University, I received a great deal of help and support, especially from two outstanding professors, Jim Fruehling and Mac Inbody.

And Mabel. Mabel Thompson made me a writer. Her love of conciseness and hatred of dead verbs had a profound impact on me.

Finally, a deep thank you to my dear wife Lois, who put up with more than anyone should have to. She read, critiqued, and offered help when I needed it. I love you.

—Tom Washington

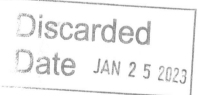

Seventh Edition

In 2000 I produced a major revision for the sixth edition of *Resume Power* with 70 pages of new material added. In 2002 I feel the most significant development in resumes has been the increased usage of web portfolios. The technology has been available for several years, but in the last two years, job seekers are more frequently recognizing a new opportunity to sell themselves. Just as artists and others have long used portfolios at interviews to demonstrate their skills, job seekers can now do this on the web in order to obtain interviews. The technology now permits not only the ability to show text documents in addition to the resume, but also photographs, art, charts, graphs, audio, and video. This new material on web portfolios appears in an existing chapter called "The Electronic Resume Explosion." Take a hard look at the possibilities.

The technology side of job hunting changes rapidly, web portfolios being a good example. Traditions relating to resumes and job hunting also change over time. My generation was used to including our height and weight as well as marital status, while our parents' generation felt compelled to indicate their religious affiliation and nation of origin. Still, the key aspects of resumes change little because human nature changes little. Employers have always wanted to know more about the applicant than just education, job titles, and years of experience—they want to know if the person is good at what he or she does. Over the past 30 years, adding results, quantified when possible, has been the major determiner of creating that impression of effectiveness. *Resume Power* has played a role in getting the word out that results count. Pages 29-50 are among the most important in *Resume Power* because that section demonstrates more clearly than any other book just how to do it.

Sixth Edition

Each of the four previous revisions have involved significant updating and additions. This sixth edition, however, has been updated, revised, and expanded from the first page to the last. This is in part due to the radical changes brought about by the growth of the World Wide Web. In the past four years its impact on job finding strategies, and resume writing in particular, has been greater than anything I've seen in the past twenty years. For that reason updates of *Resume Power* will need to be more frequent. While the principles of resume writing have not changed, I believe all job seekers should embrace the technology and allow it to help them conduct more effective job searches. At the same time, the importance of real human contact through networking is more important than ever.

In the sixth edition I was especially helped by Pres Winslow. He provided dozens of excellent suggestions for improving and updating *Resume Power*. His ideas and comments have significantly strengthened this revision.

Fran Mason and Mel Monkelis were vital in the rewrite of the Electronic Resume section. Fran and Mel both wrote key pieces. These portions enable those who are not word processing experts to produce a polished electronic resume.

Gary Kanter has been a mainstay at Career Management Resources since 1988 and has written virtually all of our resumes since 1990. He has kept us current in resume trends. Gary is an outstanding writer and a great friend.

—Tom Washington

How This Book Can Help You Get A Job

A TOP-QUALITY RESUME can net you interviews at a rate ten times greater than your competitors. This book will help you write that resume. Developing a top-quality resume is dependent not on writing ability but on knowledge and time—knowledge of how to write a resume and market yourself, and time to write, revise, and write again. A mediocre resume takes most people three to four hours to write. An outstanding resume requires six to eight hours. Those three or four extra hours could be the best investment you ever make.

A top-quality resume not only leads to more interviews, but will also produce more job offers. By taking the extra time to review your work experience and accomplishments, you'll be sharper in interviews and appear more confident. Your resume can actually guide the interview and enable you to answer questions that help make you look good. An effective job search begins with a top-quality resume.

Since 1981 I have been researching what makes effective resumes. During that time I have completed some of the first scientific research to determine what really attracts employers to applicants. To date the studies have covered secretaries, engineers, and recent college graduates. The studies have exploded such myths as the belief that resumes must be only one page in length. While more research is needed, the results of the studies already completed will enable you to write a top-quality resume. We now know, for example, that a resume with results, not just duties, will obtain more interviews. Additional findings will be described throughout the book.

RESULTS YOU CAN EXPECT

Writing a top-quality resume is not difficult, but it does take time and careful thought. This book is designed so that you can quickly absorb the information you need to write a resume that gets results. It takes you through the process step by step and answers questions as they arise. It covers key points that are not even mentioned in other resume writing books, points that can make the difference between getting or not getting an interview. If you follow my advice and take enough time to write and edit, you can obtain interviews at a rate ten times greater than competitors with typical resumes. This figure is based on an actual survey of former clients.

Happy writing!

Contents

Part Three

SAMPLE RESUMES TO USE AS GUIDES

Part Four

USING YOUR RESUME, COVER LETTER, AND MARKETING LETTER

Part Five

FINDING THE JOB THAT'S RIGHT FOR YOU

Part Six

APPENDIX

Part One
Creating A High
Impact Résumé

A Top-Quality Resume

An effective overall layout invites employers to read your resume thoroughly.

The eye is drawn quickly to your name to establish your identity.

A clear objective reveals that you are focused and creates a positive impression.

The qualifications section sells you in ways that the job description alone can't do. The section summarizes your strengths and experience and sets the tone for what the reader will discover about you.

The education section takes under a second to scan. If a job requires a degree, or a particular degree, the reader will pick that up almost instantly.

Both job descriptions are filled with results. Results sell you to an employer and reveal much more about your potential than duties alone.

The job descriptions are concise and well-written, highlighting key points. Concise job descriptions invite the employer to read thoroughly and help maintain interest.

BRIAN SANCHEZ
11918 NE 147th
Kirkland, Washington 98034
(425) 821-3731

OBJECTIVE: Management opportunities

QUALIFICATIONS

Strong management and marketing background. Experienced in controlling costs and meeting budget guidelines. Proven ability to increase sales and productivity. Recognized as an excellent trainer and motivator.

EDUCATION

BA - Business, Western Washington University (1993)

EMPLOYMENT

Arco, Seattle, Washington, 6/99-Present

Field Consultant - Work closely with ten AM/PM Minimart units to increase sales and profit margins. Hire and develop store managers. Took six corporate stores from a "poor" rating in 1998 to the top rating in 2001 and 2002. Prepare monthly and annual budgets and have full responsibility for profit and loss of each store. Have increased sales in stores over 12% per year, the second highest district average in the Northwest Region.

Eddie Bauer, Kent, Washington 9/93-6/99

Assistant Flatpack Manager - In the Eddie Bauer Distribution Center, oversaw the unpacking, pricing, and inventorying of merchandise. Directly supervised a staff of 20. Through effective training increased productivity of the unit by 18%.

The Importance Of Your Resume

THE TRUTH IS, a resume is not *just* a resume. The impact of an effective resume goes far beyond the simple act of mailing it in response to want ads. There are, in fact, at least six benefits to writing a top-quality resume:

1) You will get more interviews when responding to want ads and when sending unsolicited resumes

2) Your resume becomes your calling card and helps people remember you, while also enabling them to contact you and refer you to others

3) Knowing you look good on paper builds self-esteem and self-confidence

4) You will be better prepared for interviews

5) Because it emphasizes results, your resume will guide your interviews and enable you to focus on your most positive experiences

6) It will help your prospective boss justify the decision to hire you.

I'm going to show you how to create a resume that has real impact. You'll be making dozens of decisions as you construct your resume; the information and examples provided will enable you to make the right decisions and make them quickly. There is no single right way to do anything, but I can assure you that if you follow the advice, you will have a resume that looks good, reads well, and most importantly, has impact.

Remember, a resume is not just a resume. It represents you. Take the time to create a resume that presents the best you have to offer. A resume won't get you a job, but it can help get interviews. Or, put another way, a good resume won't get you a job, but a bad one will cost you jobs. Set your mind on spending whatever time it takes to produce a resume that truly sells you.

What Makes A Top-Quality Resume?

You never get a second chance to make a good first impression.
—Unknown

Eye Appeal

A resume must be visually appealing. Lasting impressions can be formed during the first five seconds your resume is read. That's how long it takes someone to view the layout, observe the quality of the typing and printing, and note the color and quality of the paper. Of course most of this takes place on an unconscious level. Resumes are usually scanned the first time through. If the reader detects misspellings, smudges, poor-quality printing, clumsy or verbose writing, or a confusing layout, the resume may be set aside after just ten or twenty seconds. The result—no interview.

Positive Tone

The top-quality resume presents you in the best possible light, yet does not exaggerate your qualifications. Every item is selected carefully to promote you in the eyes of the employer. Unflattering facts are not hidden, they are either left unmentioned or carefully turned into positives. The resume that concentrates on strengths helps you obtain interviews. Make positive statements about yourself; throw false modesty aside.

Impact

Write with impact. Impact is achieved with tight, concise phrases using action verbs. Impact is achieved when you accurately describe and *project* your desired image. Your full potential will come across only when you write with impact. Effective writing requires plenty of editing and rewriting—something even best-selling authors must do. The effective resume provides valuable information quickly and is easy to read. Each sentence expresses a fact, impression, or idea which will help sell you. All unnecessary words and phrases have been removed. Concise writing is appreciated by all employers and reveals much about your ability to communicate.

Results

An effective resume is filled with results and accomplishments. You've got many results, which, when described properly, will cause employers to want to meet you.

4

RESUME PRINCIPLES YOU NEED TO UNDERSTAND

The Laws of Resume Writing

There are no laws when it comes to resume writing, but there are principles that generally work. When I feel strongly about a principle or approach I'll tell you. But any rule or principle can be ignored if doing so will help sell you to employers more effectively.

One Page or Two?

At virtually every workshop I give on resume writing, someone from the audience asks, "I've heard that all resumes should be only one page, what do you think?" I usually respond by stating how that myth got started: Years ago employers realized that most resumes are poorly written, therefore they told themselves, "I'd rather read a poorly written one page resume than a poorly written two page resume." Or something like that. When a resume is well written, attractively laid out, and contains results, employers are just as happy to review a two-page resume as a one-page.

In principle a resume should be as long as necessary to sell you. I have seen executive resumes where the writer felt obligated to squeeze 25 years of experience onto one page. The person had held several key jobs yet only three or four lines were devoted to each position. After reading the resume I just didn't know much about the person, certainly not enough to know whether I would want to interview the individual.

Most of your key information should appear on page one. That means a quick scan of your first page reveals your objective, your qualifications (through a qualifications statement), your highest level of education, and a sense of your experience and accomplishments. The second page usually contains older positions as well as supplementary information that can provide valuable information when the person screening your resume reads it more thoroughly.

When I'm writing or editing a resume that goes three or four lines onto the second page I will usually look for ways to reduce it to one page. See page 88 for tips on how to do this.

By the way, most career professionals and HR managers merely suggest that most resumes be kept to one or two pages.

Occasionally a three-page resume is appropriate. This happens most frequently when a person's work consists primarily of projects. If each key project requires two to four lines, the resume may go to a third page. At that point the client and I typically discuss whether some projects could be dropped without reducing the impact of the person's broad experience. Sometimes we shorten it to two pages, and sometimes it just seems right to go with three pages. Remember, no one can put a gun to the reader's head and force them to read every word. Some employers read the first page thoroughly and then merely scan the second or third page. If you're interested, take a look at How To Create A Two-Page Resume With Three Pages on page 91.

Most of the resumes you'll see in Resume Power were originally two pages. They've been shortened so you can quickly see the key elements of these effective resumes.

How to Begin

Before your resume is completed, you will have made dozens of important decisions. This book is designed to help you make those decisions quickly and easily. Each section of a resume is explained in detail and you'll learn when and how to use each section, as well as how to write it. Examples and options are provided. You'll know what will work best for you. Examples throughout the book explain and demonstrate particular points. Read pages 2 to 80 quickly. Then return to study each section as you begin to write that portion. Highlight examples that are especially applicable to you.

How Interview Decisions Are Made

Have you ever wondered how employers decide who will get interviews after they've placed help wanted ads? A good job will typically attract 75 to 200 resumes. An employer who has a batch of resumes on her desk will usually scan each one for five to 25 seconds and place each resume in either the "I'm interested" pile or the "reject" pile. When screening resumes, people are usually looking for reasons to reject. That's why even one typo can be a killer. A resume which contains obvious typos, spelling errors, grammatical errors, or verbose writing, will most likely end up in the reject pile. Those who obviously lack the necessary background for the position will also end up in the reject pile.

Out of 80 resumes, perhaps only 20 will be placed in the "I'm interested" pile. Those 20 will be read, with one to five minutes devoted to each. Out of the initial 80 resumes, ten will generally make it through this screening process. Of the ten or so applicants who are called, perhaps six will be invited for interviews.

There is one type of resume that gets through this process nearly every time—the one that sells potential. That's the resume you need to write. I will show you techniques you can use to create a resume with this kind of impact. I'll take you through each section of a resume and show you how to pull all of the pieces together.

Stating Your Objective

AN OBJECTIVE DEMONSTRATES you are focused. For that reason most resumes should have an objective. Objectives do little good, however, if they are too general. Using an objective that states: "Position utilizing my people skills." is simply too general. It really doesn't say anything, and just won't give the employer a clue as to what you're looking for.

The following objective is a bit general, in that it lists the desire for a job utilizing certain skills, but for some people it might provide just the right information. Objective: Seek a position utilizing my administrative, customer service, and project management skills.

While most resumes should have an objective, avoid the common mistake of trying to cram too much into the objective with statements such as, "Seeking responsible accounting management position with a large progressive firm offering opportunity for growth and promotion, where skills in human relations and effective written communications will prove beneficial." These types of objectives are trying to combine an objective with a qualifications summary, but the combination simply does not work. The objective sounds trite. It's better to use a simple objective and then get creative in producing an effective qualifications summary.

Before starting your resume, write out your objective. Later you can change or delete it, but having an objective will keep you focused while you write. Objectives such as Bookkeeper, Chemist, or Construction Superintendent can be very effective.

Stating an objective on your resume demonstrates focus. People naturally respect you if you know what you want. A resume that says, "I'll do anything, just give me a job," will get you nowhere. If your objective states Sales Representative but you have never been one, everything that follows must demonstrate your *potential* for that position.

Simple objectives usually work best:

Computer Programmer
Senior Accountant
Flight Attendant
Secondary Teacher — Drama, English, ESL
Sales Manager

In the above cases, the people knew exactly what they were looking for and so they used an exact job title. If this is your case, and the title is recognized by all people in your field, use a specific job title. However, if you are considering one of several positions which are all closely related, you might try something like this:

OBJECTIVE: Office Manager/Administrative Assistant/Executive Secretary

In this example, all three types of positions—Office Manager, Administrative Assistant, and Executive Secretary—are similar. A person who is qualified for one is often qualified for all three. In fact, what one company calls Administrative Assistant, another might call Executive Secretary. This person just wants a good job with a good company, and would enjoy any of the three types of jobs. If only Office Manager is listed as the applicant's objective, however, an employer with an executive secretary opening might overlook the resume.

You should never pair unrelated job titles such as Secretary/Sales Representative, Teacher/Real Estate Agent, Flight Attendant/Bookkeeper. It's okay to be looking for both positions at the same time, but you would need two resumes with two different objectives to do so.

Instead of a specific objective, some professionals will do nicely with an abbreviation or acronym after their name which quickly indicates the type of position they are seeking. For example:

Catherine Toopsly, CPA

Jerald Riggins, CMA

Dehlia Bohannon   MPH

Jihan Refelda   PE

Those receiving these people's resumes will quickly recognize that Catherine is a certified public accountant, Jerald is a certified management accountant, Dehlia holds a masters degree in public health, and Jihan has been certified a professional engineer. While a more specific objective might work better, simply using professional designations such as these can work quite well.

In the above examples Catherine and Jerald separated their names from their professional designation with a comma. Dehlia and Jihan simply put extra spaces after their names.

Another technique works quite well:

Tom Wells
International Marketing Professional

2398 Saxon Drive
Birmingham, Alabama 35209
205/876-9867

In this case it is immediately clear what type of position the person is seeking. Here, as in any objective, you must decide whether it works best to specify a job title, or as in this case, simply indicate the career field that is desired. The job titles Tom Wells has held will then indicate the level he is seeking.

Entry-level

Some people must decide if they will use a phrase like, "Seeking entry-level chemistry position." This is almost always appropriate for a recent college graduate. It is one way to demonstrate that you are realistic about the types of positions that recent grads are considered qualified for. Don't, however, use this phrase if you believe that you might qualify for a position that is considered a step or two above entry-level.

If you are making a career shift and you have virtually no experience in the field you are now pursuing, it can make sense to state you are seeking an entry-level position. It is your way of saying, "I recognize that I'm making a career shift and that I cannot command the same salary I had in my previous profession. I want you to know that I'm flexible and willing to pay my dues, even if that means starting off with an entry-level position."

When Not To Use A Job Title

Sometimes an exact job title is *not* advised. This is particularly true in management. If you are currently a personnel manager considering positions such as Training and Development Specialist, Director of Training and Development, and Vice President of Human Resources, you might want to create an objective which incorporates all of these titles, such as "OBJECTIVE: Human Resource Management." Using the term *management* does not limit you to a specific job title, while Human Resource is specific enough that it is clear you have focus.

When To Use An Objective

Use an objective if your goal can be easily stated with a job title or a descriptive phrase. Occasionally you will find it better to omit an objective and let your cover letter and the tone of your qualifications section indicate your goal. I use an objective for approximately 85% of the resumes I help people write.

Multiple Versions Are Often Appropriate

I frequently recommend multiple versions of a resume when a person is pursuing several distinct job titles. In such cases, often the only changes needed occur in the objective and in the qualifications section. For example, if you were interested in both sales *and* marketing, you would have two versions of your resume, one with a Sales objective and the other with a Marketing objective. One resume would be directed to sales managers and the other to marketing managers.

The Qualifications Statement— Capturing Your Essence

THE QUALIFICATIONS SECTION is a summary of your background and strengths. It includes positive statements about you that would be difficult to express in any other section of a resume. Because it is designed to sell your most marketable abilities and experiences, the statements must catch and hold the reader's attention or the section will be skipped. Covering too many points will also result in the section being overlooked.

The qualifications statement can do more than any other section to create a favorable impression of you and will set the tone for the rest of the resume. It can greatly strengthen your perceived worth because employers reading your resume will constantly be asking what you can do for them. Give them positive answers in those first few seconds by creating a qualifications section which truly sells you. This section should capture the *essence* of what you want to sell. Any point which is not crucial should either be eliminated or considered for inclusion in your cover letter.

Studying the following examples will help you understand the function of the qualifications section. A job has been included with each qualifications example to help you see how they fit together.

Example 1

OBJECTIVE: Marine Sales

QUALIFICATIONS

Outstanding sales record. Highly knowledgeable in all facets of sailboats, powerboats, commercial fishing vessels, and marine hardware. Strong ability to introduce new product lines to distributors, dealers, and boat builders. Top-selling rep in the country for four major marine manufacturers.

EMPLOYMENT

Bellkirk Marine, San Diego, California 6/93 to Present

MANUFACTURERS' REPRESENTATIVE - Represent 27 lines covering California, Nevada, and Arizona. Increased the number of accounts with distributors, dealers, and boat builders from 35 to 96 and have increased sales 85%. Since 1995 have been the top-selling rep for four major manufacturers.

Qualifications example #1 includes a summary and an accomplishment. It starts off with a simple but strong statement: "Outstanding sales record." It then goes on to describe the areas of expertise. The top accomplishment (being the top-selling representative in the country for four manufacturers) has been included twice—in qualifications and the job description. It is a valuable statement worth repeating.

Example 2

OBJECTIVE: Grocery Management

QUALIFICATIONS

Strong management background. With a 21-store district, increased profits 32% and oversaw the construction of four new stores. During 17 years in management, coordinated the grand openings of 13 stores and produced some of the most profitable new stores with three different chains.

EMPLOYMENT

Fine Food Centers, Tulsa, Oklahoma 5/88 to Present

DISTRICT MANAGER 9/95 to Present. Responsible for profit and loss analysis, wage and salary administration, merchandising, store layout, advertising, and buying for 21 stores in the district. Supervised the remodeling of five stores and the construction of four stores. Developed in-house cleaning and repair services, saving $150,000 annually. Through improved merchandising and customer service, increased sales per store 28% and profits 32%.

Qualifications example #2 begins with a bold statement, "Strong management background," and then proceeds to back it up with proof. Immediately you realize this person has been very successful and you want to know more about her. One fact comes right out of her current position (the 32% increase in profits). The second statement (concerning the success of 13 store openings) is a summary that comes from her entire management background. If this summary had not been stated so clearly in a qualifications section it might have been easily overlooked, even during a careful reading of the entire resume. Because the coordination of a grand opening is an extremely valuable skill, it deserves prominence in Qualifications.

Writing Your Qualifications Section

Write your qualifications section last. It is the most difficult section to write and requires the most care. Once you have the employment section completed you will know better what needs to be included in your qualifications.

As you prepare for writing the qualifications section, review the resume and determine what points should be covered in it. Use qualifications to introduce yourself to the reader and to give an overview of why you are qualified for your stated objective. To do this ask yourself, "Why would I be good at this occupation?" Or if you already have experience ask yourself, "What makes me successful in this field?" Remember, in qualifications it is permissible to repeat or paraphrase points made elsewhere in the resume.

If you have strong work experience, you will probably want a short qualifications section. If you are seeking to break into a new field, qualifications is usually the best vehicle for bringing in related experiences and selling an employer on your potential.

While relatively short, the qualifications section is typically the hardest to write. Because it can strengthen the overall effectiveness of the resume, it deserves a great deal of attention and effort. An hour spent writing and editing your qualifications section is not too much.

11

Short, Hardhitting Qualifications Statements

I like short, hard-hitting qualifications sections. I try to capture the *essence* of what will impact employers. As a result, most qualifications sections I write are one paragraph with three to five lines. If there are two distinct areas which need to be sold then I may have two paragraphs with three to four lines each. People making career changes, or those seeking positions without having the traditional background, may need three or four paragraphs to bring out all of their related experience. Even so, the emphasis should still be on conciseness and impact. See pages 158, 173, and 185 for examples of single paragraph qualifications statements, and pages 163, 180, and 186 for examples of three or more paragraphs.

Essence is not easy to achieve, but the impact of your resume will be significantly strengthened when you succeed. Identify those qualities and areas of experience that an employer absolutely needs to know about you—those critical points. While there may be many points you want an employer to know about you, usually only two or three are critical. Sell those effectively and the employer will feel he or she must meet you.

Write A Qualifications Sketch

To write an effective qualifications section, begin by writing a qualifications sketch. List the key strengths and assets that you want to convey to employers. After writing your qualifications sketch, determine which are critical and which are not. Simply scratch out those which are not critical and use the critical ones to compose your qualifications section.

The qualifications sketch of a quality control manager might look like this:

1) Ten years in quality control. Familiar with all techniques that have been developed for the electronics industry.

2) Saved money and reduced rejects for three different companies.

3) I work well with other department heads, particularly production, and coordinate and cooperate well with them rather than work against them.

4) I've developed creative programs that really work.

5) I like my work and enjoy a challenge.

6) I'm always looking for a better method, technique, or system; I'm open to new ideas from others.

7) I'm an excellent supervisor. I train my staff well, I listen to them, I maintain high morale, and productivity is always high.

8) I'm hardworking, loyal, reliable, creative, and efficient.

The final version of the quality control manager's qualifications section might read like this:

QUALIFICATIONS

Strong experience in quality control gained during ten years in supervision and management. For three electronics manufacturers implemented new quality control programs which decreased rejects at each plant by at least 23%.

Develop excellent relations with all department heads and work well with production personnel.

Excellent supervisor. Consistently increase productivity of quality assurance personnel, and through effective staff training, increase their technical capabilities.

If you review the eight points the person originally wanted to cover, you'll notice that everything is included here either directly or by implication (points 5 and 8 were covered implicitly). By reading the qualifications section in the context of the entire resume, you would certainly pick up that he enjoys a challenge and that he is hardworking, loyal, reliable, creative, and efficient.

Tips For Writing Your Qualifications Sketch

To help you identify the points you want to make in your qualifications statement, ask yourself these questions.

1) What is the essence of what I want an employer to know about me?

2) If I could convince an employer of just one strength, what would it be?

3) What would a second strength be?

4) What are the two or three strengths that my bosses have most valued?

5) After reviewing several want ads in my field, what are the two or three strengths (that I have) that they are consistently looking for?

Once you answer these questions you will have a good idea of what you want your qualifications statement to accomplish. You're now ready to create your qualifications sketch.

In writing qualifications sections there is a tendency to use the words *strong* and *excellent,* such as "Strong experience in quality control . . ." and "Excellent supervisor." Both are excellent words, but try not to overuse them. I've searched the thesaurus and haven't found many good substitutes. I rarely use the word *good* because it just isn't strong enough. I occasionally use the word *outstanding,* but it can seem too strong, so use it selectively.

Strong, Excellent, Broad

Other phrases can also be used to make a point. If you use "Excellent experience" in one paragraph, you could use "Broad experience," "Broad background," or "Excellent background," in the next. Don't be bothered if you use the word *excellent* three times, but use substitutes to avoid using it excessively. Excellent is often the best word because it is not as humble as *good,* nor is it too strong, as *outstanding* sometimes seems.

I often start a qualifications paragraph with a short statement, such as "Excellent management experience," then back it up with further details. In this case the follow-up might be "Consistently obtain high productivity from employees," or "Consistently implement new techniques and procedures which increase productivity and lower costs." Another effective back-up statement would be: "Proven ability to turn around projects which are behind schedule and over budget." Whatever general statement you make should be explained or reinforced with details. Look at the resumes on pages 160,179, and 185 and notice how percentages or other statistics have been included in qualifications. This can be very effective but is not always necessary or possible, particularly if you are making a broad statement about your entire career.

Notice how effective the various back-up statements can be when they are paired with the beginning short statement.

> Excellent management experience. Consistently obtain high productivity from employees.

> Excellent management experience. Consistently implement new techniques and procedures which increase productivity and lower costs.

> Excellent management experience. Proven ability to turn around projects which are behind schedule and over budget.

> Strong background in trucking gained during 20 years of management experience. Recognized for ability to significantly increase market share and quickly increase profitability. At each terminal achieved one of the best on-time records in the industry.

Opening with a short statement provides impact. It hits the reader and makes the person want some evidence, which you will provide in your very next sentence. Of course, you need to be able to verify anything you say, such as "Consistently obtain high productivity from employees," either in other sections of your resume or in a personal interview.

Short, To-The-Point Qualifications Statements

For most people I find that shorter, one-paragraph qualifications statements work best. It often takes longer to write a shorter statement because it requires more time to identify the essence of what you want to sell to readers. It also usually takes more time to edit your statement until it says exactly what you want to get across.

> **OBJECTIVE:** Lending/business development position

> **QUALIFICATIONS**
> Broad banking background with strong managerial and technical expertise. Always a top producer, with the ability to establish strong, long-term customer relationships.

> **OBJECTIVE:** Marketing or Product Management

> **QUALIFICATIONS**
> Strong background in sales and marketing management. Consistently able to increase revenue, market share, and profit margin. Develop excellent, long-term relationships with key accounts, leading to better long-range planning and revenue streams.

Longer Qualifications Statements With More Points

Sometimes it takes several paragraphs to do justice to your background. The following person could have identified two or three key strengths to emphasize in one or two short paragraphs, but it seemed right to provide more information. This is another example of how important it is to determine what will best sell *you*.

QUALIFICATIONS

- Strong leadership qualities with an excellent sales and marketing track record. Consistent award winner for sales and operational excellence. Six-time President's Award winner.

- Broad experience in operations with full P&L responsibility, including margin management, sales development, forecasting, budgeting, process improvement, and quality control.

- Consistently develop market strategies that increase market share and return on investment far above the industry norm. Most recent strategic plan resulted in a 46% revenue increase over the past two years with a 285% increase in ROI.

- Able to benchmark and drive improvement on best practices throughout large geographic areas.

- Recognized for ability to establish long-term customer relationships and increase service to unprecedented levels. Won HomeGrocer.com's first Vendor Certification Award.

Qualifications Statements Without Supporting Evidence

It is always helpful to provide supporting evidence or further information to back up any claims you make in a resume. It's helpful, but not necessary. When you make statements about yourself it is because you are convinced they are true. With that in mind you must be prepared to sell that quality in an interview. In fact, any statement in your resume can result in an interview question about it, so you must be prepared to discuss it.

Let's look at two qualifications statements from two different people. Each is effective and each contains only true statements about the person.

Strong sales personality. Effectively market programs and sell ideas to key people. High-energy person with the initiative to make things happen. Excellent at assessing needs and following up to solve problems.

Sandra has held administrative positions but wants to move into sales. She has no outside sales experience but she has sales friends who think she would be great. She has the desire, personality, and drive to make it in sales. Because none of her jobs involved sales, she is using the opportunity in the qualifications statement to show her potential. A sales manager who needs someone with five years of sales experience will not give her a second look. Fortunately some sales managers actually prefer to train their sales reps. They are willing to take a raw product with lots of energy and drive and turn that person into a professional salesperson. That's the sales manager who will be attracted by Sandra.

Notice that Sandra provides no supporting evidence for any of her statements. She says she can market programs and sell ideas. She claims she takes initiative. While there could certainly be a question mark in the reader's mind, it is clear by the tone that Sandra absolutely believes that these statements are true and accurate. As long as Sandra's job descriptions show a pattern of success, with some evidence that she has taken initiative before, these statements will be believed until Sandra demonstrates in an interview that they are not accurate. That will not happen. Sandra is for real.

In the next statement, Darryl provides a short description of his real estate and land development background.

> Broad background in all phases of real estate development/investment including acquisitions, design, approvals, construction, finance, marketing, and property management. Consistently able to bring projects in ahead of schedule and under budget.

Darryl has a ton of experience and wants the reader to move right into the heart of his last two positions, but first he wants to create an impression. His goal with this statement is to quickly show the breadth of his experience. He also wants the reader to know that he has a history of completing projects ahead of schedule and under budget—absolutely critical abilities for a project manager in real estate.

Backing Up Statements With Numbers

Using numbers and statistics to provide supporting evidence of your claims can be very effective. Since you will already have written your job descriptions, ask yourself whether any of those numbers could be used. Often it is valuable to put together numbers that the employer would not have picked up on without your assistance. For example, the district manager for the grocery chain mentioned that she had managed the grand openings of 13 stores throughout her career. Here are some additional qualifications statements that have effectively used numbers to provide proof.

> (a human resources manager)

> Broad management background with strong human resources experience gained through the complete development of an HR department. Introduced systems which have increased productivity, significantly reduced turnover, and have saved over $120,000 per year in medical insurance, unemployment compensation, and training costs.

The entire statement is well written and convinces the reader that he is a very capable human resources manager. Every business would like an HR manager who can play a major role in increasing productivity, reducing turnover, and saving over $120,000 in costs. During his interviews nearly every employer asked how he had saved so much money for a relatively small, 90-employee company.

Another two examples will reinforce the value of numbers in qualifications statements. The first is a small business owner who wants to move into management with a much larger company. The second is a pharmacy manager who has a knack for attracting and keeping customers, thus increasing sales each year.

Strong management and sales experience. Build excellent relationships with customers and provide outstanding customer service. Built Kraft Windows into one of the top dealers in the Southwest by increasing sales 24% annually.

Broad pharmacy background. Recognized for strong technical knowledge and ability to effectively monitor and prevent potential adverse drug interactions. Introduced numerous cost saving measures which have increased quality and productivity standards. Have increased sales volume at each store at least 20% per year.

In both cases the numbers help convince the reader that each is a highly capable person who deserves an interview.

To write effective qualifications statements, study several examples. Analyze them to determine what makes them effective. When you're through writing a qualifications statement, compare what you have to some of the examples. If you're not pleased, set the resume aside for a day. You'll return to it later with a fresh perspective. Let others see it and get feedback from them. Don't use the qualifications section as filler. Include only those points which you really think will sell you.

A Last Resort Option

Sometimes a person just can't come up with a good qualifications section. If you fall into that category, do what you can to improve the qualifications section, but finish the resume so you can get it out to the right people. In such a case I would recommend that you wrap it up with a short summary of 15–25 words without trying to make any hard-hitting statements. Here's an example.

OBJECTIVE: Programmer/Analyst

QUALIFICATIONS

Excellent background in data processing gained during eight years in programming and systems analysis.

Even though this qualifications section lacks punch, it serves a purpose. As soon as an employer sees an objective, he immediately asks himself what makes this person qualified. By seeing the word *Qualifications* followed by a statement, the employer instantly assumes the person *is* qualified and goes on to seek evidence in the education and experience sections.

You can use this way out if you have difficulty with your qualifications, but use this approach only after you've spent at least two hours working solely on qualifications. Once you've used your resume for a while, try working on qualifications again. You'll probably have some new thoughts, and it may come together after all.

Take The Time To Make It Right

Your qualifications statement is typically the hardest part of the resume to write. Blaise Pascal, the philosopher, is purported to have sent a long letter to a friend in which he apologized for its great length. He stated, "I apologize for the length of this letter. I didn't have time to make it shorter." Something short and powerful always takes time. When you read a great ad with perhaps only ten words, the copywriter may have spent more than twenty hours to make it say exactly what she wanted. I'm not suggesting it will take that much time, but it can take over an hour. I can create a powerful five-line statement in ten to twenty minutes, but I've written hundreds of such statements. As I get to know the person I'm writing for I'm constantly asking myself, "What is the essence of what this person has to sell?" By the time I'm ready to write the statement it often just flows out. Don't expect that to occur for you, but it can happen.

Because this section is difficult for most people, I've given you numerous ideas on how to make it happen. The qualifications sketch is particularly important. Once you can sketch out the points you want to make, the statement is half written.

Be patient with yourself. Remind yourself that you are creating a portion that can easily determine whether you get an interview or not. While a qualifications statement is never required, and in fact most resumes do not use such a section, its subconscious influence on readers can be tremendous. Put whatever time into it that is required until it says just what you want it to say.

Education

EDUCATION SHOULD USUALLY APPEAR on the first page right below qualifications. If you have a college degree or a certificate in a technical field, it should be obvious why you would want education to appear early in the resume. You can design the section so that just a glance will tell the reader what degree(s) or certificate(s) you hold. Perhaps you don't have a college degree or a certificate but have very strong experience in your field. In that case, you would still place education right after qualifications because you'll want the reader to see quickly that while you don't have a great deal of education, you have a wealth of qualifying experience.

There are a number of reasons for placing education on the first page of your resume. For one thing, employers are curious about education. If education does not appear on the first page they will often flip immediately to the second page. Also, not putting your education on the first page can give the impression that you are hiding or burying your education. For these reasons, I rarely place education at the end of the resume, although it can be placed at the end of a one-page resume.

I like to see education right after qualifications. Most readers will merely glance at education and notice only that a person has a degree. The more curious will note the school, major, and year of graduation. Since employers are curious about education, and since the section takes only 3–6 seconds to read, I believe it belongs at the top.

Occasionally education is left off entirely. This most often happens when a person with 20 or more years of experience in his or her field lacks a college degree and simply decides to leave the education section off. One option is to include an education section which lists professional seminars as well as any college courses taken.

A top-quality resume must be easy to read. The first example below is easy to read and you obtain the key information almost instantly. The next two education sections are difficult to read. Notice the difference.

Easy to read:

EDUCATION

   B.A. - Business Administration, University of Washington (1978)

The above example represents the best way of describing a college degree. "B.A."—instantly a reader can see that you hold a degree. The next most important fact is your major, then your school, followed by the year of graduation.

The following bad examples show you what *not* to do:

Hard to read:

EDUCATION   <u>Butler University</u>, Indianapolis, Indiana.

Received a B.A. in Business Administration in December, 1995. Curriculum emphasized Marketing and Financial Management, with field of specialization Real Estate. Grade point average 3.21.

Harder to read:

<u>EDUCATION</u>

Central Michigan
<u>University</u>

Mount Pleasant, Michigan

September 1975   <u>Bachelor of Arts</u>, Majored in Sociology with
     to   a minor in Psychology
June 1980

Both are hard to read. The reader has to look carefully just to learn whether the person has a degree.

HOW TO BEST DISPLAY YOUR EDUCATION

The following section reveals the best way to show your education, depending on just what your educational background is. Highlight or place a mark by the one that matches your situation.

High School Graduate, No College

EDUCATION

Graduated - Roosevelt High School, Chicago, Illinois (1999)

Some College, No Degree

If you have attended college, there is rarely a reason to include your high school.

EDUCATION

University of Nevada, Las Vegas, Business, 136 credits (1974-1977)

In the example above, credits were included to show that although a degree program has not been completed, the person was at least a serious student, accumulating 136 of 180 quarter credits necessary to graduate. A major is given to show the emphasis of study. When determining what major to include, try to make sure it is related to the type of work you're seeking. If you have 20 or more credits in each of three fields, pick the one which will best sell you.

Certificate From A Technical School

EDUCATION

   Certificate - Welding Technology, Davis Technical School (1998)

or

EDUCATION

   Certificate - Computer Programming, Sims Business College (1998)
   Graduated - Norcross High School, Norcross, Pennsylvania (1994)

No Degree, Attended Several Colleges

Some people have acquired credits at four or more schools. If this is your situation, you need not list all schools on your resume; it may give the impression of instability.

EDUCATION

   Cheboit Junior College, Castlerock Community College, Riverside Community College, 98 credits.

The person in the above example actually attended three other colleges, which are not mentioned because only a few credits were obtained. The credits are included in the total, however. Attendance was very sporadic over a ten-year period, so no dates are given. There is rarely a need to mention the cities and states where the colleges were located.

No Degree, Two Colleges Attended

EDUCATION

   Northeastern Illinois University, Business, 70 credits (1981-1983)
   University of Illinois, Circle Campus, Business, 30 credits (1978)

No Degree, No or Few College Courses Taken

EDUCATION

   Total Quality Management, Dreyfuss & Assoc., 24 hours (2002)
   Implementing Just in Time, Bob Huston & Assoc., 40 hours (2001)
   The Problem Employee, Dreyfuss & Assoc., 8 hours (2000)
   Principles of Management, University of Texas, 5 credits (1998)
   Motivating Employees, Dreyfuss & Assoc., 16 hours (1998)
   Introduction to Marketing, University of Texas, 5 credits (1997)

This person has been taking seminars for years but has little formal education. He has taken college courses for personal benefit, but not with a degree in mind. By combining seminars with a few college courses, this type of education section works well and demonstrates that he is a growth-oriented person.

Degree, One Or More Colleges Attended

Unless you have a special reason for including all of your schools, list only the college you graduated from. If you got an Associate of Arts (A.A.) and then moved to a four-year college, still mention only the four-year college. Everything else is superfluous. Since you did not attend four years at the college mentioned, state only the year of graduation.

EDUCATION

 B.S. - Physics, Rhode Island University (1976)

Will Soon Graduate

If you will graduate in just a few months you might show education like this:

 B.A. - Political Science, University of Arizona (June 2003)

In the above example the assumption is that the resume has been written in the fall of 2002, and you are scheduled to graduate in June, 2003.

If you expect to graduate in the coming year, but don't know which quarter, you might express it this way:

 B.A. - Chemistry, University of Toronto (Expected 2003)

Another possibility would be:

Economics, University of Maryland, B.A. to be completed by June 2003

Bachelor's Degree Plus Graduate Studies, But No Graduate Degree

EDUCATION

 Graduate Studies, Public Administration, University of Georgia (1996-1998)
 B.A. - Political Science, University of Georgia (1990-1994)

or

 M.S. Program, Psychology, UCLA, 30 credits (1977-1979)
 B.A. - Psychology, Eastern Washington University (1972-1976)

Graduate Degree(s)

In the first two examples below the people merely listed their degrees. The third is the same except that the person chose to include his thesis. A more elaborate description of the thesis can be very effective. It could be described right after the thesis title, or an entire section could be devoted to it called *Thesis.*

EDUCATION

    M.A. - Counseling, UCLA (1972-1974)
    B.A. - Psychology, Oregon State University (1966-1970)

EDUCATION

    Ph.D. - Industrial Psychology, Stanford University (1975-1977)
    M.A. - Psychology, Northwestern University (1972-1973)
    B.A. - Sociology, Northern Illinois University (1967-1971)

EDUCATION

    Ph.D. - Physics, University of Washington (1990-1995)
        Thesis: Interlinear Regression Analysis of Wave Length Dichotomy
    M.S. - Physics, University of Washington (1985-1989)
    B.S. - Physics, University of Manitoba (1981-1985)

In addition to listing the title of your thesis, it may be useful to provide a brief description. This is especially true if you think that even people in your own field may not fully understand what the title of your thesis means. Even if they will likely understand the terms, they won't fully appreciate the value of your thesis or research without a short description.

EDUCATION
Ph.D. in Physics, University of Nebraska   1992
    Major: Theoretical solid state physics and mathematical physics
        Thesis: Analytical Solutions for Flux Phase Analysis
                 Research obtained the first analytical solutions for the
                 flux phase which was derived from high temperature
                 superconductivity models. Proved assertions from
                 early numerical calculations.
M.S. in Physics, University of Nebraska   1989
B.S. in Physics, University of Science and Technology of China   1987

You can also create a *Projects* section which would incorporate a description of your thesis as well as other projects you've worked on. In a projects section you can usually devote more space to the description than you could in the above example.

All But Dissertation

If you have completed all requirements for a graduate degree, except for the dissertation or thesis, it might read:

    Master's Program, Physics, Iowa State University, completed all but dissertation (1978-1981)
or

    Master's Program, Physics, Iowa State University, completed all coursework (1978-1981)

TIPS FOR STRENGTHENING YOUR EDUCATION SECTION

The following tips will help you put the finishing touches on your education section.

Listing Major and Minor

You may want to list both your major and minor if you believe the minor will also help to sell you. In the case below the person wanted to become a labor relations negotiator and felt the economics minor strengthened her credentials.

EDUCATION

B.A. - Major: Industrial Relations. Minor: Economics. Syracuse University (1988)

Degrees and Abbreviations

If you hold a B.A., B.S., M.A., M.S., or Ph.D., it is best to abbreviate since everyone knows what they stand for. Many people are not familiar, however, with B.F.A. (Bachelor of Fine Arts), so it is better to spell out the term. The same is true of M.P.S. (Master of Professional Studies), B.B.A. (Bachelor of Business Administration), and others. Almost everyone knows A.A. stands for Associate of Arts, but many do not know A.S. stands for Associate of Science or that A.T.A. stands for Associate of Technical Arts. If you think some people will not know what your degree stands for, spell it out.

When to Use GPA (Grade Point Average)

Generally GPA is listed only if it is over 3.0. Some experts suggest not listing it unless it is over 3.5. GPA usually is dropped from your resume after you've been out of school for five years. By that time your work record will reveal much more about you than your GPA. It's interesting to note that most follow-up studies have revealed virtually no correlation between a high college GPA and success on the job. Many who were mediocre in school begin to shine only when they enter "the real world." If your overall GPA was below 3.0, but your GPA in your major was above 3.0, you might want to list it this way:

B.A. - Geography, 3.3 in major, University of Oregon 1998

When to List Honors

If you graduated with honors or with a title like Cum Laude or Summa Cum Laude, you could include it like this:

EDUCATION

B.A. - Cum Laude, History, Brigham Young University (1978)

EDUCATION

B.A. - with honors, English Literature, George Washington University (1988)

City and State of College

The city and state in which your college is located is usually not included in your resume. This is particularly true if your college is well known in the region in which you are conducting your job search. If you think employers might be curious, however, include the city and state.

B.A. - Business, Griffith College, Austin, Texas 1989

Order of Schools

Normally schools are listed in reverse chronological order, beginning with your most recent school. Typically this would also mean that your highest level degree would appear first.

Whether to List Major

People should usually include their major, even if that major did not directly prepare them for the field they are now in. There are presidents of *Fortune* 500 companies who graduated with degrees in history or literature. I say keep your major in, but if you feel strongly about removing it, it might look like this:

B.S. - University of Calgary (1982)

Don't Claim Degrees You Don't Have

Don't fib on your education. It's the easiest part of a resume to confirm and often takes only a few minutes on the phone to learn the truth. Don't even claim you attended a college if you didn't. While claiming a year or two at an undistinguished college is unlikely to cause an employer to check your record, it just isn't worth the risk. It can and has led to terminations when it was discovered a person had lied on their application.

Including Coursework Can Add Impact

You may want to include some of your coursework to demonstrate the extensiveness of your training. If you are a liberal arts graduate seeking a management trainee position, you could list economics, accounting, and business courses. The person with a technical degree is also often benefited by listing courses. Although the reader knows your major, that information alone is not always adequate. For the person with few summer or part-time jobs, listing coursework will make your resume, and therefore your experience, look fuller.

In the following example, the person was looking for an entry-level position in advertising.

EDUCATION

B.A. - Journalism/Advertising, University of Hawaii - 3.39 GPA (1999)

Coursework included: Advertising Copywriting, Public Relations Writing, Media Planning, Media Representation, Production Graphics, Advertising Layout and Design, Media Aesthetics, Principles of Design, Principles of Color

Professional Training

LISTING YOUR PROFESSIONAL TRAINING offers one of the best opportunities to demonstrate that you are up to date in your field. If you lack the typical degrees held by people in your field, training can show that you've worked hard to compensate for that fact, so use training to sell yourself.

It is generally best to separate education from training. Training usually includes seminars and workshops, but can also include college courses taken to help you perform better in your field, but which are not part of a degree program. Seminars include those sponsored by your employer and those offered by outside consulting firms at your place of employment. You should also list seminars and workshops you've attended away from your place of employment, paid for either by yourself or your employer. Even if you have received college credit for such courses, you would normally include them under training rather than education. Glance at the example below and you'll see why it's a good idea to separate training from education.

EDUCATION

    Total Quality Control, Rainier Group (24 hours) 2002
    Terminating Employees, Human Resources Inc. (8 hours) 2001
    B.A. - Business, University of Colorado 1995
    Supervising Difficult Employees, Townsend & Assoc. (10 hours) 1993

If you hold a degree, you want the reader to spot that fact instantly. In the example above, the B.A. is hidden by the seminars. It would look better this way:

EDUCATION

    B.A. - Business, University of Colorado 1995

PROFESSIONAL TRAINING

    Total Quality Control, Rainier Group (24 hours) 2002
    Terminating Employees, Human Resources Inc. (8 hours) 2001
    Supervising Difficult Employees, Townsend & Assoc. (10 hours) 1993

Listing workshops and seminars can help demonstrate your professional growth. But as valuable as seminars are, be selective about those you choose to include—be sure they are relevant. If you took a course in estate planning, but that knowledge will be of little or no value for the job you're seeking (restaurant management, say), it's better to leave it out.

Usually you should state the seminar title, the name of the organization that put it on, and the year you attended. If most of your seminars lasted a half day or more, it would be useful to show the number of hours spent in class. If your company sent you to seminars in different cities, it can be beneficial to list those cities. It demonstrates that your company thought highly enough of you to invest in out-of-town workshops.

Some seminars have catchy titles that really don't describe their content. If "Make The Most Of Yourself" was really about time management, it should be written as: "Time Management, Simms and Associates (1989)." Feel free to alter seminar titles so the reader will understand their content. Review the following:

MANAGEMENT SEMINARS

Managing People, Harvard Business Workshop, four days (2002)
Motivating Employees, Bob Collins & Associates, two days (1999)
Management and Human Relations, California Institute of Technology,
124 hours (1997)

SEMINARS

Financial Management for Closely Held Businesses, 40 hours,
Bank of America (2002)
Construction Cost Improvement, 20 hours, Nevett & Associates(2000)
Scheduling, CPM, 20 hours, Nevett & Associates (1997)
Real Estate Syndication, 10 hours, NW Professionals (1997)
Construction Estimating, 30 hours, Lake Washington Technical College (1995)
Closing the Sale, 12 hours, Roff & Associates (1994)
Goal Setting/Richer Life, 18 hours, Zig Ziglar (1993)

Normally, training would be listed right after education. The two just go together. If your training section will take up more than eight lines, however, it is usually best to put your training at the end of the second page. One guiding principle is that you usually want to get at least your most recent job on page one and preferably at least two jobs. If your training section would allow you to get only part of your most recent job on page one, it is probably best to move training to page two.

Some people have extremely long lists of seminars that will all help sell them. In such a case you can create a totally separate page for training and simply label it Training. Or you can label it Addendum (centered at the top, bold, and 14- or 16-point type) and then skip several lines before listing Training in bold and two points smaller than Addendum. Training would be flush left. Then list all of your seminars or trainings.

I like labeling the page Addendum because that is a good way to let the reader know that you've produced a two-page resume with a one-page addendum. The word Addendum indicates that the information is being provided but that it is not essential reading. Those who are interested will quickly scan the page and those who are not will skip it. That's okay since you've included it only for those who pay attention to such things.

Below is an alternative to a long list of seminars. I rarely recommend this approach because without mentioning the specific workshops and seminars, simply saying you have lots of class hours has little impact.

Professional Training

Over 250 hours of classes and seminars in interviewing, hiring/firing, supervision, employee motivation, performance appraisal, interpersonal communications, COBRA administration, project management (list available by request)

You can also break up your training section into subject areas:

PROFESSIONAL TRAINING

Computers/Programming
Microsoft Access, Catapult, Inc., 32 hours (2002)
Microsoft Visual Basic, University of Washington, 30 hours (2001)
Intro to C Programming, Everett Community College, 60 hours (2000)
HP Basic Programming, Hewlett-Packard Education, 20 hours (1999)
Communication Skills
Presentation Skills, Decker Communications, 16 hours (2000)
Developing Effective People Skills, Jenkins & Associates, 8 hours (1998)

Employment

Every job is a self-portrait of the person who did it. —Unknown

YOUR EMPLOYMENT SECTION represents your key opportunity to sell yourself. It is your best opportunity to demonstrate the breadth and depth of your experience and to showcase your results.

For most people the employment section will be the longest section of the resume. Employment has four main purposes:

1) it reveals your career progress

2) it describes duties and responsibilities

3) it describes results and accomplishments

4) it accounts for where you've been and for whom you've worked.

Employment history should not be just a recitation of duties and responsibilities. You have a definite goal in mind: you want employers to sense your future worth to their organizations. Everything in your resume should demonstrate your ability to master the type of job you are seeking. Include whatever information will create that sense of value; exclude whatever information will not.

Describing results and accomplishments in each job you've held will do more to reveal your capabilities than anything else. Each job description should consist of concisely described duties and at least one accomplishment. The employment section should begin with your most recent position and move backward in reverse chronological order.

Writing effective job descriptions can be difficult, but I've developed techniques which will ultimately save you time and produce a better resume. The most important technique is to begin by creating a *job sketch.*

USING JOB SKETCHES TO STRENGTHEN YOUR RESUME

If I had eight hours to chop down a tree, I'd spend the first six sharpening my ax. —Abraham Lincoln

A job sketch is simply a listing of all the major duties you've performed in each job, plus a brief description of special projects, and an analysis of the results you achieved in each job.

Before you even begin to write your resume, write a job sketch for each job you intend to list in the employment section. Since developing the use of job sketches in 1981, I have seen the quality of clients' resumes improve by at least

50%. Job sketches work because they help prevent writer's block. Without a job sketch a person is forced to stare at a blank sheet of paper or a blank computer screen. Suddenly the person is under real pressure to produce. The questions come flooding in—"Where should I start, what's important, how much space should I devote to each job?"

A job sketch prevents that type of pressure and panic. Instead of beginning by staring at a blank page, you begin your resume with each job sketch in front of you. And each job sketch covers everything that could go into the resume. You produced each job sketch under low stress conditions because you were merely writing down everything that came to mind, not worrying about spelling, grammar, sentence structure, or polished writing. In other words, you were not trying to write a resume.

With your job sketch before you, it is much easier to decide what the key points really are, and what emphasis you should give to each one. Because your job sketch is so complete, you will have more information than you will actually put into the resume. But that's okay. Information that is not used may be great material to bring up in your interviews.

To produce each job sketch, review the job in your mind and then list major duties, less major duties, and even selected minor duties which might be relevant for the type of position you are seeking. Those minor duties may have taken up less than 1% of your time, but may be critical in demonstrating that you at least have exposure in a key area.

After you've listed job duties, think about any projects you worked on. Then write a brief description of them, including their results or outcomes. A project is anything that has a definite beginning and ending. Bookkeeping includes certain things that are done daily, weekly, monthly, quarterly, and yearly—bookkeeping is not a project. Analyzing the present bookkeeping system and recommending and implementing changes would be a project. Some occupations consist of repetitive duties that rarely or never involve projects. People in occupations such as engineering, programming, chemistry, and consulting continually move from one project to the next.

Thinking through all of these duties, responsibilities, and projects for all of your jobs will take one to three hours, but taking the time now can make the difference between a mediocre resume and an outstanding one. If you save each job sketch, you will never have to go through this process again, except as you add new positions.

The key to a good job sketch is to simply write whatever pops into your mind. Don't worry about grammar or spelling, just get your thoughts on paper. Go for volume. Write quickly. Don't filter out or neglect to put something down because you think it is insignificant. Remember, only a small portion of your job sketch will end up in the resume, but you need plenty of data to work with.

As you read the sample job sketches, and the job descriptions that resulted from the sketches, notice the impact that results have. After reading the polished version of the job descriptions, you will have the definite sense that these three people are very good at what they do.

The following job sketch of an insurance claims adjuster is thorough and detailed. It took about 30 minutes to write. Once this person was ready to start her resume, it practically wrote itself.

Example 1

INSURANCE CLAIMS ADJUSTER

Read each new claim file and determine which ones to act on first.

Call claimants or the insured party to clarify what occurred and set up appointment to inspect car, write an estimate, or meet injured parties.

Go to body shop to write estimate and negotiate final cost with manager. Haggle about how many hours to give for straightening frame, fender, quarter panel, etc. Use crash book figures for time necessary to remove and replace parts, to paint panels and for cost of parts. Threaten to take car to another shop if can't reach a compromise. Come up with creative and cheaper ways for car to be repaired while maintaining the integrity of the vehicle.

Totals—if totaled, use *Blue Book* to calculate value. Negotiate if necessary with claimant or insured to determine amount to be paid. Get bids from Midwest Auto Auction and award car to highest bidder. Arrange to turn over title to new owner after getting payment.

When injuries have occurred visit accident scene and draw picture, visit surrounding stores or homes to locate witnesses, get statements. Get recorded statements from claimant and insured. Go to hospital if necessary and explain that I want to make a fair settlement. Try to settle on first visit for small sum and get signature on release statement.

Collect all medical and hospital bills. Request diagnosis from treating physician. Determine real extent of injury, estimate what the case should settle for, and request an adequate money authorization from supervisor to settle.

Visit claimant and negotiate—explain why injury isn't worth as much as claimant thinks it is.

Negotiate with attorney by mail or phone. Explain any circumstances which weaken claimant's case, i.e., question of who was really at fault or extent of injury. Recognized as best negotiator with attorneys. Always well prepared for negotiations.

Results

1999 Settled the most claims in the office.

1999 Out of 15 adjusters, 3rd lowest average cost per collision settlement, 2nd lowest average bodily injury settlement.

This person had three years' experience as a claims adjuster and was looking for another claims position with an insurance company. The final version of the job description—just 77 words—is given below.

CLAIMS ADJUSTER - 6/95-7/99. Handled a full range of property damage and personal injury claims. Wrote estimates on damage to claimant and insured vehicles, disposed of total losses, and handled claims on comprehensive coverage including stolen cars and glass breakage. Investigated accidents and settled injury cases with claimants and attorneys. In 1999 settled the most claims in the office. Out of fifteen adjusters, had third lowest average cost per collision settlement and second lowest average personal injury settlement.

The job sketch below was written by an electronics technician who caught mistakes, solved problems, and constantly looked for better ways to do things. Notice how those qualities come through loud and clear.

Example 2

SENIOR TECHNICIAN

Test printed circuit boards, end items, and systems according to test procedures set by engineering. Troubleshoot down to component level.

Interface with clinical personnel if problems occur with functionality of units, kits, etc. Identify problems and suggest solutions.

Interface with design and R & D engineering regarding fit, form, or functional flaws or problems. Suggest solutions. On the Y235 scanner, suggested solutions which reduced time to produce prototype by four months. On the U454 scanner, identified a problem which would have cost more than $200,000 to fix in the production phase.

Interface with production, test, and assembly personnel to ensure a proper production flow.

Work with Quality Control on functional as well as cosmetic problems. Fix if necessary or show why QC documents are wrong or why specifications should be changed. Changes in specifications typically speeded up production by 10–15%.

Work with Material Control to ensure parts are available when needed. Expedite shipments when necessary.

Assist engineering in setting up preclinical trials for prototype products.

Check out functional test procedures for Test Engineering to ensure they are correct, practical, and understandable.

Review printed circuit board schematics and assembly drawings and make corrections where necessary.

Keep and maintain a file of all new product test procedures, drawings, specifications, and parts lists. This has improved access and use of all data and saves approximately 200 man-hours per year.

Notice how points in the final job description were taken right out of the job sketch, in some cases with only minor revisions.

SENIOR TECHNICIAN - 3/97 to Present. As Senior Technician for this manufacturer of CAT scanners, test printed circuit boards, end items, and systems, and troubleshoot down to component level. Rework failed equipment. Work closely with clinical personnel and design engineers to identify problems and suggest solutions. Identified and resolved a problem with one product which would have cost more than $200,000 to fix in the production stage. Interface with Quality Control and frequently recommend changes in QC specifications. Recommendations typically speed up production by 10–15%. Played a key role in reducing the time to produce the Y235 scanner prototype by four months.

Assist Engineering in setting up preclinical trials for prototype products. Review test procedures established by Test Engineering to ensure tests are understandable and workable. Review PC schematics, assembly drawings, and parts lists, and make corrections where necessary. Developed and currently maintain a file of all test procedures, drawings, parts lists, and specifications, which has significantly improved access and use of the data, saving approximately 200 hours per year.

In the following job sketch Sal emphasizes some great successes in the tourism industry. Once he identified his successes in the job sketch, the job description was easy to write.

Example 3

EXECUTIVE DIRECTOR

Managed and administered a statewide nonprofit association developing and promoting tourism in Idaho.

I conducted tourism seminars statewide for members of the private sector and performed lobbying duties in the state legislature on tourism issues.

I managed a staff of three, plus an intern, and reported to an elected board of directors from throughout the state.

I was the chief advocate for the private sector in tourism promotion and marketing. It required strong people skills to work with the private sector, plus gain the support of several state agencies and of the state legislature.

Increased dues-paying membership approximately 20% each year because of our success in increasing tourism. Everyone wanted to be a part of what we were doing.

Played a key role in the increase in tourism revenue which increased an average of 18% for each of the three years, versus 8–10% increases each of the five previous years. Many resort and tourism areas set records for revenue.

Our association received a $50,000 federal grant to further tourism, in recognition of the high quality of our efforts the two previous years.

In his job description Sal does a nice job of joining his duties with his results.

Idaho Hospitality & Visitors Association, Boise, ID 1989-1992

Executive Director—Administered this statewide nonprofit association in promoting tourism to and within the State of Idaho. Lobbied the state legislature and had a solid impact in both protecting and enhancing the interests of the tourism industry. Established local groups to follow up with legislators on specific issues. Obtained a key federal grant for the Regional Tourism Project in recognition of the overall effectiveness of the program.

Conducted highly regarded seminars for the private sector which enabled them to strengthen their marketing and promotional activities. Increased dues-paying membership approximately 20% per year and played a key role in increasing tourism dollars throughout the state. Supervised a staff of three.

While the data and information you produce for your job sketch are important and useful, the very process of writing the job sketch also serves several valuable functions. It makes you recall *all* the duties and functions of the job and allows you to choose the most important ones for your resume. It also causes you to relive some of the experiences and makes them more vivid. What's more, it helps you recall accomplishments and results. In addition, the very act of remembering, sorting through, and writing down all of your duties, accomplishments, and experiences prepares you for interviews.

As you write your job sketches, it is important that you make the most out of each one of your accomplishments. The next section on accomplishments will show you how to do that.

ACCOMPLISHMENTS

To write an effective resume you should look for ways to insert accomplishments into your job descriptions, special projects, and qualifications. This section will provide you with the techniques to create real impact in your resume through the use of accomplishments and results.

Accomplishments separate achievers from nonachievers. Duties alone cannot do this. Consider two people, each with ten years of experience and identical job titles. Applicant A has not had an original idea in three years. The drive and initiative that propelled A upward is gone. Applicant B, however, has demonstrated significant accomplishments each year and still exhibits great enthusiasm. Only accomplishments will distinguish over-the-hill applicant A from full-of-potential applicant B. Accomplishments make you seem more like a real person and create strong impressions. Stressing accomplishments in a resume is important for everyone, but it is absolutely critical for the person changing careers; those accomplishments will prove your potential for success in the new career.

Employers make hiring decisions based on your perceived potential. Experience is frequently used to measure potential, but it is often a poor yardstick. Employers certainly want people who can come in and handle the job from day one, but other factors are also important. Employers are willing to train someone if they feel that person has the potential to become a better employee than the one with more experience. Potential is best demonstrated through accomplishments.

Accomplishments do not have to be big, knock-your-socks-off types of experiences. They are merely experiences in which you made a contribution. An employer who clearly sees that you've made contributions that go beyond just doing your duty immediately assumes that you will continue to make contributions in the future. That's potential. But it's not enough to have achieved certain accomplishments or to possess potential. You must present them in your resume in ways that bring them to life. Your competitors, in fact, may have accomplishments even more impressive than your own, but if they fail to describe them in their resumes, it's the same as if they did not have them. And if they don't list them in their resume, they probably will not describe them in interviews. This gives *you* the advantage.

Ideally, you will list one or more significant accomplishments for each job you've held. For some jobs, however, this is not practical. Perhaps you held the job for just a short time, or didn't enjoy the job and performed below your full potential. With jobs like these, provide only short descriptions so that the reader will concentrate on the more important jobs you held.

Describe accomplishments concisely and concretely so that they'll have impact. Every employer seeks people who can increase profits, decrease costs, solve problems, or reduce the stress and pressure they face. Specific information such as percentages and dollar figures make accomplishments more tangible and impressive. Compare these two statements: "Implemented new personnel policies which increased morale" and "Implemented new personnel policies which reduced absenteeism by 27% and reduced turnover by 24%." The specific figures given in the second sentence make the accomplishment more impressive and real.

You're probably thinking, "I know my idea saved time and money, but I have no idea how much." In this section I'm going to show you how to arrive at your figures. In many cases they will be estimates, but use company records to verify your figures whenever they are available. One of my clients used printed reports to verify his 63% increase in tons of aluminum sold during a two-year period. Those figures were impressive in the resume; during interviews he was able to elaborate.

Arriving at a percentage or a dollar figure when you have no verifying figures requires creative thinking and sometimes creative guessing. You would not want to exaggerate the accomplishment, but you can calculate figures to the best of your knowledge. The following example illustrates how this can be done.

Saving Money in Alaska

Roger wanted to leave Alaska, where he had repaired heavy construction machinery. He felt he was a top-level mechanic but could think of no evidence to prove it. After talking with him a bit, I discovered he was constantly developing new tools and finding easier ways to make certain repairs. One of the tools he made helped him install a $500 part by aligning it perfectly in place. Without the tool the part was sometimes misaligned, but there was no way to tell until the part was clamped in; by then it was too late, the part would crack. Roger estimated he replaced the part 30 times per year and would have cracked two of them without the tool. In other words he saved $1000 each year by not cracking the $500 part. About 20 other mechanics with similar duties copied his tool. We figured he and the 20 others each saved about $1000 annually. So on the resume we stated that he saved $20,000 per year with his tool. Actual savings may have ranged from $18,000 to $25,000 per year; we chose $20,000 as the most likely. If an employer asks Roger to verify the figure, he can explain how it was calculated. Employers have always been satisfied with his explanation. In an interview all you need to do is explain how you arrived at the figures and state that they're accurate to the best of your knowledge.

Ideas For Identifying Accomplishments And Results

To identify results, you should first identify your accomplishments. Each accomplishment will have at least one result. Here are some questions to ask yourself and some techniques for identifying accomplishments.

- What are your accomplishments? An accomplishment is any experience where you did something well, you were complimented for it, you enjoyed it, you got satisfaction from it, or are proud of it. If any one of these five occurred or all of them, it is by definition an accomplishment. Not all accomplishments will end up in the resume, but the first step is to identify them.

- Did you create, reorganize, or establish any effective procedures or systems?

- Did you streamline a process or increase productivity?

- Did you oversee or participate in a special project that had a good outcome?

- Have you done anything that saved money, simplified a process, or solved a problem?

- Are you a good supervisor or trainer whose people get promoted faster and farther than your fellow supervisors?

- Did you win any awards or get special recognition from a boss or the company itself? Did you get recognition from an industry association, from a local organization thanking you for special efforts, or from a national body that recognizes people such as the Emmy in television and the Pulitzer Prize for journalism? Did you receive a lifetime achievement award from an organization you belong to?

Take time to go through each of your jobs or volunteer experiences and pose these questions to yourself. Jot down the thought as soon as it comes into your mind. Do not filter out experiences just because they don't seem big enough to you. You may eventually not include it in the resume but you should list it because one memory will then trigger another. You need as long a list as possible so you can choose just the right ones to put in your resume.

Almost any award is worth mentioning. It does not have to be a lifetime achievement award.

Using Results To Create Impact

It's great when you've got computer printouts or company documents to prove what you are claiming, but few people have that type of documentation. In such cases it will be necessary to "guesstimate." This is a very acceptable practice. When estimating it is good to be a little on the conservative side so that in an interview you can state that the actual improvement was probably greater. I have never had a client tell me that his or her claims were not believed. To be accepted you merely need to explain what you did and how you did it.

Accomplishments which cannot be translated into dollars or percentages can still have impact. Statements such as "Selected as employee of the month," or "Brought the product to market five months ahead of schedule," can have a powerful effect on employers.

In the following sample job descriptions, notice that accomplishments are described very briefly. Elaborate on your accomplishments during the interview, not in the resume.

In the Memory Academy example below notice the impression you gain, even though no figures are used. You will quickly recognize that she is responsible, creative, hard working, and an excellent supervisor and trainer. She is the type of person who is always looking for ways to improve programs and systems.

Memory Academy, Dallas, Texas, 5/92 to 6/95

> **Office Manager/Executive Instructor** - Office manager of a 14-person office with direct responsibility for ten. Developed and wrote detailed manuals for each position and created a smooth functioning office. In 1994 redesigned the teaching techniques of the memory course. Instructors immediately experienced better results and received enthusiastic ratings from clients.

Her key accomplishment came from improving the teaching techniques at the Memory Academy. With the recognition of an accomplishment comes a better understanding of her as a person. You know that she cared about her job and invested her energy in making the business more effective and successful.

Accomplishments are loaded with powerful information. One fifteen-word accomplishment can say more and have more impact than one hundred words of a job description. Look at the following two examples and notice the impact of the accomplishments. Imagine what the impact would be without them. I have italicized key parts of the accomplishments.

Des Moines Trust & Savings, Des Moines, Iowa, 9/94 to Present

> **Branch Operations Manager** - Managed operations at three branches and supervised 20 employees. *Overcame serious morale problems* by working closely with the branch staffs and providing better training and supervision. Within the branches *absenteeism was reduced 42% and turnover 70%.* Customer service and marketing of bank services were strengthened. Based on customer surveys, the *customer service rating improved from 74% good or excellent to 92%.*

Central Mortgage, 5/96 to Present

> **Division Manager**, Missoula, Montana, 8/98 to Present. Opened the Missoula office and set up all bookkeeping and office systems. Within ten months *became the number-one home mortgage lender* in the Missoula area and *obtained 31% of the mortgage market and 44% of all construction loans.* During five years *have averaged 48% profit on gross income, the highest in the company among 33 offices.*

The following example vividly illustrates the need for accomplishments. The first version lacks both accomplishments and impact. The revision ultimately sold the person into a good position.

Before

Sales Representative - 2/97 to Present. Develop and service established accounts as well as new accounts. Set pricing structures after determining the market. Responsible for the district's western Orange County territory. Sales have increased each year.

After

Sales Representative - 2/97 to Present. In the first three years moved the territory from last in the district to first among ten territories. Aggressively went after new accounts and have significantly increased market share in the territory. By 2000 became the number one sales rep in total profits and have maintained that position. Profits have increased an average of 30% annually.

Is there any question which resume would result in an interview? In the second job description, you get a sense of a salesperson who is successful, works hard, has excellent product knowledge, and knows how to get a sale. It makes an employer want to meet him to learn if he is as good in person as he seems on paper.

Notice that the impression you get of the person is much stronger in the second version, yet it required just one more line than the first. This powerful effect can be created by presenting *what* you've done in jobs, rather than *how* you've done it. Tell *what* resulted from your efforts, but devote little or no space to describing *how* it happened. Accomplishments speak for themselves and you rarely need to go into detail regarding all the things you did to get your results. Save the details for an interview.

Sometimes you will want to allude to what was done without providing details. The bank branch operations manager presented earlier provides a perfect example. She said, "Overcame serious morale problems by working closely with the branch staffs and providing better training and supervision. Within the branches absenteeism was reduced 42% and turnover 70%." How she got her result is merely alluded to with the statement, "Overcame serious morale problems by working closely with the branch staffs and providing better training and supervision." She did not go into detail about the morale problem, but simply stated it existed. And, she only alluded to *how* she solved it—working closely with staff and improving training and supervision. An employer who wants to know more will have to interview her.

In the resume below, a bank controller's job description does not do him justice. Because this was his most recent and most responsible position, more detail is required to show his potential. Although the second job description is longer, it is well-written and concise. It does not contain any unnecessary words. Everything mentioned is designed to sell him and give an employer a full view of his experience.

Before

Controller - Managed accounting department, seven-person staff; prepared financial statements and filed various reports with state and federal agencies; assisted and advised senior management concerning regulatory accounting and tax ramifications of decisions and policies; worked with savings and loan divisions on operational and systems design; served as primary liaison with computer service bureau in Los Angeles.

After

Controller - Managed a seven-person accounting department and significantly increased productivity by simplifying procedures, cross-training staff, and improving morale. Prepared financial statements and advised senior management on regulatory, accounting, and tax ramifications of new policies and programs under consideration. Heavily involved in the research and planning of an investment "swap" program which resulted in a $5.3 million tax refund. Successfully directed the Association's response when the refund resulted in an IRS audit.

As financial division representative, worked closely with both the savings and loan divisions to increase interdivision cooperation related to new systems, operations, and customer service. Significantly improved communications with the Association's service bureau and implemented modifications in the general ledger system which streamlined operations and saved more than $20,000 per year.

The accomplishments he included were his increase in productivity, finding a unique approach for justifying a large tax credit and then defending it before the IRS, increasing cooperation among divisions in the bank, improving relations with the computer service bureau, and saving money on computer services. These accomplishments are likely to pique the interest of a targeted employer.

Results Sell People

Below are additional statements which effectively convey accomplishments. Read them to give you further ideas on how you might present your results.

Quantified:

Developed a new production technique which increased productivity by 7%.

Through more effective recruiting techniques, reduced terminations company-wide by 30% and turnover by 23%.

Edited a newsletter for an architectural association, with readership increasing 28% in one year.

Organized a citizen task force which successfully wrote a statewide initiative, adopted with a 69% favorable vote.

As chairperson for fundraising, developed a strategy which increased funds raised by 26% while reducing promotional costs.

Set a record of 46 days without a system failure.

Nonquantified:

Awarded Medal of Merit for contributions to the community.

Established a voluntary labor-management forum that significantly reduced tension between labor and management.

Developed a self-managed quality program that substantially reduced noncompliant parts.

The advertising tie-in with Star Wars was credited with building strong name recognition for our new toy line.

Received a letter of appreciation from the Chairperson of the Ballard Community Council for bringing together 20 local businesses, which provided seed money for a community center.

Played a key role on a task force that recommended over 20 ways to improve plant safety. Not only have injuries been significantly reduced, but morale has improved as production personnel recognized that the company valued and respected them.

Which/Which Resulted In

Accomplishments and results are powerful. Everything you've done on a job has had a result. When the result is positive *and* significant, it belongs in the resume. Train yourself to look for results. Remember, you don't need computer printouts to verify your results. Your own honest estimate is sufficient. If asked about it during an interview, just describe how you arrived at the figure and then go into more detail concerning how you accomplished it. Results sell you.

I've developed a simple technique which will help you identify your results as you write your job sketches. As you list a duty or a project, add the words *which*, or *which resulted in*, and then ask yourself what the duty or project resulted in. For example, "Wrote an office procedures manual" becomes, "Wrote an office procedures manual, *which* decreased training time and billing errors." After you've taken time to quantify the results and to explain it more accurately, it will become, "Wrote an office procedures manual, which decreased training time of new employees by 25% and reduced billing errors more than 30%."

Later, after completing your job sketches, go through the process one more time. Review each duty and project to see if you forgot to list a result as you were writing.

The words *which* and *which resulted in* force you to take all of your activities and accomplishments to their logical conclusion. With each duty or function you list, ask yourself whether you did it as well or better than others. If better, ask yourself how you know. This process will lead you to the logical end result. You should keep going back until you have determined what the most basic result is. Once you've identified all of the results from a particular experience, you can then determine which ones will have the most impact in your resume.

The problem I've observed is that people are often quite satisfied to come up with just one result from a duty or project. Many times, however, three or more results are actually lurking in that project just waiting to be discovered. Each one is important. Even if not all of your results get into your resume, they can become highly valuable in interviews.

When describing an accomplishment, be sure to include concrete information about its effect. Don't stop short. People often write in a way that they think demonstrates a result, but does not. For example, one person wrote, "Developed a scheduling system to better schedule production and reduce late deliveries." Through the use of the word "to" the person is merely implying that the *goal* was to improve scheduling and decrease late shipments. The statement does not tell us for sure that it was accomplished. Look what happens when we add *which*: "Developed a better scheduling system, *which* improved production scheduling and virtually eliminated late deliveries." This is a stronger statement.

There is now no doubt that the new system accomplished its goal and had a real impact on the operation.

Don't assume that just because a result does not come to mind immediately, that there is no result. People are often amazed when they go over their job sketches a second time, or when a friend helps out, that there were many more results than were initially visible.

Virtually all projects which had a successful conclusion contain at least one result. Some duties, however, do not have results; you simply did the work but did it no better and no worse than others. Still, you need to pause as you look over each of your duties from all of your jobs and ask yourself whether there could be a result hiding in there. The more you find, the more interviews you'll get, and with those interviews you'll sell yourself to the fullest.

Identifying Results Within An Accomplishment

The trick is to identify the result or results first and then seek to quantify them by using the hard data you have available or by estimating the result. Also, don't stop with just one result or benefit. Many of your best experiences have had several results, so take the time to identify them. Although not all of your results will end up in the resume, you'll be able to select the ones that will have the greatest impact in the resume. Your other results will come in handy during interviews.

Let's look at a project that produced multiple results. When I first helped Sam identify his skills and results in this experience, I had no idea we would identify so many results. It takes a little work, but the results will remain hidden without this effort. Identifying as many results as possible has a great deal to do with building your confidence for the job search. No one enters a job search with too much confidence. Take the time to identify your results to create the strongest resume possible and to prepare for interviews. Note: The material below did not come from Sam's job sketch but from his extensive writing on past accomplishments. Most job sketches would not include such detail on a single project or accomplishment.

> In my position as lobbyist for the Detroit Realtors Association, I was very active in building coalitions with the homebuilders, the Economic Development Council of Detroit, and other housing groups. As part of these coalitions, I was asked to co-chair an affordable housing committee. From the Realtors perspective, government regulations were a major problem. So I pulled together an all-inclusive committee, including representatives from General Motors, Housing Coalition of Detroit, and the Detroit Housing Authority, as well as county and state officials. We brought in local experts on a variety of topics and asked for recommendations for reducing or streamlining unnecessary government regulations. We came up with over 80 recommendations and presented it at a regional event sponsored by the mayor and county executive as well as the Detroit Free Press. It was publicly well received, and because of the quality of the recommendations and the breadth of the coalition, over 30 key recommendations were adopted in the past year, with more to follow I'm sure. By streamlining permit and building processes, builders are saving about $600 per home.

Sam demonstrated numerous skills in this project as well as several results. Let's examine the results and quantify them if we can.

> Brought together a coalition of groups that usually oppose one another.

Persuaded government organizations and agencies to remove unnecessary government regulations.

Reduced the cost of building a home by over $600 each.

Reduced the average time to obtain construction permits from 120 days to 75 days.

Developed strong relationships with government agencies by showing that we Realtors didn't oppose everything they recommended, and worked with them to actually strengthen some regulations.

Developed allies that we never had before. (With many we both knew that we wouldn't agree on many issues, but we found that we could work with them on some issues.)

This array of businesses and organizations learned the importance of really listening to what each group was saying and of taking the time to learn what was most important and critical to them.

Got the ear of the mayor, who previously would not listen to us.

I personally gained great visibility by being interviewed by three major newspapers and by the CBS and ABC local affiliates.

Received a $5,000 bonus from the Realtors.

Everybody wins. More affordable housing units can be constructed so more new homebuyers can get that first home. The city and region win because the changes did not compromise the quality of the homes or their energy efficiency.

In the first year the percentage of new homes purchased by minorities increased from 28% of all homes to 38%, a 36% increase.

When we first started identifying Sam's results I quickly saw about four, but I had no idea we would come up with this many. In the resume Sam can decide which results to include. He would virtually always mention that the cost of building homes was reduced by $600. That may not seem like much, but it was accomplished exclusively by eliminating some unnecessary regulations. Part of the cost reduction came by reducing the time required to obtain building permits. When land has been purchased with loans, every day that a home has not been completed (and sold) adds cost in the form of interest. If the profit on a $95,000 starter home would be about $9,000, then $600 equals 6% of the total profit. That's substantial.

It takes some time to come up with results and to quantify them. Sometimes it can take an hour or more. You may have the data necessary to quantify the result, but the information may be spread among several different sources. Of course sometimes the numbers are readily available and have already been calculated.

This should be a reminder to you for the future. As you start a project or look for a way to improve a particular process, figure out how you will measure your success. First you have to determine what you hope to accomplish. Then you have to determine what the current status is. If you are going to improve training in hopes of reducing turnover and errors, then you need to know what the current turnover and error rate is. If those rates are not currently being measured, then you'll have to do it. This effort is worth it because you can obtain a great payoff: you can bring it to the attention of your boss through a memo.

You don't have to ask your boss to respond. As long as your boss does not dispute your results, it means he or she accepts them. Of course your results could help you get a raise, a promotion, or a bonus. But you have to let the key people know what you've done. Don't let yourself be a well-kept secret.

To Versus That

In their resumes people often make statements like, "Developed new procedures to increase office productivity." The statement is not bad, after all, the person is trying to demonstrate a result. The problem is, it's weak. It's much stronger to say, "Developed new procedures *that* increased office productivity." Notice the difference? When you say *to*, you're really only saying the goal was to increase productivity, it does not say the increase in productivity actually happened. When you say *"that* increased office productivity," you're saying unequivocally that the increase indeed happened. This may seem a bit subtle, but put this idea into practice. Go through your resume when it's finished and look to see if you have any *to* statements that should be *that* or *which* statements.

CALCULATING RESULTS/GUESSTIMATING

To make the most out of your results you need to know how to quantify them. One reason we don't see more statistics in resumes is that people don't know how to calculate results, and then don't know how to use or describe them to their best effect. Usually all it takes is simple arithmetic and a little logic. I'm going to show you the methods for calculating percentages. Try to follow along, but if it gets confusing don't worry. There are people out there who can help you. If you are at least able to pull some estimates together, you can locate friends or relatives who can help you in this critical area. I work with statistics frequently, but I still have to think twice before I can remember how to do the calculations. So, let's begin.

In the process of calculating results the first step is to identify all benefits, whether it was something improved, increased, or decreased. Start with the assumption that if you can identify it, you can quantify it. Quantifying results may require some guesstimating, but you can do it.

Review your job sketches to see what clues they might give you. Were there any functions that were left off the sketches that you now think might be valuable? Were there any projects that were not mentioned in your sketches? If a project achieved its goal, it almost assuredly had a result. That result can probably be quantified. Even if you think a particular result was too small to mention in the resume, still spend some time with it because it might be helpful in an interview. Since you are going to discuss a lot of things in interviews that are not included in your resume, you need lots of additional experiences to discuss. Being able to quantify them will enable you to score points.

Suppose you know that an action you took improved something—sales, profits, productivity, turnover—but you don't have computer printouts to prove it. Let's say that the matter is turnover. When you came into the department morale was down, and people were continually leaving out of frustration. When you joined the department there were 16 people. During the year you were assistant supervisor, you saw five people leave and one get fired, for a total of six. That represents 38% turnover.

With a turnover rate that high, productivity was bound to be low because people didn't stay around long enough to really learn the job. In addition, the supervisor had to devote a lot of time to training new people and correcting their mistakes. Eventually your boss was fired and you were promoted into the position. According to your observation, your boss never adequately trained people, got angry at them when they made mistakes, and never supplied positive feedback. As a result, people quit out of frustration.

So when you became supervisor, you worked closely with the core group. This took a lot of overtime on your part, but you made sure they knew what they were doing. You gave them strokes and they appreciated that. During your first year on the job four people quit, the next year two people quit, and the following year two people quit. Your turnover rate for the first year was 25% (4 divided by 16). The second and third years it was 12% (2 divided by 16). It appears that things had definitely stabilized.

Now you need to determine the percentage by which you reduced turnover, and what other benefits accrued as a result. The turnover rate has been reduced from 38% to 12%. Just an approximation will tell you that the reduction is about two-thirds, or 67%. To get the actual figure you would subtract 12 from 38, to get 26, and divide 26 by 38 to get 68%. As valuable as reducing turnover is, that is still not the end result. Because your people are now better trained they make fewer mistakes, get more done in a day, and provide better customer service. So, next you would measure the quality, productivity, and customer service improvements. The resume might read, "Developed an effective training program, which reduced turnover from 38% to 12%. As a result of the program, productivity increased more than 14%, and customer complaints were reduced more than 75%." Such a statement will have real impact on employers.

In the process of calculating results, the first step is to identify all the benefits of an action you took. Start with the assumption that if you can identify it, you can quantify it. Quantifying results may require some guesstimating, but you can do it.

EXAMPLES

Determining An Average Annual Increase

Often a person will bring about improvements over a period of several years. A good way to express this figure in a resume is to show the average annual increase. Selling something would be a typical example. The following example shows how one client used an increase in sales to its best effect.

Susan increased sales in her territory over a five-year period. Sales the year prior to her coming to the territory were $200,000. Her first year she increased sales to $240,000, then $275,000, then $300,000, then $310,000, and finally $350,000. Her first year increase was 20% since her increase of $40,000 is 20% of $200,000.

Mathematically it is figured this way:
$$\$240,000 - 200,000 = \$40,000$$
$$40,000 \div 200,000 = .20 \text{ or } 20\%$$

The second year her increase was 14%:
$$\$275,000 - \$240,000 = \$35,000$$
$$35,000 \div 240,000 = 14\%$$

The third year the increase was 9%, the fourth 3% (a recession year), and the fifth 13%.

Over the five years she increased sales 75%. To get the average annual increase add the increases from each year and total them (20+14+9+3+13 = 59). Then divide by the five years to get the figure (59 ÷ 5 years = 11.8%) of an 11.8% average annual increase. For a resume it would be rounded off to 12%, or in the resume it could be stated, "Increased sales an average of 12% per year." Although she increased sales a total of 75% you cannot divide 75 by 5 to get the average annual increase.

Once the figures have been determined, a decision has to be made as to the strongest way to present the information. Sometimes the best way is simply to present the raw figures. In this case it would be, "In five years took sales in the territory from $200,000 to $350,000." If those figures did not have the impact she wanted she could say, "Took over a mature territory and increased sales 75% in five years," or "During a serious economic downturn in the region, increased sales an average of 12% per year."

Simple Increases

Simple increases can be figured according to the following method: In 1990 advertising revenue for a magazine had been $2,560,000. By the end of 1992 it had increased to $3,180,000. The percent of increase is 24% (3,180,000 - 2,560,000 = 620,000; 620,000 ÷ 2,560,000 = .242 or rounded off to 24%).

The formula for calculating increases is: $\frac{b-a}{a}$ where a is the original number and b is the new number after the increase.

Simple Decreases

Simple decreases can be figured and expressed similar to the example below: A manufacturing supervisor reduced rejects (parts which did not meet specifications and were therefore rejected by quality control) from a rate of 6% to 2%. On resumes people often miscalculate such figures and might report that they reduced rejects by 4%, simply subtracting 2 from 6 and getting 4. Going from 6% to 2% actually represents a 67% reduction in rejects, however. The proper way to calculate this is 6 - 2 = 4; 4 ÷ 6 = .6666 or 67%.

The formula for decreases is: $\frac{a-b}{a}$ where a is the original number and b is the new number after the decrease.

Another common problem occurs if something was reduced from, say, 15 to 7. We'll say that the average daily absenteeism in a department has been reduced from 15 people per day to 7. Some will subtract 7 from 15 getting 8; then dividing 8 by 7 getting 1.14, which they translate into 114%. On the resume it might read, "Reduced absenteeism 114%." But nothing can ever be reduced by more than 100%, or to be more accurate, 99.9999%. Reducing something from 15 to 7 equals 53% (15 - 7 = 8; 8 ÷ 15 = .53) Logic tells you that absenteeism was cut by a little more than half so you know it will be slightly above a 50% decrease.

Large Increases

With large increases you must be careful when calculating percentages. Let's say production in a plant went from 10,000 units per year to 30,000 over a five-year period. It is easy to see that units tripled, so one would tend to say that production increased 300%. The problem is that it actually represents a 200% increase. Going from 10,000 to 20,000 was a 100% increase, and going from 20,000 to 30,000 was another 100%, for a total of 200%.

The formula for increases works just as well for large increases as it does for small ones. Remember, the formula is $\frac{b-a}{a}$. So 30,000-10,000 = 20,000; 20,000 ÷ 10,000 = 2, or 200%.

If calculating numbers is still difficult, don't simply decide not to include your results—get help. Those who know how to calculate such things will enjoy helping you.

Provide Proof Of Results When Possible

The value of including results, especially quantified results, has already been established. In addition to including a quantified result, it is very helpful to provide proof. The proof might include figures produced by your company, numbers that you produced but which were approved or acknowledged by your boss, or figures produced by some outside agency. Large companies in particular will often have research firms provide information for them. Companies, for example, often want to know their market share and they will use these research firms to provide it. If you were a sales manager or a regional manager and you had information indicating that on your watch market share went up significantly, you would want to mention that. Such proof can be indicated in several ways. Listing awards is one excellent way to show that your employer recognized the quality and value of your work. Below you'll see a couple of examples.

> **Mechanical Engineer**—For this $45 million manufacturer of latex surgical gloves, designed a total quality management program that has saved $1.5 million in the first year as documented by an internal management audit.

> Or

> **Operations Manager**—Designed a cost saving program in the areas of shipping, warehousing, material flow, and just-in-time purchasing. Received the Corporate Gold Medal award for one of the top-five cost saving programs among the 25 plants nationwide.

ASSISTED IN/TEAM RESULTS

In most cases, if you were the key person, or one of two people heading up a taskforce, you would simply make a statement that you accomplished something: Planned, organized, and implemented a cost-saving program that reduced production costs 6.5%. If you want to share credit in your resume you might say, "As part of a cross-functional team, played a key role in reducing productions costs 6.5%." If you feel uncomfortable taking primary responsibility for a project, you can use the phrases, *instrumental in, key person in, played a key role in,* or *played an important role in.* It might read, "Played a key role in implementing a management-by-objectives program, which increased productivity 14%." Other terms that can work include co-authored, collaborated with, or co-led.

In resumes I often see the phrase *assisted in.* I rarely use it because it tends to dilute the person's actual contribution. For example, Fred wrote "Assisted in developing a quality control program which reduced rejected circuit boards 24%." In this case, the other person working on the program was a peer who contributed less to the success of the program than Fred. A more appropriate description would be, "Developed a quality control program which reduced rejected circuit boards by 24%." During an interview Fred could explain that he was the primary but not the sole developer of the program.

WRITING YOUR JOB DESCRIPTIONS

Job descriptions must be concise yet complete. A common problem of resumes is that the job descriptions are too short and do not adequately describe duties, experience, level of responsibility, or accomplishments. As you begin, don't be concerned about limiting the resume to one page. While it is often assumed that a resume should be no longer than one page, my studies have verified that so long as it is well-written and concise, a two-page resume is perfectly acceptable, and for many people, essential.

Once you've completed your job sketches with duties, projects, and results, you're ready to write a rough draft of your resume. Start by stating your objective. Although the wording of the objective may change later, you know that everything which appears in the final draft must demonstrate your capability of performing the work defined by your objective.

Begin by reviewing your job sketch for your current or most recent position. What are the most important things an employer should know about the job? Try to eliminate some of the less important duties, but don't worry if your first draft seems a little too long. When you rewrite, you will be able to identify points that should be deleted or summarized more briefly.

From your resume the employer should be able to sense your positive attributes, such as diligence, efficiency, cooperation, effectiveness, and intelligence. Your duties must be adequately covered so that the employer will recognize the full range of your experience. The types of positions you will be seeking will determine which duties should be given the most attention. If employers will have no interest in a certain duty, it should be mentioned only briefly or not at all. Describing your duties effectively will help employers immediately realize that you are ready for more responsibility. Results and accomplishments will be the frosting on the cake that makes the employer want to meet you.

The examples below demonstrate these points. Read the job descriptions as the person had originally written them, then read the revision. Notice how the revisions were made and how they affected the impact of the information being presented.

Compare the following two versions of one woman's employment section. Notice how in the first version her descriptions are concise, but lacking in detail compared to the second version. Her second version provides a fuller, more vivid description of her experiences.

Also, as you study the revised job description, ask yourself what you know about the person that you didn't before. The revised job description is longer, but it had to be to adequately describe what she had done and to give an employer enough details to fully appreciate her capabilities.

Version 1

EMPLOYMENT

Employer	Wiggins Sportswear 2001 to Present
Position	Marketing Coordinator
Responsibilities	Coordinate the entire clothing program
	Creating and utilizing Excel spreadsheets for marketing, production, and finance projections
	Market research
	Coordinating advertising with publications
	Work with outside contractors on special projects
	Fabric and notion research/purchasing
	Calculated preliminary and final costing of garment
	Approved bills relating to the clothing program
Employer	Broadway Department Store 2000 to 2001
Position	Salesperson
Responsibilities	Sales
	Interior layout and display
	Opening and closing the department
	Handling customer complaints and problems
	Issuing merchandise transfers

Version 2

EMPLOYMENT

Wiggins Sportswear, San Diego, California 4/01 to present

Marketing Coordinator - Coordinate the production and marketing functions for a new line of active sportswear. Came into the project when it was two months behind schedule and in serious trouble. Worked with the designer to select colors, designs, and fabrics.

Purchased fabric and accessories. Negotiated with two garment manufacturers to produce small lots, thus reducing the required unit sales to reach a break-even point. Worked out schedule arrangements with manufacturers and authorized any changes in specifications. Line was introduced on schedule with final costs 20% lower than originally projected.

Coordinated the production of the annual sales catalog. Designed order forms, verified prices, and consulted with graphic artists and printers. Had authority to make all necessary changes.

Set up the company's first computerized systems, using Excel and other software to provide the first accurate year-to-date sales figures, as well as highly useful marketing, financial, and manufacturing projections.

Broadway Department Stores, San Diego, California 9/00 to 4/01

Salesperson - Sold women's clothing and had interior layout and display responsibilities. Selected as Employee of the Month for December in this store of approximately 190 employees. Selected on the basis of sales, favorable comments from customers, and taking on added responsibilities.

The revised version is longer than the original, but because it provides more background, you get a clearer picture of her capabilities. By mentioning a project that was behind schedule and in serious trouble, her ability to complete it on schedule and under budget makes the accomplishment especially meaningful. Her original resume contains only a brief list of duties and gives you no information regarding whether she had been successful. The revised job description conveys a sense of her potential. It shows that she was given a lot of responsibility and that she handled it well. It suggests to the reader that she has some very interesting stories to tell about her experiences at Wiggins; but those details will be saved for the interview.

The experience at Broadway did not receive as much space because she has no intention of returning to retail work. The experience does, however, demonstrate valuable background which pertains directly to her career in marketing. It is important that she was able to demonstrate that she was successful even though it was a short-term job. Simply listing her duties provides no clues about the quality of her work, and could lead an employer to believe that she did not do well since she stayed such a short time. Mentioning that she was employee of the month proves that she was valuable. By mentioning the basis for the award—sales, comments from customers, and taking on responsibility—she demonstrates to the employer that she was judged outstanding in each category.

As you write your resume, look for ways to tell your story that convey your value and your successes. Even if you were fired from a job it is possible to show that you were valuable. Do that by stressing what you did well; simply ignore your problem areas.

The next job description comes from a youth counselor. One of his earlier positions was as supervisor for a parks department. In the first job description you get nothing but a dull list of duties. He is a very interesting person with an excellent background, but the first version of the job description fails to convey this.

Version 1

> **Supervisor** — Portland Park Department, Portland, Oregon. Overall responsibility for staff, facility, and program at a neighborhood community center; supervising, hiring, training, and recruitment; program planning, implementation, and evaluation; record keeping, budgeting, grant writing, and analyses; work with schools, local, state, and federal agencies in a variety of capacities; direct service including teaching, training, and work with adults and youth in social, educational, cultural and athletic programs; community and business presentations.

As you read the revised job description below you'll get the sense that here is a person worth meeting. There's a personal touch evident in this version that is lacking in version 1.

Version 2

Portland Park Department, Portland, Oregon

> **Supervisor** - Developed and promoted social, educational, cultural, and athletic programs for the community. Contracted with consultants, instructors,

and coaches to provide instruction in dozens of subjects and activities at the Browser Community Center. Interviewed and hired instructors, and conducted follow-up assessments to ensure top-quality instruction. Personally taught several courses and coached athletic teams. In three years tripled participation at the Center and took it from a $1,400 deficit to a $12,000 profit.

The revised job description presents a person who has goals and ideals. It's clear that he really cared about what he did: he got involved, he took action, and he got results. This more vital, caring tone is created by using action verbs like *developed* and *promoted.* You feel the action. The programs that the community really wanted didn't exist so he went out and *developed* them. Since people don't come flocking to programs they don't know about, he *promoted* them. And he not only planned programs, he also taught some. He even coached several athletic teams. This demonstrates that he is an action-oriented person in good physical shape. The ultimate result of all this effort was a tripling of participation, yet his original job description did not even mention it.

Writing a top-quality resume takes time. From these examples you can see why. Also, describing oneself in positive terms is difficult for most people, yet it is necessary. Write your job descriptions and then keep editing until they approach the examples you find in this book. Everyone can do it, but it will take time and thought. Just remember that taking the time will pay off in interviews and job offers. And that's what you're after.

AN EFFECTIVE EMPLOYMENT FORMAT

The format you choose for your employment section can make a big difference in the visual appeal and readability of your resume. I have tested formats extensively and find that the format below is the one that most employers prefer.

EMPLOYMENT

Balboa's Steak House, 7/95 to Present

General Manager, Miami, Florida, 10/01 to Present. Took over a troubled restaurant which had had six managers in two years and had incurred losses each month during that time. Resolved serious morale problems, instituted an effective training program, and redesigned the menu. During the first nine months increased lunch revenue 38% and dinner 29%. Losses were eliminated within two months and a consistent profit margin of 14% has been maintained.

Assistant Manager, Ft. Lauderdale, Florida, 7/99 to 10/01. Redesigned the menu and helped introduce wine sales. Provided extensive staff training that enabled the restaurant to become number one in wine sales in the chain of twenty restaurants. Purchased all food and supplies.

Saga, Inc., Tallahassee, Florida, 9/97 to 7/99

Student Manager - For this college cafeteria, prepared food, scheduled part-time workers, purchased supplies, and oversaw lunch and dinner lines.

Following are sample treatments of various types of work histories. One of them should conform fairly closely to your own.

Same Company, Three Positions, All in the Same City

EMPLOYMENT

Douglas Bolt Company, St. Louis, Missouri, 8/83 to Present
    V. P. Purchasing, 7/92 to Present. ....
    ....
    Directory of Purchasing, 5/89 to 7/92. ....
    ....
    Manager, Stock Parts Purchasing, 8/83 to 5/89. ....
    ....

Same Company, Three Positions, Three Different Cities

EMPLOYMENT

Horizon Gear, 8/82 to Present
    Regional Sales Manager, Houston, Texas, 7/93 to Present ....
    ....
    District Sales Manager, Atlanta, Georgia, 3/89 to 7/93. ....
    ....
    Sales Representative, Little Rock, Arkansas, 8/82 to 3/89. ....
    ....

In a situation like this you might want to indicate where the headquarters is located. In that case you would show it as: Horizon Gear, Chicago, Illinois, 8/78 to Present.

One Position With Each Company

EMPLOYMENT

Shannon Electric, Garden City, Michigan, 5/91 to Present
    Installer - ....
    ....

Preston Electric, Detroit, Michigan, 6/88 to 5/91
    Installer - ....
    ....

Work for a Subsidiary or Division of a Major Company

EMPLOYMENT

    Antac, Inc., Subsidiary of A&R Industries, Buffalo, New York, 5/86 to Present

It is seldom necessary to specify the parent company. If you choose to, however, this is the easiest way to do it.

PRIOR EMPLOYMENT

A prior employment section is particularly useful if you are trying to shorten your resume or de-emphasize your earlier jobs. A prior employment section is an effective way to explain how you've gotten to where you are without making the employer spend a lot of time reading about it. Other titles for this section include *Previous Employment, Prior Experience,* or *Additional Experience.*

The example below shows the most commonly used format for the prior employment section. The Assistant Purchasing Manager position is the sixth job description position on his two-page resume.

> **Assistant Purchasing Manager** - 3/81-5/82. Set up and developed an inventory control program to reduce inventory and operating costs. Over the next year reduced inventory by 20%.
>
> PRIOR EMPLOYMENT
>
> **Counterperson**, Zenith Electronics, Los Angeles, CA, 3/80-3/81
> **Expediter**, Hughes Aircraft, Los Angeles, CA, 4/78-3/80
> **Parts Manager**, High Lift Equipment, Long Beach, CA, 9/76-4/78

In the example above, the person has included title, name of company, city and state, and dates. Generally this information would be included. In the remaining examples, however, you will see how personal taste varies. I generally include city and state, but if it seems like unnecessary detail for some distant jobs, feel free to leave city and state off.

In the example below, the person provides the job title, name of employer, and dates, but not the city and state.

Example (starting with the person's fifth position on a two-page resume):

> National Computer Stores, Spokane, WA, 5/86-6/87
>
> **Sales Representative** - Sold hardware and software for this IBM authorized dealer. Consistently exceeded monthly sales goals.
>
> PRIOR EXPERIENCE
>
> Food Service Specialist, Johnson Nursing Home (8/84-5/86); Cook, Boyd's Restaurant (7/82-8/84); Cook, Iron Pig Restaurant (6/81-7/82)

In the following example the individual did not feel it necessary to give specific time periods or list the names of employers.

Example (starting with the person's seventh position on a two-page resume):

> Xytelin Electronics, Mountain View, California, 1971 to 1975
>
> **Internal Auditor** - Discovered weaknesses in the parts inventory control procedures and recommended remedial action. Responsible for quarterly and yearly audits.
>
> Prior Experience, 1964 to 1971: Airline Internal Auditor, Cost Clerk, Production Scheduler.

In the example below, the person listed dates, but did not list employers.

Example (starting with fifth position on a one-page resume):

Department of Social Services, Winston-Salem, North Carolina, 3/74 to 4/75

ELIGIBILITY SPECIALIST - Assisted families in obtaining all of the Medicaid benefits they were legally entitled to. Provided psychological and social support services.

Previous Experience:

CASHIER/HOSTESS, 1/73 to 3/74; SALES CLERK, 6/72 to 1/73; LONG DISTANCE OPERATOR, 7/70 to 6/72.

The remaining examples will simply give you more options.

PRIOR EMPLOYMENT

CASHIER - Pay Less Drugs, Elgin, Illinois, 1974-1976
CASHIER - Don's Rexall, Carbondale, Illinois, 1972-1974
STOCKER - Jewel Foodstores, Peoria, Illinois, 1971-1972

Previous Employment

TRUCK DRIVER (1967-1971); WAREHOUSEMAN (1967); MACHINE REPAIRMAN (1966-1967)

Sometimes a person will choose not to describe all the positions with a particular company, especially the first one the person worked for. The person below has worked for Boeing since 1976.

Production Inspector - 3/84-4/86. Performed final interior, flight line modification, and wing line inspections on Boeing 737 aircraft. Verified that the production department installed assemblies according to specifications.

Prior Boeing positions: Assistant Production Inspector, 4/81-3/84; Tooling Inspector, 5/79-4/81; Jig Builder, 3/76-5/79.

TIPS FOR WRITING EFFECTIVE EMPLOYMENT HISTORIES

The Job Description Summary

It is often helpful to begin your job description with a summary, or an overview of what you did. It typically consists of a string of items and is very effective in helping a reader quickly understand what you did. A job description summary might look something like this:

Research databases and create surveys to analyze trends and to identify opportunities for improving customer support strategies.

For this sign manufacturing company, prepared financial statements and supervised payroll, billing, and accounts receivable personnel.

Directly responsible for all phases of investment analyses, development, and management of properties.

Coordinated all aspects of the Early Childhood Special Education Program, including hiring and training of staff and support professionals, and the design and implementation of curriculum.

Supervised and trained a lending staff of four in credit and business development efforts.

Interviewed, counseled, and educated patients and families preceding and following open-heart surgery.

Even before learning the details in the rest of each job description, the reader has a good overview of what the person did. It is fine to start off with "Responsible for ..." but don't overuse it. Notice that only one of our examples used "responsible for ..."

Several Jobs Within One Company

Sometimes a person will have five or six changes in job title within one company, during a four- to six-year period. Frequently the person was promoted and kept all or most of the previous responsibilities, and then added others. To describe each job separately would be redundant and unnecessary. Look for any two jobs that were *essentially* the same, and treat them as one.

What To Call Your Employment Section

There are a variety of words and phrases you can use to head your employment section: *Employment, Employment Experience, Work Experience, Professional Experience, Employment History, Work History,* and *Experience* are all good terms. I typically use *Employment,* and sometimes *Professional Experience.* Each of the terms is a good term so pick the one that feels right for you.

If all of your work has been in one major field, and you intend to stay in that field, you can use that term when listing your work experience. You could call it Healthcare Administration Experience, Automotive Experience, Engineering Experience, or Financial Administration Work History.

Dates

Dates should be used on nearly all resumes. If you have no time gaps between jobs or short gaps, you should usually use the months and years you started and left. If you have long gaps, you can indicate the year you started and the year you left.

When to use month and year (example: 5/87-3/93):

1. No gaps in employment.
2. Short gaps of less than five months.
3. One gap of more than five months, several years ago.

Employers prefer to see month and year and may wonder if you are hiding anything by omitting months. On the other hand, if you reveal long gaps between jobs, employers may question your perseverance and dedication. With this in mind, decide what is best for you.

Location Of The Job

Your resume should indicate the city and state you actually work in, not the location of your company's national headquarters. If you work out of your home, include your city as your location; if you live in a suburb, include either the name of the suburb or the more familiar name of the large city you live near.

Clarifying What Your Company Does

If you work for General Motors, General Electric, or Boeing, there is no need to explain what the company does. If your employer is Eastside Masonry Products, it is also unnecessary to elaborate because the company name explains its type of business. If you work for SLRC Corporation, though, you may want to explain in the resume. Handle it this way:

SLRC, Inc., Boston, MA 1996-1999

> **Sales Rep**—For the second largest distributor of electronic components in the Northeast, increased sales over 20% each year.

Or

> **Sales Rep** for the Northeast's second largest distributor of electronic components. Increased sales over 20% each year.

Or

> **Sales Rep**—Increased sales over 20% each year for SLRC, the Northeast's second largest distributor of electronic components.

You can also use such phrases as these to explain what business your employers were in:

> For this social service agency...
> For this social service agency providing help for the homeless...
> For this agency responsible for eliminating chemical hazards in the work place...
> For this not for profit company...
> For this software development firm

Scope Of The Job

The scope of a job includes such things as the products and services of the company, size of company in terms of gross sales, the size of your department in terms of people and dollar budget, the budget you personally work with, and the number of people supervised. It is useful to include the scope of the job if doing so will clarify your level of responsibility or any other key point. To describe the scope of a job you might say, "Managed all finance, accounting, and data processing functions for this $80 million manufacturer of outdoor equipment." Or you might say, "Supervised a staff of four supervisors and managed a department budget of $1.2 million."

How Much Detail And Space Should You Give?

Principles (not laws) to keep in mind:

1) Your current or most recent position is described in the greatest detail as long as it is similar to the type of job you are seeking. Each preceding job is described in slightly less detail.

2) If the job you held three jobs ago is closest to what you're seeking, devote the most detail to it.

3) Jobs held many years ago and jobs that have nothing to do with what you want to do in the future can usually be described in two or three lines, or handled as *Previous Employment* or *Prior Employment*. See page 52 for more on Prior Employment.

How Far Back Should Your Descriptions Go?

If you are a college graduate, go back as far as your first full-time job after graduation. If you went to work right after high school, go back to your first serious full-time job. If you've had a lot of jobs, you can write about your four to six most recent positions, but also include a previous employment section, which merely lists prior positions without descriptions.

Although some of your earlier jobs may not be applicable to your current occupation, employers are still curious about where you've been. Such positions require only a very straightforward two- or three-line description of duties. Or, you might present this information in a prior employment section where you would include your job title, employer, and dates, but would not use any job descriptions.

If you feel certain that it would be detrimental to include all of your jobs, simply do not list those in the most distant past. If you do so be sure not to show dates for education, or any other information which would give away your age or would indicate that some positions are missing.

Current Job Is Less Relevant Than A Prior Job Or Prior Jobs

Generally, it's wise to devote less space to a current, but less relevant job, and more space to an earlier, more relevant job. Another option can be effective: you can separate your experience into two segments, calling one *Related Experience* and the other *Additional Experience*. Instead of Related Experience it could be given a name. For example, if a real estate agent wanted to return to the field of Training and Development, she would call the section Training and Development Experience rather than Related Experience or Relevant Experience.

The related experience section would come first and would generally have the greatest detail. Except for the fact that you have two employment sections, Related Experience and Additional Experience, it is a standard reverse chronological resume. Within each category you should list jobs in reverse chronological order and show the correct dates. Showing the information in this way makes it clear to the employer that even though you are using an atypical format, all jobs have been covered. More importantly, it means that the employer will read your relevant experience first.

Avoid Long Sentences

An effective job description combines short, medium length, and longer sentences. A common mistake in resume writing is to create one long job description using a series of semicolons. It makes the resume hard to read. There is simply no reason to create such a job description. The following will show you why:

Duties: Writing all local copy for top-rated contemporary radio station involving: Dealing with a broad range of advertisers from fashion to food; supervising flow of ad materials from sales through production to on-air status; communicating with advertising agencies re: national advertisers; voicing special news reports, ski reports and various commercials; and overall, maintaining efficient station continuity and copy excellence enhancing advertiser/station relations and decreasing commercial errors.

Quite a mouthful, isn't it. Below is a more readable version. With a little editing here and there, it also has more impact.

Write all local ad copy for this top-rated contemporary radio station. Deal with a broad range of advertisers from fashion to food and supervise the flow of ad materials from sales through production to on-air status. Communicate with advertising agencies regarding national advertisers. Provide special news reports and act as on-air voice for numerous commercials. Have significantly improved advertiser relations by improving copywriting, reducing on-air commercial errors, and making station operations more efficient.

Repetitive Jobs

There are times when you may have had virtually the same job with two or three separate organizations. Take, for example, a real estate agent who has worked for three real estate companies. The duties will not have changed so the agent will want to explain the duties only once and then show what makes him or her effective. You don't have to write, "Same duties as above," which seems awkward. It might look like this:

McKenzie Real Estate, Seattle, WA; ReMax Real Estate, Bellevue, WA; Cole Real Estate, Redmond, WA   1989-1997

Real Estate Agent—Developed a strong real estate referral base by specializing in home listings throughout northern King County, selling homes ranging from $450,000 to $2.5 million. At each branch became either the number one or number two producing agent. Developed a reputation for holding deals together and getting full price for home sellers.

Or

McKenzie Real Estate, Seattle, WA
ReMax Real Estate, Bellevue, WA
Cole Real Estate, Redmond, WA

Real Estate Agent, 1989-1997—Developed a strong real estate referral base by specializing in home listings throughout northern King County, selling homes ranging from $450,000 to $2.5 million. At each branch became either the number one or number two producing agent. Developed a reputation for holding deals together and getting full price for home sellers.

Emphasizing You Were Recruited

Sometimes it's a nice touch to emphasize that you were recruited, indicating your employer sought you out either directly or through a recruiting firm. It also implies that you were happy in your previous job, were not actively looking, and that you left only because a great opportunity was presented to you. At the beginning of your job description you might write, "Recruited away from previous employer by the president of XYZ," or "Recruited away from previous employer and given a mandate to turn around sales and improve quality."

Including Volunteer Experience

Sometimes volunteer experience provides more supporting evidence of your ability to succeed in a new field than any paid experience. Or, if not more valuable, then at least valuable enough that you would want to include it among your work experience. If you choose to include volunteer experience among your work experience, you do not need to label it volunteer. Generally you should just treat volunteer experience like a job, listing the organization and dates as you would if it was employment. Of course, if you feel it is important to indicate that it was volunteer work, you can say so. A good way to handle it is right after the job title by stating, "In this volunteer role, had responsibility for ____, ____, and ____. When incorporating volunteer experience into your work experience, call your employment section *Experience* or *Work History* rather than *Employment* or *Employment History.*

You're Overqualified For Your Job Objective

Perhaps you're seeking a position with a $20 million company and you recently held a senior position with a $250 million company. Coming from a larger company is often considered a bonus by a potential employer, but if you think it will hurt you, simply don't mention the size of your previous employers. Another option is to call your company "a multimillion dollar company" instead of a $250 million company. If you led a department or branch of 120 employees in your previous position and you're likely to have only ten in the job you're seeking, you might change it from "Managed department staff of 120" to "Managed a large department and had full responsibility for meeting production quotas."

Job titles can also be intimidating. If you want to tone down your background, determine whether it might be appropriate to also tone down your job title. This works best in organizations that really don't rely on job titles or where people have more than one title.

The primary way to tone down your resume is in the job description. The premise in resume writing is that everything you write must be true. It is your right, however, to withhold certain information. With that in mind you can simply choose to not mention some of your duties or not indicate your full level of responsibility. Rather than describing your strategic responsibilities, you might concentrate on the tactical side. If you had full P&L responsibility for a branch, you might simply exclude that piece of information. Mention the more mundane aspects of your job.

The real dilemma is what to do with your results. If you cut production costs 8%, saving $45 million and you want to join a firm with total sales of $45 million, you would just mention the 8% reduction. If you have a major result in an area that would unlikely be part of your responsibility, you might choose to not mention that result.

Another form of overqualification comes when you are seeking a position that is at least one level below your last experience. Perhaps you're a project manager for a software development group and you'd rather step back to simply being a senior programmer without all the headaches of project management. Or perhaps you're an engineer who has risen to management and you've determined that you prefer the hands-on work of a design engineer. Even in your management job description, you would emphasize whatever design work you did during that time.

Giving this advice is difficult for me because I believe so strongly in selling your results and your potential. Unfortunately sometimes you can overwhelm people with your background. They may assume you would quickly become bored with their little company or that you would quickly tire of having less responsibility than in the past. It is also possible to intimidate people and cause them to feel that you would quickly be seeking their position. Write your resume in such a way that a hiring manager will not feel intimidated by you nor feel you would quickly become bored. In the cover letter and later in an interview indicate why you find the job attractive. If the hiring manager truly believes you want the job, you will likely not receive the income you enjoyed in the past, but you may end up with a nice job that you really enjoy.

Gaps Of Six Months To One Year

Job seekers are typically ultra-sensitive to any perceived problems with their work history. This often includes concern over gaps in employment. Most gaps are non-issues and don't deserve any concern or thought.

It is true, however, that if you've been unemployed for six months or more, some employers will begin to question why. They may wonder why an organization has not hired you by now.

Look for ways to cover the gap. If you did a little consulting on the side you could mention that. You will need at least one real client, however, because employers will typically ask about your consulting, partially out of interest, and partially out of curiosity as to whether you actually did some consulting. You could even provide some consulting for free just to cover that time, even though your primary focus has been job hunting.

If a 4–12 month gap occurred prior to your current or most recent job, it is generally best to simply ignore it. There's nothing you can do about it and some employers won't even notice it. Certainly you should not make dates prominent. Those who do notice the gap may be mildly curious, but if you have recounted your successes, the gap will have virtually no impact on your being invited to an interview. Sometimes it will be both helpful and appropriate to simply list the starting year and ending year of employment instead of month and year. Frequently this will cover your period of unemployment.

If you are currently unemployed, and have been for over six months, determine if just using a year-to-year format will help you. If so, that is the first thing you should do.

Gaps Of One Year Or More

I had a client who hiked the Cascade Crest trail from Canada to Mexico and took a year off work to do it. Hiking through the Cascade Mountains down into the Sierras is a huge undertaking, one that many start but few complete. He was proud of his accomplishment, but it was important to fill that time with something valuable if possible. We called it a sabbatical and then took one sentence to describe what he did. It was perfect.

If you have gaps of over one year you can choose to ignore them or try to fill them in.

Women should often simply ignore the gap. Employers often assume that you took time out to care for children. You may in fact have been desperately looking for work, but the reader does not need to know that.

Perhaps you were doing several things during a two-year work hiatus, including taking care of an ill relative. Maybe you had been laid off and were looking hard for work when your relative became ill. You may have been a full-time caregiver or perhaps you dropped in every day for an hour or two. In either case you could show that on your resume:

Home care provider for terminally ill relative   1997-1999
Full-time home care provider for a terminally ill relative   1997-1999

Other options include:

Independent travel to Asia and Africa   2001-2003
Personal travel   1996-1997
Adventure travel   1996-1997
Travels to Indonesia and Thailand   1995

Full-time parent and PTA volunteer at Robert Frost Elementary   1991-2002
Full-time parent   1991-2002
Home management   1991-2002
Family management   1991-2002

Independent study   1994-1997
Professional development   1994-1997
Personal growth and development   1994-1997
Student   1996-1998

Volunteer   1993-1995
Volunteer with Habitat for Humanity   1993-1995

The key thing is to determine what you were doing during that work gap and then determine what is the best way to present it. Whatever you state, be prepared to answer questions about what you actually did during that time period when you go to an interview.

Indicating that you consulted during that time period often helps fill in the time. It is important that you actually had some clients since employers will often ask about that. Your consulting may actually account for only a few weeks out of a one year period, but at least on the resume the time is covered. Be prepared to discuss it in telephone screening interviews and face to face interviews. If the employer discovers that you've really only had two one-day assignments, the feeling will be that you were deceptive in the resume.

Work Through Temp Agencies

If you worked for a significant period of time through temporary agencies, it is generally best to simply mention the one you got the most assignments from. If you had a long-term assignment with one organization you could choose to list only that organization and not the temp agency that placed you there.

If some of the organizations you provided temporary services for are well known, you might want to mention some of them.

Blaylock Temporary Services   1996-1998

Office and Administrative Services—Provided clerical services for local firms with assignments ranging from one to twelve weeks. Functions included project management, developing improved systems, desktop publishing, reception, bookkeeping, and collections. Worked for such firms as Merrill Lynch, IBM, Nordstrom, State Farm Insurance, Matthews & Sons, and Jones & Jones Construction. One of the most highly sought temps with Blaylock because of ability to quickly learn existing systems and procedures.

Below is a section of a resume of a person who was seeking permanent employment in the human resources field. Much of her HR experience was gained while working through temp agencies. She felt no need to list the temp agencies since she wanted to put the emphasis on these longer term projects that were more HR oriented. Her shorter stints and those that had nothing to do with HR are simply not mentioned.

LONG-TERM CONTRACT SERVICES   1992-1996
Projects typically ranged from 6 to 15 months. Major projects:

Regal Insurance Group—Employment Specialist

• Provided recruiting services for technical and administrative personnel, including offer letters and reference verification.
• Performed periodic EEO surveys and ensured all goals were met.
• Researched and worked with Corporate Counsel in a training awareness program for supervisors regarding the Americans With Disabilities Act.

Digital Equipment Corporation—Employment Specialist/Recruiter

• Recruited qualified candidates for a hardware design program. Interfaced with department managers and Corporate Relocation Services. Authorized and explained appropriate relocation benefits to managers.
• Provided employee counseling and problem resolution.
• Promoted, planned, and coordinated the Software Business System personnel database, which significantly increased personnel data available to management. Participated in the design of a redeployment plan.
• Developed, implemented, and directed a Reward and Recognition program for a 500-person project, with the award budget totaling $150,000. Program was well received by management and employees.
• Designed a new-hire orientation for the Northeast region.

Unisys—Transition Team

• Initiated and facilitated employer relocation and outplacement services for 95 engineering and manufacturing people. Provided job search training, skills assessment, career counseling, and advocacy.
• Coordinated with 45 high-tech firms to arrange employment interviews both locally and out-of-state. All employees successfully transitioned to other positions with Unisys or outside companies.

IBM—Employee Benefits Office

- Researched, interpreted, and communicated benefit-related issues to coworkers and clients. Acted as liaison between employees and insurance companies to resolve claims.
- Worked with insurance companies to effectively introduce new programs to employees. Assisted in new-hire orientation, 401(k), medical, vision, and dental programs.

Bullets Versus Paragraphs

One debate in the world of resume writing is whether job descriptions should be bulletized or composed using paragraphs. There are fairly strong arguments for both sides. I will cover the arguments for both sides and then explain why I prefer paragraphs.

Like many controversies this one has no simple answers. You need to know the arguments for both sides so you can decide what will work best for you. That is always at the heart of any issue concerning your resume. You don't care what has worked best for others. Your only concern should be whether doing something a certain way will benefit you.

Bullets—The primary argument used to justify bullets is that it makes your resume easier and quicker to scan. In addition, it is usually cited that employers typically devote only 20–30 seconds scanning a resume before deciding whether to place it in the reject pile or in the to-read pile. For that reason it is believed that the bullet resume passes the first test more frequently.

Paragraphs—The argument for paragraphs runs like this: If the paragraphs are kept to 3–7 lines, they are actually easier to read than bullets because most of the text we read—books and newspapers—uses paragraphs rather than bullets.

Let's look at the two arguments. Both bullets and paragraphs can work well for a person. The most important issue is using them properly. If you have too many extremely short bullets, or numerous bullet points of two or three lines, the benefit of bullets has been negated. If you use paragraphs and most are 8–12 lines, such a large block of text will not invite the employer to read the resume. Eye appeal is important in a resume, but neither bulletizing nor using paragraphs is automatically the most eye appealing.

The biggest problem I have seen with bulletized resumes is that they tend to provide too little information. Because the job seeker believes employers want short resumes that can be fully reviewed in thirty seconds, the job descriptions tend to be extremely short. The bullet resume often succeeds well in the first phase of scanning resumes, when the reader is merely determining whether the job seeker has the basic experience that is sought. When the person does have the right experience it will usually end up in the "I'll read" pile, also known as the "I'm interested" pile. So out of 80 resumes, often only 20 will make it to the "I'll read" pile.

Out of the 20 that make it through the scanning phase, only about ten people will be called. The problem for the overly brief, bulletized resume, is that it often lacks supporting evidence and the details that the employer needs to determine who has the right qualities in addition to the right experience. Usually all 20 people who are in the "I'm interested" pile have excellent backgrounds and are very capable people. The reader is now seeking additional information to determine which ten really have everything or nearly everything desired. The reader is also trying to assess other qualities such as the work ethic, whether the person will fit into the work group, and whether the person has the potential to succeed and get promoted.

The problem at that point of the selection process is that the bullet resume often lacks sufficient detail. Most bullet resumes concentrate on listing past duties and tend to be devoid of results. Because of this the bullet resume often does quite well in the screening stage, but it often gets filtered out in the more detailed evaluation phase. There is simply too little information. The reader just doesn't know enough to decide whether the individual should be brought in for an interview.

The problem with the paragraph resume is that it is often verbose. The writer often fails to produce a solid second and third draft, and as a result, is sending out a bloated resume. When it is visually unattractive and hard to scan, it rarely makes it through the scanning stage.

So, the problem is not so much one of style but presentation. My bias, however, is that a well-written and well-designed paragraph resume will usually outsell the well-written, well-designed bullet resume, but not by much. That is why *you* should decide which one you believe will work best for you. As long as you follow all of the recommendations for producing a top-quality resume, you'll do fine.

The job description below is a well-written and visually attractive paragraph-oriented job description. There are no unnecessary words—everything included helps demonstrate that he is an experienced and effective store manager.

Store Manager—4/01-Present. For the third largest music retailer in the Midwest, maintain profitable store operations. Supervise 16 employees and execute corporate sales programs. Evaluate inventory levels and order CDs that will sell in our market. Record and track store sales and overhead costs. Maximize retail sales through effective space allocation, merchandise presentation, and signage.

Recognized as a highly effective trainer and manager. Six of my trainees have been promoted to store manager. Exceeded the monthly revenue plan 23 of the last 24 months. Improved video sales 120% in the first year of a marketing program I developed and tested for the region. Increased store profitability by increasing sales 27% in 2001 and 24% in 2002, while at the same time decreasing labor costs 4% and reducing theft 65%.

The example below is identical except that it uses one large block of text instead of dividing it into two paragraphs. Just the simple process of breaking up the text with two shorter paragraphs and providing more white space makes the above job description more inviting.

Store Manager—4/01–Present. For the third largest music retailer in the Midwest, maintain profitable store operations. Supervise 16 employees and execute corporate sales programs. Evaluate inventory levels and order CDs that will sell in our market. Record and track store sales, payroll, and overhead costs. Maximize retail sales through effective space allocation, merchandise presentation, and signage. Recognized as a highly effective trainer and manager. Six of my trainees have been promoted to store manager. Exceeded the monthly revenue plan 23 of the last 24 months. Improved video sales 120% in the first year of a marketing program I developed and tested for the region. Increased store profitability by increasing sales 27% in 2001 and 24% in 2002, while at the same time decreasing labor costs 4% and reducing theft 65%.

Now let's look at this job description in a bullet format.

Store Manager—4/01–Present.

- For the third largest music retailer in the Midwest, maintain profitable store operations.
- Supervise 16 employees and execute corporate sales programs.
- Evaluate inventory levels and order CDs that will sell in our market.
- Record and track store sales, payroll, and overhead costs.
- Maximize retail sales through effective space allocation, merchandise presentation, and signage.
- Recognized as a highly effective trainer and manager. Six of my trainees have been promoted to store manager.
- Exceeded the monthly revenue plan 23 of the last 24 months.
- Improved video sales 120% in the first year of a marketing program I developed and tested for the region.
- Increased store profitability by increasing sales 27% in 2001 and 24% in 2002, while at the same time decreasing labor costs 4% and reducing theft 65%.

The above bullet format looks good and is easy to read. It provides valuable information with all the bullet points being either one or two lines in length. The example below uses most of the same information, but it has been intentionally shortened to reflect how a typical bulletized resume reads. In this case the writer ends up making the job description too short and simply does not give the reader enough information. In this version the resume loses its heart and soul. Although the key results have been kept in this version, you no longer get a real sense of the person. He just seems more like a set of duties.

Store Manager—4/01–Present.
- Maintain profitable store operations.
- Supervise 16 employees.
- Execute corporate sales programs.
- Evaluate inventory levels and order CDs.
- Record and track store sales and overhead costs.
- Maximize retail sales.
- Recognized as a highly effective trainer and manager.
- Exceeded the monthly revenue plan 23 of the last 24 months.
- Improved video sales 120%.
- Increased profitability by increasing sales 27% in 2001 and 24% in 2002.

From this you can see that both the paragraph format and the bullet format can work well. How well you write each job description ultimately has more to do with the success of your resume than whether you use paragraphs or bullets.

Shifting Careers Or Industries

Any time you make a career or industry shift, you face disadvantages. By definition you're lacking knowledge or experience that most of your competitors possess. Somehow you must overcome these deficits.

First, thoroughly study the career field and industry. Read back issues of the trade journals that people in your new field or industry read. Learn the jargon and learn about the issues that have received the most attention in the past three years. Locate a textbook that covers all aspects of your chosen career field.

Textbooks are great because they're comprehensive. For example, I loan a textbook to clients who want to enter human resources. It covers virtually every aspect of the field without going into too much detail.

Next, talk to three or four people in your desired field or industry. From your reading you should determine areas in which you hope to gain clarification. Pose your questions to these people and get advice on how to enter the field. Ask who the best organizations to work for are. It is also good to say something like, "My background is this and this and my strengths are this and this. Is there anything that will prevent me, or make it difficult for me, to enter this field?"

Once you have the confidence you can make it in the field, you're ready to start your resume, or take your current resume and adapt it to your new field or industry.

Adapt is the key word. Perhaps your current resume mentions a certain duty. Based on your research you realize that in your new field that same duty is known by a different name or term. You would use the term best recognized in your new field.

You should also have been studying job postings you've found in newspaper ads, Internet sites, and on company websites. What are they generally looking for? Are there some areas of knowledge and experience that keep popping up? If so, and if you have that knowledge and experience, make sure it is fully covered in your resume and cover letter.

If you're missing a key piece of experience, but you've done similar things, describe it in such a way that a hiring manager or recruiter will recognize the similarity. Even if your accomplishments come from quite a different field, make the accomplishments prominent because it is critical that an employer can see you've been successful in the past. Employers recognize that those who are successful in one field will likely be successful in another.

Sometimes it works well to have a section labeled *Highlights*, where you would pick out key projects or experiences which used critical skills needed in your new field. Or you might want to consider a functional resume that also utilizes fairly extensive job descriptions.

Special Projects/Activities/Awards

A SPECIAL PROJECTS SECTION can be especially effective for a person with valuable experiences that did not occur on a job. Career changers, recent college graduates, and women reentering the work force can benefit from including a special projects section. The section can also be labeled *Selected Projects, Accomplishments, Achievements, Activities, Projects, Noteworthy Projects, Selected Accomplishments,* or *Noteworthy Accomplishments.* Volunteer experiences with clubs and associations, as well as special projects performed as part of a course, can be presented in this section.

Use these examples as guides to determine whether a special projects section will strengthen your resume.

In the example below, the person had been at home rearing children since 1989. Her special projects section helps make it obvious that she is very capable and energetic.

SPECIAL PROJECTS

As President of PTA, increased parent participation by 26% and funds raised by 34% over the previous year. (2002)

As a United Way fundraising team leader, exceeded the quota by 22%. Honored at banquet as Team Leader of the Year. (2000)

A project or accomplishment seldom requires over 45 words—20–30 words is usually best. Do not try to describe the project in detail—concentrate on results. When writing out each accomplishment in the first draft, feel free to describe it in 50–70 words. Then rewrite it by concentrating on results and include just enough detail so that the reader will understand what you did. Save all other details for an interview. List the projects and accomplishments in reverse chronological order and include the year.

The person below had been active in community affairs for several years and was seeking the directorship of a city-run agency for youth. His employment experience alone would not even have gotten him an interview.

SELECTED PROJECTS

Wrote news articles and special features for *Troy Herald, Outdoor News,* and *College Forum.* (2000-2002)

Lobbied for and obtained Troy city council support for three community parks. Played a key role on the planning committee and helped obtain matching federal funds for this model project. (1998)

Participated as a guest expert on disadvantaged youth for a public affairs radio talk show. (1997)

Organized a basketball camp for disadvantaged youth in Troy and obtained $55,000 in corporate and city funding. Got four coaches and seven college players from three surrounding colleges to donate one week to the program. (1995)

Below is a special projects section used by a 40-year-old woman reentering the work force after completing an MBA. She had held just one part-time research position ten years earlier.

SPECIAL PROJECTS

Developed and coordinated budgets for YWCA and Big Sisters Program, Newark, 1995-2002.

Developed highly successful parenting, exercise, and personal growth programs for the Newark YWCA, 1994-1997.

Planned and coordinated programs for the League of Women Voters, Newark, 1992-1996.

Chaired The Mayor's Conference on Aging, Newark, 1991.

The following example was written by a teacher who was seeking a position in private business and needed to demonstrate non-classroom abilities.

SPECIAL PROJECTS

Interned for Omaha National Bank during the summer of 2002. Received assignments working with retail credit, corporate loans, and trust departments. Developed and completed a survey that determined customer needs. (2002)

Supervised the senior class store that sells school supplies, tickets, jackets, and sweaters. The store maintained a profit each year under my management, something it had never done previously. (1990-1999)

Supervised the research and publication of the Omaha "Volunteer Directory," which helped draw new volunteers into dozens of agencies. (1998)

Developed an intern program to allow students to work in nursing homes and schools for the disabled. Dozens of students gained new skills and several now work in geriatrics. (1989-1995)

Organized record-breaking blood drives and won trophies each year from 1990 to 1994. No other school came close to matching the high percentage of students who donated blood. (1990-1994)

Sometimes other section titles such as *Honors and Awards, Publications,* or *Activities* will work better than *Special Projects.* This recently graduated college student had only one special project to describe so she combined it with an award and called the section, *Awards and Publications.*

AWARDS AND PUBLICATIONS

Chairperson, Task Force on Teaching Quality. Investigated teaching evaluation methods at Reed College and published position paper which helped initiate change in tenure decision policies. (2002)

Senior Class Inspirational Person-of-the-Year Award. (1998)

Licenses/Certificates

ANY LICENSES you hold that are necessary or valuable in the field you are seeking should be listed. Be selective, though. Only list certificates and licenses which are relevant to the new position. Mentioning a real estate license when you want to be a purchasing agent for a tool manufacturer would not add to your qualifications and might cause the employer to wonder whether your preferred career was selling real estate or purchasing.

LICENSES

First Class FCC Radio Telephone Operator (1984)
Commercial Instrument Pilot rating (1983) 840 hours flight time
Private Pilot (1982)

(Electronics technologist and sales rep who flies to see customers)

LICENSES

General Electrical Administrator Certificate - California (1982)
Journeyman Electrician License - California, Nevada, Arizona (1981)
Commercial Instrument Pilot's License (1980)

(Electrician who would like to do some flying for his employer)

LICENSES

FCC, 1981

(Broadcast journalist who needs a Federal Communications Commission license to operate on the air)

LICENSES

CPA - New York, New Jersey, California

LICENSES

Professional Engineer, Mechanical Engineering - Colorado (1989)

CERTIFICATION

Standard Elementary and Secondary, Idaho (Lifetime 1986)

(Teacher)

CERTIFICATE

Personal Coaching, The Coaching Institute (1999)

CERTIFICATE

Human Resources Management, Continuing Education, University of Washington (1997)

Associations/Memberships/ Professional Affiliations

INCLUDING ASSOCIATIONS and memberships can demonstrate you are keeping up to date in your profession and that you have developed useful contacts. For the person making a career change, listing memberships can demonstrate you are serious in making a shift in career direction. Use these categories only if they are relevant and will help you. An engineer might use the following:

PROFESSIONAL AFFILIATIONS

American Chemical Society (1982-Present)
American Institute of Chemical Engineers (1980-Present)

Belonging to associations and professional organizations may mean only that you paid the annual dues, or it could mean that you are active in the organization. If you want a one-page resume and you are three lines over, affiliations can be sacrificed. The section provides interesting, but not usually crucial, information. List any offices held. The examples below can be used as guides. Do not list an affiliation unless you believe its adds credibility or value to your resume. Organizations you are no longer a member of or no longer active in are usually not mentioned, unless you held an office.

Use the examples below as guides for presenting information regarding affiliations.

MEMBERSHIPS

Pacific Northwest Personnel Managers Association (1986–present)
American Society for Personnel Administration (1985–present)

ASSOCIATIONS

Homebuilders Association, member 1984–present
   Officer 1992–present
   Associate of the Year 1996
Board of Realtors, member 1986–present
   Chairperson, Legislative Committee 1992–1996
   Chairperson, Political Affairs and Education 1989–1991

ASSOCIATIONS

Southeast Community Alcohol Center
   President, Board of Directors (1995)
   Member of Board (1992–present)
Northwest Nurses Society on Chemical Dependency
   Treasurer (1995–1998)
   Member (1989–present)

You should rarely mention associations that indicate religious affiliation, political identification, ethnicity, or race. Bias and prejudice are alive and well in the United States and Canada. Don't give people excuses for not meeting you. When we meet people in person we are often able to overcome stereotypes—do everything possible to get that interview.

If you want the reader to know your politics, religion, ethnic background, or race, then by all means indicate the association. You would do so, however, only if you are quite sure that by including that information you have increased the likelihood of obtaining an interview. Don't do it with the rationale that you don't want to work for them if they don't like that part of you. Everyone is biased, much of it on an unconscious level. Get the interview, get the job offer, and then decide if you want to join that organization.

Being active in an association often provides opportunities to demonstrate leadership, program management, and project management skills. As an officer or as a committee chair or cochair, you may have gotten some excellent results in that capacity. As Program Chair, perhaps you brought in the best speakers in the past several years and, as a result, attendance at meetings picked up significantly. You may have, for example, recruited minority mechanical engineers and thus increased membership and the diversity of your organization. You may have coordinated a highly successful conference.

If you've been an officer or a committee chair, ask yourself what you accomplished. How did the organization benefit from your participation. Even if you later choose not to put that in your resume, you have just added stories you can share in interviews.

Once you've identified what your results were, or those results you were at least partially responsible for, determine if mentioning those results will help sell you. If yes, just begin writing.

Memberships

Association of Mechanical Engineers, member—1989–present
    Board Member—1992–1999
    President—1996
        As president, developed a recruiting program that increased minority membership from less than two percent of total membership to over ten percent.
    Treasurer—1994–1995
        Recommended selling booth space for the first time at the state convention and recruited over 45 vendors. This brought in $15,000 in additional revenue, equal to 10% of total association revenue for the year. The number of vendors and revenue have grown significantly each year since.

This section works well for this engineer. His job descriptions do a nice job of selling his technical skills, but he is now seeking to move from senior engineer where he oversees projects and guides younger engineers, to a true management position. The fact that he was an effective president and treasurer helps an employer picture him in a management role.

Publications

A LIST OR DESCRIPTION of publications can be used to demonstrate expertise in a particular field. Listing publications can also demonstrate your abilities in researching, interviewing, and writing. If you are widely published, include only your most relevant articles.

Publications include articles in newspapers, magazines, trade journals, professional journals, school papers, anthologies, or just about anything in printed form with a circulation larger than 50. If you have many publications, but are including only some of them, call the section *Selected Publications*.

PUBLICATIONS

"The Arts in Seattle," *The Weekly*, July 27, 1999
"Marketing A Symphony," *The Conductor*, April 1997
"Will Bach Be Back?" *Symphony News*, November 1995

PUBLICATIONS

"The Dismantling of Student Loans," *University of Kentucky
Daily*, 1999
"Tenureship Under Attack," *University of Kentucky Daily*, 1999
"An Hour With G. Gordon Liddy," *University of Kentucky Daily,* 1998

PUBLICATIONS

"Robots and Production," *Chrysler Employees Newsletter*, 1998
"Automation and Its Impact on Blue Collar Workers," paper presented
at the annual Industrial Psychologists Symposium, 1996

If you are going to use a special projects section and have only one publication, you could include the publication with your projects. For example:

ACTIVITIES

Volunteer Probation Counselor, King County - 1990 to Present
Authored an environmental article published in *Ecojournal* - 1997

Personal Information

USING A PERSONAL DATA SECTION has become outdated. During the 1970s and '80s resumes moved from virtually always having a personal data section, which included such information as age, marital status, height and weight, and health status, to an almost total extinction of such a section. Women began excluding it from their resumes about 20 years ago and men have followed suit. Equal Employment Opportunity legislation also helped hasten the trend. It was never a very helpful section, but it was traditional to include it.

In the 1930s and '40s it was traditional to include religion and the national origin of parents in a personal data section. It was assumed that employers wanted to know and therefore it should be included. Actually, including this information merely gave employers greater opportunity to discriminate.

My recommendation is to exclude it as a section. Sometimes, however, it is useful to use a section called "Personal." It can be used to cover bonding, security clearances, citizenship, willingness to relocate or travel, and any other aspects that might not fit in other categories of a resume.

Include personal information only if you believe the points covered will help sell you.

With that in mind, do not include the old personal data information such as age, height, weight, marital status, and health status. Also, do not include information that reveals age, religion, political affiliation, or ethnicity.

Bonding

Mention you are bondable if your type of work requires it. Essentially, anyone who does not have a prison record is bondable. Bonding is a type of insurance employers take out on employees who handle large amounts of money. If an employee heads to Mexico with thousands of dollars, the employer collects from the bonding company.

Security Clearance

Many people in the military, and civilians working on military projects, have been given security clearances, typically "Secret" or "Top Secret." After leaving the military, it quickly lapses and a new investigation is conducted before reestablishing a security clearance. By including your security clearance, however, you're really saying, "My honesty and integrity were verified by a very thorough investigation; you, too, can trust me." If you held a security clearance within the last ten years, it may be helpful to mention it. Indicate the years it was active. An alternative is to mention your security clearance in your military job description.

Citizenship

Include this information only if you believe an employer might question your citizenship, or if you especially want to let an employer know that you are a U. S. citizen. If you are not a U. S. citizen, you may want to state "Permanent Resident" or indicate your status. There is no need to specify "Naturalized U.S. Citizen;" simply say "U.S. Citizen," or possibly "U.S. Citizen since 1978." Other terms could be "Canadian Citizen since 1959," or "Valid Green Card."

Health

I suggest not listing your health status. Everyone always states "Excellent Health" anyway, so it really has no purpose.

Relocation

If you are willing to relocate and you are contacting national or regional firms, state this in the personal section or merely state at the bottom of the resume, "Willing to Relocate." Do not include a statement in the resume or cover letter that you are unwilling to relocate. Save that for the interview or after you get the job offer.

Travel

If the job is likely to require extensive overnight travel, and you're willing to do so, consider stating that in a Personal section, or in the cover letter. If you are unwilling or unable to travel, or if you could travel only one night a month, say nothing in the resume or cover letter about travel. Be prepared to discuss it in the interview, however.

Languages

If you want to sell your language skills you can create a category called Languages or you can include it within a Personal section. It would typically look like this:

LANGUAGES

> Fluent in reading and writing French
> Conversational in Spanish
> Able to translate and interpret in Russian

See below how languages can be incorporated into a personal section.

Activities

List only those activities that you are heavily involved in and knowledgeable about. More than one person lost a job opportunity because an employer who truly was active in that endeavor simply asked a few questions to compare experiences, only to discover the person knew virtually nothing about it. As small as it seems, none of those people were able to recover in the interview. All credibility had simply been lost.

Personal

Languages: French (12 years of study); Spanish (2 years of study)
Hobbies: Reading literature and business subjects, piano, horseback riding
Willing to relocate

Whether you should include activities or interests is open to debate. Some insist that anything not demonstrating work-related skills or background should be excluded. Others feel a discussion of activities can become an interesting topic of conversation and helps the candidate to be remembered. Both sides make good points. I sometimes include activities because it can make a person seem more real. Select your interests and activities carefully; use only those in which you really are active. Jogging is an excellent activity to include, but don't list it if you run only occasionally.

With each activity you select, ask yourself what impact it will have on an employer. Unless you believe most employers will view it positively, do not include the activity.

Give a consistent picture of yourself. Decide what image you want to convey and then select the appropriate activities. Office workers are wise to state interests that indicate a highly energetic personality.

ACTIVITIES

Strong involvement in marathon running, skiing, and scuba diving.

ACTIVITIES

Actively involved in golf, jogging, and camping.

INTERESTS

Enjoy making exotic breads, creating stained glass windows, and dance exercise activities.

Saying It With Impact

PRODUCING IMPACT through your words is crucial in a resume. Knowing which action verbs, adjectives, and adverbs to use and how to use them will significantly strengthen your resume. This section will cover all of these points and show you how to bring it together in your resume.

ACTION WORDS

A resume should sound alive and vigorous. Using action verbs helps achieve that feeling. "I changed the filing system" lacks punch and doesn't really indicate if the system was improved. "I *reorganized* and *simplified* the filing system" sounds much better and provides more accurate information.

Review the sentences below to get a feel for action words. Then quickly scan the words in the following list and check any you think you might want to use in your resume. Don't try to force them in; use them when they feel right.

Conducted long-range master planning for the Portland water supply system.

Monitored enemy radio transmissions, analyzed information, and identified enemy strategic and tactical capabilities.

Planned, staffed, and organized the intramural sports program for this 1,200-student college.

Produced daily reports for each trial and made sure documents and evidence were handled properly.

Presented seminars to entry-level secretaries and worked to increase the professionalism of secretaries in the county system.

Improved the coordination, imagination, and pantomime techniques of adults through mime and dance training.

Allocated and dispensed federal moneys to nine counties as board member of the CETA Advisory Board.

ACTION VERBS

accelerated	active in	advised	answered	arranged
accomplished	adapted	advocated	anticipated	articulated
accounted for	added	aided	applied	ascertained
accumulated	addressed	aligned	appointed	assembled
achieved	adhered	allocated	appraised	asserted
acquainted	adjusted	altered	apprised	assessed
acquired	administered	amplified	appropriated	assigned
acted (as)	advanced	analyzed	approved	assimilated
activated	advertised	announced	arbitrated	assisted

assured	compelled	derived	established	harmonized
attached	compiled	designated	estimated	harnessed
attained	completed	designed	evaluated	hastened
attended	composed	detailed	examined	headed
attracted	compounded	detected	exceeded	heightened
audited	compromised	determined	executed	helped
augmented	computed	developed	exhibited	hired
authored	conceived	devised	expanded	identified
authorized	concentrated	diagnosed	expedited	illustrated
automated	conceptualized	diagrammed	experienced	imagined
awarded	conciliated	dictated	experimented	implemented
backed	concluded	directed	explained	impressed
balanced	condensed	disciplined	explored	improved
bargained	conducted	discovered	expounded	improvised
bid	confined	discussed	expressed	incorporated
blended	conserved	dispatched	extended	increased
boosted	consoled	dispensed	extracted	indexed
bought	consolidated	displayed	fabricated	induced
braced	constructed	disproved	facilitated	influenced
briefed	consulted	dissected	familiarized	informed
broadened	consummated	disseminated	fashioned	initiated
brought	contacted	dissuaded	filed	innovated
brought about	contracted	distributed	finalized	inspected
budgeted	contributed	diverted	financed	inspired
built	controlled	documented	fixed	installed
calculated	conversed	dominated	focused	instigated
campaigned	converted	doubled	followed up	instilled
canvassed	convinced	downsized	forced	instituted
capitalized on	cooperated	drafted	forged	instructed
cared for	coordinated	dramatized	forecasted	insured
carried out	corrected	drew up	formalized	integrated
catalogued	correlated	drove	formed	intensified
caught	corresponded	earned	formulated	interfaced
caused	corroborated	economized	fostered	interpreted
centralized	counseled	edited	found	intervened
certified	created	educated	founded	interviewed
chaired	criticized	effected	fulfilled	introduced
championed	critiqued	elected	functioned as	invented
charted	culminated in	eliminated	funded	inventoried
checked	cultivated	employed	furthered	invested
clarified	customized	empowered	gained	investigated
classified	cut	enabled	galvanized	judged
closed	dealt	enacted	gathered	justified
coached	debated	encouraged	generated	kept
coined	decided	endorsed	governed	kindled
collaborated	decorated	enforced	graduated	launched
collected	decreased	engineered	grew	lectured
combined	defined	enhanced	grouped	led
comforted	delegated	enlarged	guaranteed	liaised
commanded	delivered	enlisted	guarded	lifted
commended	demonstrated	ensured	guided	listened
communicated	demystified	equipped	halved	litigated
compared	depicted	escalated	handled	lobbied

localized	participated	recruited	served	synchronized
located	perceived	rectified	served as	synergized
logged	perfected	redeemed	serviced	synthesized
lowered	performed	redesigned	set	systematized
magnified	persuaded	redirected	set goals	tabulated
maintained	phrased	reduced	set up	targeted
managed	piloted	reeducated	settled	taught
manipulated	pinpointed	reevaluated	(disputes)	terminated
manufactured	pioneered	referred	shaped	tested
marketed	placed	refined	shifted	took over
mastered	planned	reformed	shipped	traced
maximized	played	regulated	shopped	tracked
measured	positioned	rehabilitated	shut down	traded
mechanized	precipitated	reinforced	simplified	trained
mediated	predicted	rejuvenated	sketched	transacted
mentored	prepared	related	sold	transcended
merchandised	prescribed	remarked	solicited	transcribed
merged	presented	remedied	solidified	transferred
met	presided	remodeled	solved	transformed
minimized	pressured	removed	sorted	translated
ministered	prevented	rendered	sourced	transmitted
mobilized	printed	renewed	sparked	treated
moderated	prioritized	repaired	spearheaded	triggered
modernized	processed	rephrased	specified	trimmed
modified	proclaimed	replaced	spelled out	tripled
molded	procured	reported	spoke	triumphed
monitored	produced	represented	sponsored	troubleshot
motivated	programmed	researched	stabilized	turned around
multiplied	projected	reshaped	staffed	tutored
navigated	promoted	resolved	standardized	uncovered
negotiated	proposed	responded	started	underwrote
netted	protected	restored	stated	unearthed
nominated	proved	restructured	steered	unified
nourished	provided	resulted in	stimulated	united
nursed	publicized	retailed	stipulated	updated
nurtured	published	retrieved	straightened	upheld
obliged	purchased	revamped	streamlined	urged
observed	quadrupled	reversed	strengthened	upgraded
obtained	questioned	reviewed	stressed	utilized
offered	raised	revised	stretched	vacated
opened	ramrodded	revitalized	structured	validated
operated	ran	revived	studied	verbalized
optimized	ranked	revolutionized	substituted	verified
orchestrated	realigned	riveted	succeeded	vitalized
ordered	realized	routed	summarized	voiced
organized	reassured	safeguarded	supervised	won
originated	received	saved	supplemented	won over
outlined	reclaimed	scheduled	supplied	worked
overcame	recognized	screened	supported	wrote
overhauled	recommended	secured	surpassed	
oversaw	reconciled	selected	surveyed	
packaged	recorded	separated	swayed	

DESCRIBING RESULTS WITH KEY ACTION VERBS

The typical resume merely lists duties and does little else to sell the person. One of the best ways to sell yourself is to describe accomplishments in terms of *results*. While duties are often represented by phrases such "Responsible for...," results are frequently conveyed by using the verb *developed*. For example, one might say, "Developed a secretary's manual which explained hundreds of procedures and significantly reduced clerical errors." This person's duties were typing, filing, and answering phones, so to show that she stood above the rest, she demonstrated results.

When describing projects and results, one of the best words to use is *develop*. More than any other word, it seems to be so useful and it clearly expresses what a person wants to convey. While *develop* is an excellent word, when used three or four times in a resume it becomes overworked and loses impact. You'll need substitutes. The most common are:

created	instituted
designed	introduced
established	set up
implemented	

Other verbs that may be appropriate substitutes for develop in certain circumstances would be:

built	elaborated	generated	planned
composed	enhanced	installed	prepared
constructed	fabricated	organized	produced
coordinated	fashioned	originated	refined
cultivated	formed	perfected	revamped
devised	formulated	pioneered	

Here are examples that demonstrate how to describe results in various situations. In parentheses are words that could have been used instead of *develop*.

Developed (devised, prepared, produced) a creative financing/purchasing package to obtain 1900 acres of prime California farmland.

Pioneered a mime program for gifted children age 8-12.

Developed (designed, established) training programs for new and experienced employees and supervised the new employee orientation program.

Set up apprenticeship programs for five skilled trades at the Physical Plant Department.

Developed and implemented an information and referral service for consumer complaints and human rights issues.

Coordinated the company marketing effort, including advertising and promotions.

Another set of action verbs is particularly useful when you are describing a result and plan to quantify the result:

achieved	increased
cut	produced
eliminated	saved

VERB TENSES

Describe your current job in the present tense. For all previous jobs, write in the past tense. You may need to describe an event in your current job, such as a project that has already been completed. In that case, use the past tense to describe the project while using the present tense in the remaining portions of your current job.

Example:

STORE MANAGER - 6/90–Present. Oversee total operation of the store, supervise and schedule employees, and complete monthly profit and loss statements. <u>Designed</u> a new inventory system which has saved over $10,000.

Since the inventory system was designed over a year ago, it must be described in the past tense.

USING ADJECTIVES AND ADVERBS

Adjectives and adverbs are words that describe things and actions. Used appropriately, they can enliven a resume and describe more accurately what you did. While using adjectives and adverbs can add sparkle to a resume, if overused, they can actually weaken a phrase. Notice how they change the tone of the sentences below. In each example the second sentence has more impact.

1. Worked with industrial engineers.

   Worked <u>closely and effectively</u> with industrial engineers.

2. Initiate and develop working relations with local, state, and federal agencies.

   Initiate and develop <u>outstanding</u> working relations with local, state, and federal agencies.

3. Establish rapport with customers.

   <u>Quickly</u> establish rapport with customers.

Here are more examples of how to use adjectives and adverbs effectively:

Dealt <u>tactfully</u> and <u>effectively</u> with <u>difficult</u> customers.

Presented technical material in <u>objective</u> and <u>easily understood</u> terms.

<u>Consistently</u> maintained <u>high</u> profit margins on all projects.

<u>Significantly</u> improved communications between nursing administration and staff.

Completed <u>virtually</u> all apartment units ahead of schedule.

<u>Continually</u> streamlined policies and procedures to create a more reasonable work schedule.

A list of adjectives and adverbs is given below. Review the list and check the ones you think may be useful to you. Try to include them but don't force it. Don't use a word or phrase unless it really fits your personality and strengthens your resume. After writing each draft, go back through the list to see if still another word or two might be useful.

accurate/accurately
active/actively
adept/adeptly
advantageously
aggressive/aggressively
all-inclusive/
   all-inclusively
ambitious/ambitiously
appreciable/appreciably
astute/astutely
attractive/attractively
authoritative/
   authoritatively
avid/avidly
aware
beneficial/beneficially
broad/broadly
capable/capably
challenging
cohesive/cohesively
competent/competently
complete/completely
comprehensive/
   comprehensively
conclusive/conclusively
consistent/consistently
constructive/
   constructively
contagious
continuous/
   continuously
contributed toward
decidedly
decisive/decisively
deft/deftly
demonstrably
dependable/
   dependably
diligent/diligently
diplomatic/
   diplomatically
distinctive/distinctively
diverse/diversified
driving
easily
effective/effectively
effectually
efficient/efficiently

effortless/effortlessly
enthusiastic/
   enthusiastically
entire/entirely
especially
exceptional/
   exceptionally
exciting/excitingly
exhaustive/exhaustively
experienced
expert/expertly
extensive/extensively
extreme/extremely
familiar with
familiarity with
firm/firmly
functional/functionally
handy/handily
high/highly
highest
high-level
honest/honestly
imaginative/
   imaginatively
immediate/immediately
impressive/impressively
incisive/incisively
in-depth
industrious/
   industriously
inherent/inherently
innovative/innovatively
instructive/instructively
instrumental/
   instrumentally
integral
intensive/intensively
intimate/intimately
leading
masterful/masterfully
meaningful/
   meaningfully
natural/naturally
new and improved
notable/notably
objective/objectively
open-minded
original/originally

outstanding/
   outstandingly
particularly
penetrating/
   penetratingly
perceptive/perceptively
pioneering
practical/practically
professional/
   professionally
proficient/proficiently
profitable/profitably
progressive/
   progressively
quick/quickly
rare/rarely
readily
relentless/relentlessly
reliability
reliable/reliably
remarkable/remarkably
responsible/responsibly
rigorous/rigorously
routine/routinely
secure/securely
sensitive/sensitively
significant/significantly
skillful/skillfully
solid/solidly
sophisticated/
   sophisticatedly
strategic/strategically
strong/strongly
substantial/
   substantially
successful/successfully
tactful/tactfully
thorough/thoroughly
uncommon/
   uncommonly
unique/uniquely
unusual/unusually
urgent/urgently
varied
vigorous/vigorously
virtual/virtually
vital/vitally
wide/widely

Resume Tips

IN THIS SECTION, many important points are covered to help you make the most out of your resume.

Making It Readable

Since resumes are often skimmed the first time through, it must be easy for the reader to pick up key pieces of information quickly. Using long paragraphs of over ten lines or using heavy blocks of text can cause readers to quickly put your resume aside.

Honesty

Throughout your resume you should be honest and accurate—but positive. Whatever is stated should be true, but you do not need to tell everything. Both in resumes and in interviews you have a right to withhold certain information.

Never claim to have a college degree if you don't have one. Neither should you claim a degree from a college other than the one that bestowed it on you. This is the easiest information for employers to check. I know a person who was just 20 credits short of a degree and chose to indicate that he had the degree. He received an offer for a very good position, but it was rescinded after it was discovered he had lied. He received a tongue lashing from the executive who had befriended him and recommended that he be hired.

For the same reasons, do not claim responsibilities that were not yours, nor job titles that would inflate your actual level of responsibility.

Also, do not exaggerate your accomplishments. There is virtually never a need to do so. Do your best to state your results as accurately as possible and in an interview, be prepared to discuss how you accomplished those results. Results do not have to be stupendous in order to mention them. Simply showing how you improved a procedure or process is good enough. The size of the improvement is less important than demonstrating that you are always looking for better ways to do things.

Do not claim that you did something when it was really done by someone else. If you were part of a team, then you can share in the results of the team. Emphasize your primary responsibilities and then describe both your specific results and the results of the team.

Of course, if you're a supervisor, you can take credit for the successes of your team. In an interview be sure to describe your role in your team's results, then show that you are a good supervisor by giving team members credit for the outcome and indicating that you couldn't have done it without their teamwork, creativity, and energy.

Studies by search firms and reference check firms indicate that 25% to 35% of all applicants lie on their resumes or job application forms. To counter this trend of inflating the truth, many firms are going to great lengths to verify information provided by the top two candidates. Don't become a finalist only to be eliminated because you stretched the truth. It isn't worth it.

What To Call It

It's not necessary to type *Resume, Qualifications Brief, Profile,* or any other such title at the top of your resume. Everyone will know it's a resume just by glancing at it.

Color And Type Of Paper

While paper is available in a variety of colors, textures, weights, and sizes, there are some standard guidelines you should follow. The color of paper you choose can definitely make a difference in the number of interviews you get. White is always a safe color, but my studies reveal that buff or off-white paper provides even better results. (Keep in mind that if you believe the resume will be scanned it should be white or a very light off-white.)

The best paper I have found so far is the 20- or 24-pound classic linen made by several paper manufacturers. (I do like the classic linen in white—it is very classy.) Many people also like classic laid. Both classic linen and classic laid have a texture that implies quality without overdoing it. If you prefer a paper without a textured surface, choose one with a "rag" or cotton fiber content of at least 25%. For those seeking management positions a light gray can be effective. Blues and greens have not tested well. Color should have a positive effect; this will nearly always mean you should use light shades. Dark grays and browns or bright colors are not effective. Twenty-pound paper is always a safe standard. A slightly heavier paper is fine, but avoid heavy stocks. Monarch size paper (7" x 10") is fine for thank you notes, but stick with 8½" x 11" for your resume. Good papers have a watermark, so make sure it is right side up if you print it or copy it yourself. Photocopy shops usually check for this, but it's wise to double check this yourself.

You can buy all types of fancy papers with borders and other nifty stuff. It's pretty, but I wouldn't use it. It feels like overkill and typically distracts from you and what you've said about yourself. Most employers are not impressed.

Just as I would not buy paper with preprinted borders, I would not use your word processing capabilities of putting in borders or boxes around text in the resume. If you are pursuing an artistic type of position, the resume can provide an opportunity to demonstrate your design ability. Even then I would keep it simple. Consider including photocopies of a few key examples of your artistic or graphic work.

Avoid Overusing Word Processing Features

One danger of using today's feature-laden word processing programs is that people are tempted to overuse such features as different fonts, bolding, underlining, and italics. This produces a resume which looks busy and is overdone. The example following is exaggerated to help you see what I mean; you'll notice your eyes going all over the place, unable to read or concentrate on the job description.

GENERAL MOTORS, Detroit, Michigan 10/97-Present

> <u>SENIOR ENGINEER</u> - As part of a team of **Software Quality Assurance Engineers,** evaluate <u>CAD/CAM</u> software and *make* recommendations for improvements before software is made available to users within the company. Review <u>functional specifications</u> to *ensure* all portions are testable and fully meet **user needs.** REDUCED time necessary to fully evaluate software from **45 days** to **18 days.**

As a rule of thumb regarding the use of such features—keep it simple.

Size of Type

There are three sizes of type which are typically used for resumes: 12-point, 11-point, and 10-point. I generally recommend using 12-point, because it is a little larger and more readable than 10-point. If you are using 12-point and your resume just barely goes over a page long, you may want to make minor adjustments to make it all fit on one page. Widening the length of the lines may be all you need, or you may choose to reduce the top and bottom margins. Reducing the type size to 11-point may do the trick, and it is also very readable.

If you suspect your resume may be scanned into an employer's databank, use 11- or 12-point. With 10-point the scanner and OCR software will make more errors and will diminish the quality of your resume. For more on scanning see page 134.

Photographs

Photographs should rarely be submitted with resumes, although they may be appropriate for models, flight attendants, performers, and media personalities. Many organizations are leery of receiving photographs with resumes because it increases the likelihood of age and race discrimination charges. Employers are nearly unanimous in preferring not to receive photographs.

Confidentiality

Employers who receive your resume will rarely inform your current employer. Even if they know your boss, they understand the importance of confidentiality. I would say that only if your boss or company has a reputation for firing people for "disloyalty" should the steps listed below even be considered. If you are truly concerned about confidentiality, your options include:

1. Write "Confidential" at the top of your resume.

2. At the bottom of the resume type and underline, "Please do not contact employer at this time."

3. Replace the name of your present employer (and possibly your next-to-last employer) with a description such as, "A major manufacturer of automotive parts," "A Fortune 500 Corporation," or "A National Retail Chain."

4. Utilize an executive recruiter (headhunter). A recruiter will sell you to an employer over the phone without revealing your name and will send your resume only if the employer is particularly interested.

If your boss suspects you are looking, but you know you are considered a valuable employee, you have nothing to worry about. You are more likely to get a raise than to get into trouble. In one sense, everyone is looking for another job—some are just more active than others. When headhunters call regarding truly great jobs, I guarantee you, virtually everyone is willing to talk. The World War II saying was "Loose lips sink ships." That's good advice at work also—do not tell even your most trusted friends at work that you're actively looking.

Salary

Salary history and salary requirements should virtually always be omitted from a resume to avoid giving anyone a cause for eliminating you.

Want ads frequently ask for desired salary or salary history. I would recommend ignoring the requested information. In this country what a person earns is one of the most personal and confidential bits of information we possess. Not only are you giving away your bargaining position when you state your current salary or salary requirements, but you are giving private information to people you don't even know.

If you feel compelled to acknowledge the request, you might simply write in your cover letter, "Salary is negotiable." Another option when asked for desired salary is to indicate a large range. For someone seeking $40,000 it might state, "Seeking $37,000 - 47,000 depending on responsibilities." For someone seeking $80,000, a $15,000 range might be used.

Relocation

If you are seeking a position with a national company, you'd better be prepared to relocate. Since many people are unwilling to relocate, a statement under "Personal" or "Additional," stating "Willing to Relocate," will make you stand out in a positive way. If you don't have a personal section, merely type it in at the end of the resume.

Reason For Leaving

Everyone has a reason for leaving a job, but the resume is rarely the place for stating it. Invariably an attempt to explain the reason will simply raise more questions than it answers. Save the explanation for an interview where the issue can be handled much more effectively. The only time I ever mention in the resume the reason for leaving is if the company or department moved out of state or the company went out of business. Even then it's best to mention it subtly, so that it just seems to be a part of the resume. Below is an example:

Lead, Order Entry Department—Responsible for scheduling, training, and supervising four employees. Delegated work load, resolved customer problems, and coordinated with other departments. Developed procedures which increased order entry accuracy by 35%. Left due to a merger with NOP Industries when the order entry department was moved to Chicago.

This explanation works well. The emphasis would always be on the job description and demonstrating your successes. The reason for leaving is simply tagged on at the end and it provides useful information. On the person's resume the reason for leaving two earlier positions was not provided. Other reasons given can include:

Left when the company downsized and position was eliminated.

Company went out of business in 2002.

The key point to make when a downsizing occurs is to state that the position was actually eliminated. That clarifies that they weren't dissatisfied with your work, terminated you, and then replaced you with someone else. Although explaining that you left during a downsizing is acceptable, I will rarely mention the reason for leaving when it is due to a downsizing. It is usually better to explain the situation during an interview.

I will often mention the reason for leaving when it was due to a plant closure, the company went out of business, or when a plant closes and moving 80 miles or more was required to keep your job.

Abbreviations

Avoid abbreviations that may cause confusion to readers who are not familiar with them. As a rule of thumb, if you are certain that *everyone*, from the personnel clerk who may screen the resume to the person with power to hire you, will recognize and understand it, then consider using the abbreviation. Keep in mind, however, that words are more visually attractive when spelled out. For this reason I generally recommend spelling out the names of states, particularly in the address at the top of a resume. The trend, however, is to use the two-letter abbreviation for states used by the Postal Service. In essence you can't go wrong if you spell out the states or use the two-letter abbreviation. The key is to be consistent throughout the resume. Some abbreviations such as "B.A.," "M.A.", and "Ph.D." are preferred over spelling them out.

If you are going to use an abbreviation or acronym more that once, spell it out the first time it is used and then put the acronym in parentheses. From that point on you can use the abbreviation or acronym. An example would be: Introduced a Total Quality Management (TQM) program which reduced rejected parts by 22%.

Know The Tradition Of Your Field

Learn what is traditional and accepted for resumes in your industry or field. Although I have tried to give you the principles for writing a powerful resume, I can't talk about, nor do I know, all the traditions in all fields. While I recommend limiting most resumes to two pages, the four or five page curriculum vitae (the term for resumes used by academics), is perfectly acceptable. There may also be certain formats which are most accepted and expected in particular fields. When you find that is the case, go along with that tradition unless you have a compelling reason not to.

Creative License

In some ways my advice about resumes follows tradition, in some ways it does not. A conservative, tried-and-true approach often works best. This, for example, is why I recommend off-white paper. At the same time I also encourage you to be creative. Can you think of something which might just give you an edge over your competition? When you come up with an unusual idea, ask yourself, "Will it work for me; can I pull it off with my personality?" An approach tried by someone with an artistic, flamboyant personality might be readily accepted, while that same thing attempted by a more conservative, traditional person would not. If you are about to try something rather unusual or "far out," get the opinions of others first, or try it out in a few cases to see what kind of response it gets.

I mention the creative side because over the years clients have suggested trying things which I never would have thought of. Sometimes I caution against the idea, but more frequently I give my full encouragement. When clients use these creative ideas, they've usually worked.

Selecting A Format

The format is essentially the layout of the resume. Many of the sample resumes included in *Resume Power* use the layout that I prefer, after having tested many during the past 15 years. An example is found on page 187. I like the format because it is easy to scan and it makes excellent use of space. Throughout the resume there is a balance of white space and text. There are literally dozens of formats with dozens of variations. Flip through the resume section from page 155 to page 216 and you'll probably find a format you like. If you've found a format in the past that you like, and feel it would do a good job of presenting your background, by all means use it. If you do not have a preferred format, you cannot go wrong if you use the primary format used in most of the sample resumes. It is time tested and well accepted.

Always Be Careful About Always And Never

Resume books are often filled with advice such as *always* do this, and *never* do that. I rarely use always or never, because there are exceptions. Much better to suggest *usually, almost always, rarely,* or *almost never.* Listen to my advice and that of others, but ultimately you must do what you feel will work best for you in your situation.

Effectively Show Your Name, Address, Phone, Cell Phone, E-mail Address, and Web Site

A reader's eye virtually always goes to the top of the resume to see a person's name and address. For this reason, the very first impression of you is created by the appearance of your name and address at the top. Naturally you want this to create a favorable impression.

My favorite heading:

Rob Thomas

23654 Savoy Lane
Houston, TX 77058
(713) 483-0098 (H)   (713) 476-0093 (C)
rthomas@mind.com

I like this heading. Everything is centered and the name is 2-3 point sizes larger than the rest of the text. In this case the text is 11 point and the name is 14 point. The name stands out, but it is not so much larger that it visually blasts the reader. I prefer not to bold the address.

If you have a cell phone and will keep it on most of the time during your job search, go ahead and list it. It is highly useful to have voice mail or to have a recording device on your home phone. When trying to reach you, most employers will leave a message asking you to call them. Including your e-mail address is especially useful. If you have created a web portfolio you would also include your web address, usually on the same line as your e-mail address.

Below are some variations. I've used 12 point for the name and 10 point for the rest.

Rob Thomas	**ROB THOMAS**	**ROB THOMAS**
23654 Savoy Lane	23654 Savoy Lane	23654 Savoy Lane
Houston, TX 77058	Houston, TX 77058	Houston, TX 77058
(713) 483-0098	713-483-0098	713/483-0098
rthomas@mind.com	rthomas@mind.com	rthomas@mind.com

In the first example the name uses upper and lower case while the second uses all caps. In the third example the name uses "small caps." After the first letter, the remaining letters in the first and last name are also capitals, but they are slightly smaller than the capitalized first letter. The only other differences are in the phone number. The first uses parentheses for the area code while the second sets the area code off with a hyphen and the third example uses a slash. Some people show the phone number this way: 713.483.0098. All are appropriate.

These days most people use the Postal Service two-letter state code, such as TX for Texas, but if you like, feel free to spell it out.

In each of the examples above I've included the person's e-mail address. If you have an e-mail address, include it. Some employers find it to be the preferred way to communicate, while others would contact you by e-mail if they failed to reach you by phone after one or two attempts.

Show your name at the top the way you want to be called. I'm Thomas Fuller Washington, but I go by Tom and few know my middle name. If your resume says Robert you'll be called Robert even if you prefer Rob or Bob. If you write Elizabeth but prefer Liz, write Liz. There is no reason to include your middle name or middle initial.

All of the examples in this section had everything centered. That is the most common way to present your name and address but there are other ways as well. For additional ways to create a heading turn to the following pages: 174, 186, 196, and 209.

In virtually all cases your name should appear at the top. Visually that's the best place for your name. When resumes are scanned into an electronic resume databank it becomes critical. Some systems automatically assume that the top line is your name. For that reason it is best to stick with tradition and put your name at the top, with nothing else on that line except your name.

Showing Work Numbers On Your Resume

If it would be virtually impossible for you to carry on a conversation with a recruiter or employer while at work, it is best to leave your work phone number off the resume. Nearly all such calls however, that come in during work hours last only a few minutes. As long as you keep your calls short you should not be concerned about using company time.

Justified Left And Right Or Ragged Right?

Books and magazines are virtually always printed using a justified right and left format. This means all of the type starts in a straight line on the left and all type ends at the same spot on the right. This paragraph is justified left and right.

With your word processing software you can choose either a justified right format or a "ragged" right format. With a ragged right format, the lines do not end at the same spot. Research is said to have demonstrated that print is easiest to read when it is ragged right. I've never seen the results of any research on this matter, but this has been the standard wisdom for a long time. If it is true, why do books and magazines prefer a justified left and right format? By the way, this paragraph uses ragged right. Typically I have used a ragged right format for resumes, but I believe a justified right format looks fine also. It's your choice. See pages 158 and 163 for a ragged right and pages 187 and 210 for a justified left and right resume.

Simple Tricks To Use With Your Word Processor

Word processing is a wonderful tool, particularly for those of us who remember using typewriters, Whiteout, and carbon paper. There are two particularly helpful tricks that you can do with a word processor: You can use the cut and paste features, and you can manipulate both the font size and margin settings to get your resume to the right number of pages.

Copy and Paste. I strongly encourage you to tailor your resume for each job you apply for. This can take anywhere from two minutes to an hour, but usually can be done in under a half hour. Any time you add new points to your resume, save them in a file labeled Copy & Paste. Once you accumulate numerous sentences you will find that when responding to an ad, you may already have covered that point in a previous resume. In that way you can save time by not always having to create a new sentence when you already have a good one.

To put a sentence in a Copy & Paste file, highlight the sentence and click on the copy icon on your toolbar. Then open the file you've already labeled Copy & Paste, and simply click on the paste icon. The text will appear. Then click on the save icon.

When you're responding to an ad and you already have a great sentence or paragraph to add to your standard resume, go into the Copy & Paste file, highlight it, click on copy, go to the resume you're working on, put your cursor where you want it to go, and click on paste.

Another way is to keep a printed copy of what is in your Cut & Paste file. When you see a sentence you like, simply key it in where it is appropriate.

Changing font size and margins to squeeze more on a page. Sometimes you face a situation where you want a one-page resume, yet several lines of type have spilled over to a second page. Try changing the top and bottom margins. You can often reduce your top and bottom margin to .6 inches and still have plenty of white space. A one-inch margin is nice but not necessary. If I started with one inch at the top and bottom and I had just two lines to get onto page one, I would immediately reduce the top and bottom to .8 inches. If that did not work I would decrease the top and bottom margin in increments of one tenth of an inch.

I might also reduce the right and left margins unless I believed that the resume was likely to be scanned. Although I like one-inch margins left and right, I sometimes reduce them to .7 inches.

A third way to get more words onto a page is to reduce the font size. For readability and scannability, a 12-point font is best. Sometimes, however, just reducing the font size to 11.5-point will do the trick. If not, reduce the font size in half-point increments. Highlight all the text you intend to reduce in size, then click on the font size icon on your tool bar, key in the font size you want, then hit the enter key and the font size will instantly change.

Do not go smaller than 10-point type. An 8- or 9-point font is difficult to read and it scans poorly for resume databanks.

A fourth way to get more on a page is to reduce the space between paragraphs. If you are using a 12-point font, every time you do a double space, it will make a 12-point space between lines. After you've finished the resume, those spaces between lines can be changed from 12-point to 8-point or even 6-point. There will still be sufficient white space between paragraphs.

If you want to try this with Word, here's how to do it. Put the cursor on the first paragraph symbol you want to reduce in size. (There will be paragraph symbols throughout your resume if you are using that function. If you don't see the paragraph symbol, go up to the tool bar and click on the paragraph symbol. Instantly your resume will be filled with paragraph symbols and there will be a dot between each word.) Leave the cursor there and click on the font size. Then just key in 8 or 6. Hit the enter key and the space will be reduced. Move the cursor to the next paragraph symbol and hit the F4 key (the repeat key). Go through the resume pressing the F4 key any time you want to reduce the font size.

Don't Rely On Spell Check

As great as spell check is for those who don't spell well, you must still proofread all of your documents before sending them out. Spell check will catch both typos and misspellings, but it does have a weakness. It cannot determine if the properly spelled word you used is truly the correct word. In other words if you wrote a sentence stating, "I went their for my vacation and returned there pillowcase." Spell check would not catch the two errors. It should actually read, "I went there for my vacation and returned their pillowcase." Both *their* and *there* are real words in the dictionary of any spell check program, but the wrong words were used. Many examples of similar problems could be used. If the correct word was *waste* and you spelled it *waist,* spell check would not catch the error. If you intended to type *as* but actually typed *at,* a spell checker would not pick that up.

By all means use spell check. It's great for picking up misspellings and words that have letters reversed in them like *worte* instead of *wrote,* missing letters like *lttle* for *little,* or too many letters like *tellling* instead of *telling.* Mistakes like this are often difficult for proofreaders to pick up.

No Typos, No Errors

Whether or not you use spell check, you must produce a resume with no errors and no typos. This virtually always requires at least three readings on your part, and readings by two to three other people. Make sure one of your readers is a grammarian so that commas are where they should be and tenses are correct throughout.

Your cover letter is an important document and should be perfect as well. If you tailor each cover letter to each ad, you're going to be making many changes and additions to it. This makes perfection considerably harder. My recommendation is still to proofread each letter three times and let one or two others read it as well. A spouse or close friend will generally catch errors that have gotten past you.

Put Your Name At The Top Of Page Two

It is usually a good idea to place your name at the upper left corner of page two and also indicate it is page two. Sometimes pages get separated and having your name at the top would help get page one and page two back together again. It would look like this:

Joe Stephens
Page Two

If space is tight you can save a line like this:

Joe Stephens—Page Two

If you absolutely have no room, eliminate your name from the top.

Skip The Clip Art

There's a lot of clip art available from clip art books and from the Internet. On a brochure or newsletter the art can add a nice touch. Such art virtually never belongs on a resume unless you're the artistic type and are using the art to show your graphics ability. Preparing a graphically appealing resume is all most people need to do to demonstrate they have nice taste.

Learn The Jargon

Every occupation has its own jargon and buzz words. Learn the jargon and make sure you use terms correctly. Then look for ways to get those words into your resume and cover letter. Not only will this help when a recruiter is doing a key word search to find your resume in an electronic resume database, but it will also help when a real live person is reading it. Using the right buzz words creates the impression that "you're one of us." Without it you seem like more of an outsider. Outsiders rarely get called for interviews. Make sure you use the jargon in appropriate places—don't force it in.

Use Simple Words

Some people believe that the four-syllable word is always superior to the two-syllable word. It is often believed that longer words demonstrate intelligence and a strong vocabulary. Actually, good writing consists of using just the right word that says exactly what you want it to say. That often means a one- or two-syllable word. Keep your writing simple and straightforward. If a two-syllable word captures the thought you want, it's better than a longer word.

Use Only Words You're Familiar With

The problem writers often face with using long or unfamiliar words, is that they frequently use them incorrectly. Your resume is rarely the place to try using new words. For one, it's rarely necessary, and two, using a word incorrectly will seriously damage that all-important first impression of you.

Keep Your Key Information On Page One

Qualifications, education, and your two most recent jobs usually belong on page one. If the employer scans your resume and does not find enough of interest on page one, the person will often set it aside before looking at page two. If your most important or valuable experience took place three or more jobs ago, see Current Job Is Less Valuable Than A Prior Job on page 56 on how to bring your key experience to the forefront.

How To Create A Two-Page Resume With Three Pages

It is usually best to keep a resume to two pages. Two pages have become the standard length and a third page could cause some employers to be less inclined to read the resume. If the resume is well written and each point is as concise as possible, however, most readers will have no trouble with three pages. Nevertheless, sometimes it is best to have a three-page resume that is really just a two-page resume with a one-page addendum.

Here's how it works. Some people have long training sections containing 10-25 workshops or courses that are worth mentioning. With a long section like that I would never put it on the first page. When it goes on the second page it will sometimes spill over onto a third page. When that occurs I will take the entire training section and move it to a third page. At the top it will be called Training Addendum. With this wording you have just created a two-page resume with a one-page addendum. In the employer's mind it is a two-page resume. Addendum means supplemental so the reader knows that the information contained on that page may be valuable but is not essential.

If you have two or more categories to put on the third page, such as Training and Publications, you would simply type Addendum at the top and then include the material for the two categories. You would typically bold the titles of both categories.

Claiming It Doesn't Make It So

Just because you say something or claim something doesn't mean the employer will automatically accept it or be impressed. Back up your claims with evidence whenever possible. Evidence or proof is not always necessary to cause a person to accept or believe a point you are making, but it sure helps. See page 46 for more on providing evidence.

Determine What You Want To Emphasize With Your Job Descriptions

Use bold type for what you most want to emphasize whether it be your title or the name of the organization. I usually bold the job title. If you want to emphasize dates (something I virtually never recommend) put them out to the far left.

A Useful Font

There is a font style known as small caps. It gives you another format for listing employer names or job titles. Here's what it looks like:

Exeter Manufacturing
Exeter Manufacturing
EXETER MANUFACTURING

The middle version uses the small caps in bold. Notice that the first letter E in Exeter is a full-sized capital letter. The remaining letters in Exeter are also capitals, but they are slightly smaller. It's just a nice touch that can be used. It also looks good for your name.

How you create small caps may vary depending on your word processing software. With Word 97 and Word 2000 in your tool bar, click Format. Then click Font. Under Effects you'll see one that says Small Caps. Click on the box, hit OK, and start typing in small caps. Use the cap key just as you normally would if you want the first letter to be a full-sized capital letter.

Multiple Resumes

In order to sell you, a resume must demonstrate focus. If you are considering more than one type of job, you may need two or more resumes. In this case you may want to write only one resume, but give it more flexibility by using more than one objective, leaving everything else the same. This is easy to do with word processing.

An example will help. Jim is a very good computer salesperson with no desire to leave sales, but we created three different objectives for him to use in three different versions of his resume: "OBJECTIVE: Computer Sales;" "OBJECTIVE: Electronics Sales;" and "OBJECTIVE: Sales." Nothing else in the resume was changed. Computer companies got one resume, electronics companies got another, and if Jim saw something interesting outside those two industries, he sent the one that said "Sales."

Changing the objective, however, may not be adequate if the types of jobs you are seeking are considerably different from each other. Writing a new or modified qualifications section for each objective will often do the trick. Far less frequently, you may need to make small changes in the employment section. Typically that consists of adding an area of experience which was a very small part of your job, but one which will help sell you with that particular objective. You would also look for ways to get the right buzz words in.

Using Cover Letters For Flexibility

A cover letter should accompany each resume you mail out and should be individually typed. The cover letter provides an excellent opportunity to mention points you know are important to that particular employer, but are not mentioned in the resume.

Answering Want Ads

When a want ad provides specific job requirements, there are a number of ways to respond. You can

1. Send your resume with a standardized cover letter;

2. Send your resume with a custom-written cover letter discussing key points mentioned in the ad; or

3. Customize your resume to hit all the important points in the ad *and* write a creative cover letter.

Obviously the third approach is most likely to provide the best results, and it really doesn't take much more time.

As you customize your resume, you may find that the job descriptions require few if any changes, while the qualifications section might require substantial changes. The entire process of rewriting might take one to two hours. If you are really interested in the position and know you could handle it, consider the time as an investment. Taking time to redo the resume will not guarantee you an interview, but it can *double* your chances. If you lack certain desired skills or experience that were mentioned in the ad, simply ignore those points and really sell what you do have.

Printing Your Resume

Print your resume on a high-quality, 600-dpi (dots per inch) laser printer if at all possible. Most laser printers sold since 1999 are 600 dpi. A resume printed on a 300-dpi printer will look just fine as well, but will not be quite as sharp.

Ink jet printers simply cannot produce the same high quality. If you're thinking of upgrading to a laser printer, a job search is just the excuse you've been looking for. Laser printers are also more economical to operate because their cartridges last longer. Most studies show that ink jet printers cost about nine cents per page versus about five cents per page for a laser printer. Laser printers are also several times faster than ink jets and significantly quieter.

Because they are fast and relatively inexpensive per copy, most people with laser printers print out originals of their resume rather than using photocopies.

If you can't upgrade your ink jet printer, go to a copy shop that has computers and laser printers and make an original. Then have numerous copies made from a photocopier. Use your ink jet to produce your cover letters and to get a resume out quickly when you're in a pinch. Most people cannot tell the difference without looking closely.

Reproduction

Reproduction quality will have a lot to do with the visual impact of your resume. There are a number of advantages to having your resume reproduced at a professional photocopy shop. For one thing, the top-of-the-line copying equipment used in such shops will produce high-quality copies that are crisp, clear, and almost as good as the originals. The quality of photocopiers most have at home or in the office cannot compete with the equipment at a copy shop.

For another thing, copy shops have a variety of high-quality papers to choose from. You can produce your original resume on a plain white bond and have it copied on your choice of paper.

And finally, copy shops are fast—you can usually be in and out in about ten minutes. They are inexpensive as well. Photocopying will cost you five to eight cents per copy plus eight to eleven cents per sheet for special paper. Many people buy extra paper so their cover letter paper will match their resumes.

Producing originals from a laser printer will also produce a high-quality resume.

Mailing

Traditionally resumes are folded in thirds and sent in a standard number ten business envelope. That is still perfectly acceptable, but consider spending a little more and sending the resume in a 9" x 12" envelope so the resume does not need to be folded. It is not a big thing, but if it is not folded it will look nicer in the stack.

For a really hot job consider having it delivered by an overnight delivery service. For a super hot local job, consider having a messenger service deliver it. The extra effort is one way of saying you want the job. Priority mail also works well. While two- or three-day service is not guaranteed, most letters do get delivered anywhere in the country within three days for $3.85 (as of 2002) for up to one pound.

In these days when many organizations scan resumes, sending the resume without folds takes on greater importance. Sometimes the fold will cause a scanner to misread the resume.

Read Those Reject Letters, Then Toss Them

Most reject letters are form letters that tell you that though you have a fine background, they had many excellent candidates, and they have selected several for interviews who have just the right experience. Go ahead and read such letters and then toss them. Make a note on your sheet that contains the clipped-out ad you responded to and simply write "No" or "Reject." Then move on.

Occasionally you'll get a reject letter that indicates that the recruiter liked you, but you simply didn't have the credentials or experience that some others had. Such statements are rarely made just to make you feel better. It indicates that this is an organization you should stay in touch with. Write the recruiter thanking him or her for the nice note. You could follow up a week later and ask for advice on how to break into the organization, assuming you really are interested in it.

When the Recruiter Calls

When a headhunter, corporate recruiter, or hiring manager calls you to arrange an interview, listen to all the person has to say and take notes. After agreeing to an interview, ask the person for more details about the position. Since you are keeping track of all ads you respond to, you would try to find the ad while you are speaking on the phone. Since the recruiter may have found your resume posted on an electronic resume database, it is possible that you would have no information about the job prior to the call. So, whether you have an ad to look at or not, ask further questions about the position. The more you can learn about the position, the better prepared you will be for the interview itself. Questions you could ask include:

Could you tell me a little more about the position?
You indicated that the person would do (a duty), could you elaborate a little on that?
Who does the position report to?

Sometimes the headhunter will be calling you without having seen your resume. Perhaps you were referred by someone who knows you or the headhunter found your name in a local newspaper article. If you show interest in the position, the headhunter will ask you to send a resume. By having extensive information about the job, you can then tailor your resume and cover letter to fit the exact requirements of the position.

Maintain a File For All Ads You Respond To

When an employer calls you in response to an ad, you should be able to quickly locate it so you can scan it as you speak. If the person says his or her name so quickly that you don't catch it, or you don't catch the name of the organization, ask the person to repeat it. It is as simple as stating, "I'm sorry, there was some noise in the background and I didn't catch your name or the name of your organization, could you repeat it?" No one will ever be offended by a question like this.

With the name in hand you should quietly flip through your pages with the attached ads, as you try to find the appropriate one. Having that information will help you ask further questions about the position and will put everything into context.

If You Don't Have Your Own Computer or Have Internet Access

Some people do not own a computer, and many who do don't have Internet access. If you have a computer, I would strongly suggest you obtain Internet access so you can visit company websites and utilize many other job hunting tools that the Internet now offers. Having Internet access will also enable you to start using e-mail. This can be a real help. Just as job seekers often consider an interviewing suit a necessary investment, the same could be said for owning a personal computer.

If you don't have a computer, consider investing in one. It doesn't have to be the latest and greatest. An adequate computer can be obtained for about $600. The only additional software you really need is Microsoft Word for word processing. I recommend Word because it has become the de facto standard. You may find occasions when you will want to send an e-mail with an attached resume, and since most computers are either using Word or can read Word documents, it is the safest word processing software to use.

You will also need a printer. A decent ink jet printer will cost around $200. If you can afford to spend $400 on a printer, I would suggest getting a low-end laser printer. They are quieter and faster than ink jets and the print quality is sharper. Laser printers also cost considerably less to operate because their cartridges print far more pages.

If you simply cannot purchase a computer, virtually all libraries offer computers and Internet access. They may limit the time you can use the computer, but one will be available. Figure out the best times to use the library's computer to minimize your wait when others have gotten there ahead of you. You can also use these computers to get your e-mail if you have an e-mail account with one of the free e-mail services.

In addition to libraries, your state Job Service or One Stop Center will have computers available. Generally you must be unemployed to use the services, but that may not be the case with some government services. Certain nonprofit agencies, particularly those designed to help low-income or unemployed folks, will have computers available. If you don't know how to use a keyboard, or how to use the word processing program, the library or agency may have software available to help you learn on your own.

Using a friend's computer may be the answer for you. Friends are often willing to help out by sharing their computer with you and may even be willing to show you how to use their word processing software. Just remember to be aware of their needs for the computer and let them know you really appreciate their help.

Free E-Mail

There are many free e-mail services including:

Yahoo Mail (www.yahoo.com)
Hotmail (www.hotmail.com)
Lycos (www.lycos.com)
Mail.com (www.mail.com)

Not only are these e-mail services free, but you can access them from any computer that has an Internet connection. Juno offers free e-mail (www.juno.com) which you can access even if you do not have Internet service. You will, however, need a web browser such as Internet Explorer.

Don't Expect Responses To Your Resume

It's nice to get a card from an employer acknowledging that your resume has been received. It alleviates that little fear we all feel, "What if they didn't get it?" Yes, an acknowledgment is nice, but not necessary. You also won't get many. Most organizations simply do not feel that it is their responsibility to confirm receipt of your resume. It is both expensive and time consuming of company resources—that is, HR staffers. My advice, don't waste two seconds complaining about or even thinking about that resume you sent last week. Over 99.98% of all letters reach their correct destination within a reasonable time. We may like to criticize our Postal Service, but it really does a pretty good job delivering the mail. So, simply assume it got to the right people and that they will call you if you appear to be a top candidate. Actually, you should be so busy with your job search and have so many irons in the fire that you don't have time to worry about the resumes you've sent out.

Before You Fax Or E-mail That Resume

Most faxes and e-mails go through just fine to the appropriate destination. Some have problems, however. Perhaps your fax comes out the other end looking really crummy. Or, maybe your e-mailed resume has turned to gibberish. As a smart precaution at the beginning of your job search, send a faxed resume to a couple of people and e-mail your resume to at least two others. Then ask them to mail back to you what came out on their end. If they look good, you can be pretty sure that everything will work for you. You can also e-mail a resume directly to yourself and accomplish virtually the same thing.

Matching Envelopes Are Fine But Not Necessary

When you buy a nice quality paper for your resume, you can also buy matching envelopes. My own bias is that matching envelopes are fine, but not necessary. I would personally just use white, number ten envelopes, which is the standard business-size envelope.

Avoid Common Faux Pas

It is not recommended to photocopy your resume at work. It is improper to use company resources for personal benefit, especially when making a job switch. Also, people have been known to remove their copies and leave their original in the copier. You shouldn't work on your resume at work. Bosses have walked by the desks of subordinates only to discover the employee's resume on the screen.

Usually you would not include a fax number on your resume because most people will not seek to communicate with you by fax, particularly if you have voice mail. Also, if you use a fax machine that is shared by several people at work, you wouldn't want someone seeing a message faxed to you regarding your job search.

You Can't Please Everyone

No matter how hard you try, you can't please everyone. For every hundred people you talk to about resumes, you'll find a hundred different opinions on what makes an effective resume. Everyone disagrees. Since it's impossible to please everyone, why worry about it? Okay, you say, I won't worry about it, but what should I do? My suggestion is to determine what you're trying to accomplish.

Generally it's best to create a resume that is well-written, sells your strengths, and will be disliked by very few. The things I've suggested throughout *Resume Power* will accomplish that. We also know the formats (layouts) that people generally find pleasing. All of the sample resumes in *Resume Power* fall into that category. Yet, you can follow all of the suggestions and you'll still find some people who won't like something about your resume. Of course you hope it isn't so serious that it prevents them from seeing how capable you are. Fortunately, if you follow the advice throughout *Resume Power,* that will rarely happen.

So, the first point is that usually you should create a resume that nearly everyone likes. The second point is that there are exceptions. Sometimes your background is unusual enough that only a few people would be able to use the strengths that you want to emphasize. If that is the case it may be appropriate to try some unusual things. After all, you only need to grab the attention of a few people. If you try something unique in your resume, you may turn off a few people, but perhaps those were the ones who weren't going to call you anyway. Those open-minded, more daring people, however, might really like your creativity and gumption. Those may be the only ones who were going to be interested in you anyway. And remember, it takes only one good offer. I'm not suggesting that you intentionally turn off 99 people on the off chance that the hundredth will really like it. But sometimes it makes sense to take some risks.

To show you how irrational some people are, I'm going to tell you about an anonymous hiring manager out there who uses an irrational approach to resumes. When narrowing the list from 30 applicants to only six to invite for interviews, this person frequently discovers that two or three people are tied for that sixth spot. In order to select that sixth person, she will measure the borders of the resumes of the people who are tied, and will select the one that has exactly one inch margins top and bottom and on the sides. It doesn't make sense, but she does it anyway.

The Types of Resumes

ESSENTIALLY THERE ARE THREE TYPES of resumes—Chronological, Functional, and Qualifications/Chronological. Chronological and functional resumes have both advantages and disadvantages, while the qualifications/chronological resume offers the advantages of both the chronological and functional resumes, but none of the disadvantages.

Chronological resumes describe a person's work experience in reverse chronological order, with the most recent job appearing first. Traditionally they have emphasized dates, job titles, duties, and names of employers. The primary advantage of the chronological resume is that employers are used to reading it. They know how to scan it quickly and get what they need from it. Its major disadvantage is that it is difficult to show employers the "themes" which run through your experience.

The functional resume, on the other hand, excels at bringing out these themes or functional areas of experience. The job seeker identifies key areas of experience, or "functions," and labels those functional areas with titles such as Management, Design, and Computer Programming. The writer then describes the experience the person has had in those areas. The major drawbacks of the functional resume are that it is more difficult to read, and the employer typically does not know when or where the experience being described took place. For this reason it can be confusing.

The qualifications/chronological resume is essentially a chronological resume with a qualifications section included at the beginning. It combines the best attributes of both of the other types of resume, but has virtually none of their drawbacks. The qualifications section of a qualifications/chronological resume is usually shorter than the functional portion of a functional resume, but it covers the most crucial areas of experience and provides a quick introduction to the strengths of the individual. The job description section, the other main part of the resume, emphasizes results rather than just duties, making it extremely effective.

On the next three pages you'll see excellent examples of a chronological resume, a functional resume, and a qualifications/chronological resume. Following the examples you will find a complete description of the functional resume, how to write it, how to determine whether you should use it, and samples to give you ideas.

Chronological

JUAN LOZANO
19301 Whispering Road
Phoenix AZ 85044
(602) 535-2809

OBJECTIVE: Restaurant Management

EDUCATION

AA—Liberal Arts, Frost Community College   (1989)

RESTAURANT MANAGEMENT TRAINING

Restaurant Management Training School, 300 class hours, Gaucho Restaurants (1994-1996)

EMPLOYMENT

Gaucho Restaurants, Phoenix, AZ   6/93-Present

GENERAL MANAGER - 6/97-Present. Took over a troubled restaurant in the chain that was experiencing high employee turnover, poor service, and a loss in the customer base. Within nine months stabilized the operation. Resolved serious morale problems, instituted an effective training program, and developed a strong support staff for consistent service. During the first nine months increased sales 18% and reduced staff turnover 50% and labor costs 10%. Provided excellent wine training for the staff and significantly increased wine sales.

In 1998 increased sales 15% and profits 21%. In 1999 increased sales 14% and profits 18%. Named Regional Manager of the Year in 1998 in a region of 21 fine dining restaurants.

ASSISTANT MANAGER – 6/93-6/97. As assistant manager oversaw one of the highest volume restaurants in the chain and was responsible for reducing turnover and regaining customer confidence through training and development of floor staff. With stronger training and better marketing, increased sales 11%, achieved tighter budgets, and produced a level of service that brought strong compliments from customers.

La Casa Restaurant, Phoenix, AZ   4/89-6/93

ASSOCIATE MANAGER – 4/91-6/93. For this well-established restaurant, responsible for maintaining high standards related to service, food quality, personnel training, cost control, and sales. Introduced a method of analyzing previous sales figures that better predicted staffing needs, cut labor costs, and increased food and beverage sales.

MANAGEMENT TRAINEE – 4/89-4/91. Learned all aspects of the restaurant industry with assignments in purchasing, food preparation, wait staff, and hosting.

Functional

SUZANNE HALL
18852 52nd S.E.
Bothell, Washington 98011
(206) 481-2756

OBJECTIVE: Personnel Management

QUALIFICATIONS

Personnel Management - Six years experience in personnel, with three years as Personnel Manager of a store with 230 employees. Supervise and train a staff of four. Significantly increased morale among store personnel and successfully fought off a unionizing effort.

Recruiting, Interviewing, Hiring - Very effective interviewer. Screen and hire all sales, supervisory, clerical, and support personnel. Over 80% of all people hired have remained with the store at least one year. Turnover has been reduced 22% by careful screening and by implementing other improvements throughout the store.

EEO - Perform periodic surveys and ensure all goals are met as required.

Wage and Salary Administration - Identified unfair wage differentials between recent hires and those with longer service. Removed pay scale discrepancies and nearly eliminated turnover among more experienced staff.

Promotions - Work closely with supervisors to determine those ready for promotions. Write all final recommendations for promotions.

Terminations - Arbitrate in all firing situations and participate in all firing interviews. Conduct exit interviews and identify causes for termination. By taking quick action, several terminations have been averted.

Manpower Planning - Predict staffing needs for Christmas and major sales and hire necessary personnel.

Career Counseling - Provide extensive career path counseling to store employees.

Training and Development - Developed and conduct a 16-hour training program emphasizing customer service and job training. Turnover and customer complaints have been reduced substantially since the program was increased from 8 to 16 hours. Supervise additional training during the probationary period.

EMPLOYMENT

Briggins Department Stores, Seattle, Washington (1983 to Present)

Personnel Manager (2000 to Present)
Assistant Personnel Manager (1997 to 2000)
Schedule Coordinator (1989 to 1997)
Credit Manager (1987 to 1989)
Credit Adjustment Processor (1984 to 1987)
Sales Associate (1983 to 1984)

EDUCATION

Attended Bellevue Community College (35 credits)

Qualifications/Chronological

ROBERTA JENNINGS
1121 Peach Drive
Atlanta, Georgia 30601
(404) 574-8769

OBJECTIVE: Airline Management

QUALIFICATIONS

Excellent management and supervisory capabilities. Highly respected by subordinates and able to obtain high performance levels from employees. Established one of the best on-time performance records in the airline industry.

EDUCATION

B.A. - Business, University of Southern California (1986)

EMPLOYMENT

Air Florida 3/92-Present

Customer/Ramp Service Supervisor, Atlanta, Georgia 6/98-Present. Opened the Atlanta airport facility for Air Florida and have created one of its most efficient and effective operations. Supervise and train 30 Customer Service Agents and Ramp personnel. Responsible for all day-to-day operations decisions and handle all crises related to weather, passenger deaths and illnesses, bomb threats, and hijackings.

Established one of the top records in the industry by successfully loading planes and preparing them for departure in twenty minutes or less, 97% of the time. Effective planning and scheduling permit up to four planes to be serviced simultaneously. Lost time due to illness has been reduced by 68% and industrial accidents by 71%.

Customer Service Agent, Miami, Florida 3/92-6/98. Functioned as Ticket Sales Agent, Boarding Agent, and Customer Service Representative. Provided the type of service and concern for customers which made Air Florida one of the fastest growing airlines in the U. S. Became adept at solving problems and satisfying customers' complaints. Consistently maintained monthly sales in the top 10%.

Alaska Airlines, San Francisco, California 1/87-3/92

Customer Service Agent - Worked closely with customers to provide the best connecting flights and make each flight an enjoyable experience.

THE FUNCTIONAL RESUME

The functional resume offers some people the best way to get their story across to employers. If your strengths can readily be put into categories, then you should seriously consider using a functional resume.

In its purest form, a functional resume includes only functions—job titles, dates, and names of employers are omitted. I rarely recommend a pure functional resume because it usually raises more questions than it answers. When dates and employers are omitted, hiring authorities tend to wonder if the applicant is hiding something, such as a long gap in employment. If you have strong reasons for not revealing details of your employment, however, consider a functional resume.

As you will notice in Suzanne's resume (page 101), employment was included but job descriptions were not. This is common in functional resumes and helps employers feel more comfortable with the functional format. The functional section in Suzanne's resume is devoted entirely to her duties as personnel manager and assistant personnel manager. Those were the only jobs which were relevant to the position she was seeking. In a chronological resume it would have been difficult to have devoted so much space (24 lines) to just two positions. For Suzanne the functional resume was a perfect choice.

Read the following sample functional resumes to get a feel for how they are constructed and what makes them effective. Although the backgrounds of the people will differ from yours, you should be able to determine whether your experience is better suited to the functional format or the qualifications/ chronological format illustrated and discussed throughout the book.

A functional resume worked well for Paul Shupbach (page 105) and enabled him to go into much more detail about his areas of experience. His job descriptions also add important information.

David Goldman's resume (page 106) could be labeled a functional resume, but it is really a combination of a functional and chronological resume. It demonstrates that by remaining flexible and creative you can produce something which works best for you and your particular situation.

Jason Ryerson's resume (page 107) enabled an ex-military officer to sell his experience in basically nonmilitary terms. He started with a traditional chronological resume that overemphasized military terminology. Only with a functional resume was he able to avoid the military jargon and use civilian-oriented terminology. Once that was accomplished he quickly found a position with an aircraft manufacturer.

There are literally hundreds of categories that can be used in functional resumes. Begin by trying to identify the categories that will work best for you. Some might be very specific to your field or industry. An art supplies salesperson might use three primary categories called "Sales Experience," "Customer Service," and "Art Supplies Background." The first two are generic categories and the third is specific to the industry.

The following list may contain categories that will work well in your resume.

Functional categories

Accounting
Accounts Payable
Administering (Programs)
Administration
Advertising
Analysis & Preparation
Auditing
Behavior Modification
Benefits
Brochure Design
Budget Controls
Budget Management
Business Law
Buying
Caseload Supervision
Client Relations
Communications
Community Relations
Community Resource
   Utilization
Company Benefits
   Programs
Computer
Computer Programming
Computerized Accounting
Conflict Resolution
Construction
Consulting
Contract Bid Preparation
   and Administration
Contract Negotiations
Cost Accounting
Cost Controls
Cost Effectiveness
Cost Effectiveness Studies
Cost Estimating
Cost Saving
Counseling
Creative Writing
Credit and Collections
Credit Management
Crisis Intervention
Curriculum Development
Customer Service
Customer Training
Data Processing
Database Management
Design
Display Design
Editing
Employee Relations
Engineering
Engineering Proposals
Equipment Acquisition
Equipment Repair And
   Maintenance
Environmental Impact
   Statements

Expediting
Facility Management
Finance
Financial Management
Financial Statements
Full-Charge Bookkeeping
Fundraising
Government Contracts
Grant Proposal Writing
Group Therapy
Growth Planning
Human Resources
Industrial Security
Initial Public Offerings
Internal Auditing
Inventory Control
   Management
Information Management
Inspection
Interviewing (Techniques)
Investor Relations
Invoice Processing
Job Costing
Labor Negotiations
Labor Relations
Leadership
Learning Disabilities
Legal
Manufacturing
Management
Management Consulting
Management Information
   Systems
Managing (Projects)
Market Penetration
   (Strategies)
Marketing
Material Support
Media Relations
Mediation
Merchandising
Mergers & Acquisitions
Negotiations
Office Management
Operations
Organizational
   Development
Organizational Theory
Payroll
Personnel Administration
Personnel Management
Planning
Policy Development
Presentations
Problem Solving
Procedures Development
Product Design
Product Development

Production
Program Coordination
Program Development
Project Engineering
Project Coordination
Project Management
Production Planning
Production Management
Progress Reports
Promoting
Public Relations
Public Speaking
Publishing
Purchasing
Quality Control
Quality Assurance
Re-engineering
Records Control
Recruitment
Repair Procedures
   Development
Research
Research And Design
Research And
   Development
Retail Management
Safety
Safety/Accident Prevention
Safety/OSHA Standards
Safety Procedures
Sales
Sales/Customer Service
Sales Personnel Training
Scheduling
Security
Security Procedures
Shipping and Receiving
Staff Development
Staff Evaluating
Statistical Analysis
Strategic Planning
Supervision/Training
System Design
Systems Analysis
Tax Analysis
Taxes
Technical Report Writing
Technical Writing
Technology Acquisition
Technology Transfer
Telecommunications
Theft Control
Training
Troubleshooting
Turnover Reduction
Vendor Negotiations
Vendor Relations
Writing

PAUL SHUPBACH
2917 S. E. 112th
Pittsburgh, Pennsylvania 15203
(412) 579-0002

QUALIFICATIONS

Technical Expertise - Hands-on person. Capable of operating and trouble-shooting virtually any piece of equipment. Understand the problems faced by machine operators and utilize engineering knowledge to effectively solve those problems.

Proposals, Contracts and Negotiations - Have written and developed dozens of proposals and negotiated over 40 major contracts. Heavily experienced in all types of contracts, including DCAS, ASPR and DAR. Consistently negotiate the most favorable terms for Cost Plus, Cost Sharing, Cost Plus Incentive Fixed, and R&D Contracts.

Cost Management, Cost Analysis, Cost Control - Over fifteen years of cost management experience with all types of products and components, including processing equipment, fiberglass, and sheet metal parts. Establish program financial controls which pinpoint manufacturing problems and prevent cost overruns. Expert in Value Engineering.

Cost Estimating - Experience covers all facets of manufacturing including machined parts, sheet metal, plastics, fiberglass, and software. Highly experienced in all methods of estimating including parametric estimating.

Vendor Selection - Inspect and analyze vendor facilities, equipment, capabilities, and quality. Recommendations to use a vendor have virtually always been adopted.

EDUCATION

B.A. Industrial Management, University of Pennsylvania (1971)
B.S. Industrial Engineering, University of Pittsburgh (1969)

EMPLOYMENT HISTORY

Davenport Engineering & Consulting, Pittsburgh, Pennsylvania 1995 to Present

Industrial Engineering Consultant - Work on assignments ranging in length from 3 to 12 months in the areas of Bidding, Estimating, Selecting Vendors, Cost Management, and Manufacturing Planning. Enabled one manufacturer to obtain their first ever contract with U. S. Steel and to expand production from $40,000 to $140,000 per month with no increase in personnel. Researched and adapted a new technology which allowed the firm to consistently underbid all competitors.

Pennsylvania Division of Purchasing, Scranton, Pennsylvania 1981 to 1995

Specification Analyst - Developed quality standards, specifications, and test procedures for many raw, semi-processed, and processed materials. The capabilities and sophistication of the Division were substantially increased through these efforts.

U. S. Steel, Pittsburgh, Pennsylvania 1971 to 1981

Cost Analyst - Estimated and analyzed costs of machined parts, hydraulic components, and mechanical systems supplied by vendors. Negotiated prices and engineering changes.

DAVID GOLDMAN
2430 Stoneway North
Little Rock, Arkansas 72202
(501) 254-3242

OBJECTIVE: Project Management

QUALIFICATIONS

Supervising. Took over a district with high turnover and low morale and created one of the top teams in the company. Work closely with individuals to enable both company and personal needs to be satisfied.

Negotiating. Negotiate contracts that are fair, workable, and satisfactory to customer and manufacturer. Work hard to get the best for both.

Coordinating/Planning. Installations have always been completed on schedule. Maintain close contact with customers, manufacturing, and field engineering to deal with all problems as they arise. Able to get commitments and support from those not directly responsible to me.

Computers. Excellent training and broad work experience installing and maintaining computer systems.

EMPLOYMENT

Data Systems, 1985 to Present

Senior Project Manager, Little Rock, Arkansas, 1999 to Present. Negotiate contracts, schedule deliveries, and troubleshoot all phases of computer installations. Work closely with customers to determine their needs, then gain contractual commitments from manufacturing and field engineering to install systems by specific dates. Monitor factory schedules and software support schedules to ensure delivery schedules are met. Despite many difficulties, all deliveries and installations have been completed on schedule.

District Manager, Field Engineering, Los Angeles, California, 1994 to 1999. Supervised and scheduled the work of 18 field engineers installing and maintaining computer systems. Took over a district with high turnover, low morale, and a poor reputation for customer service. Within one year turnover was reduced from 35% to 8% annually. Response time to down systems was reduced from six hours to two hours. Functioned as Project Manager for the installation of a branch on-line system for Security Western Bank (180 branches). All installations were completed on time.

Field Engineer, Washington, D. C., 1985 to 1994. Installed and maintained systems for banks, hotels and airlines. Customers were kept very satisfied because of extremely low downtimes.

U. S. Air Force, 1981 to 1985

Computer Tech - Maintained and serviced on-board aircraft computer systems. Supervised a five-man team.

EDUCATION

Computers
Field Engineering, Data Systems Manufacturing School - 6 months, 1988
Computer Repair, Computer Learning Institute - 6 months, 1987
Electrical Engineering, Old Dominion University - 1 year, 1985-1986
Computer Tech School, U. S. Air Force - 9 months, 1981

JASON RYERSON
14568 NE 9th Street
Redmond, Washington 98053
(425) 877-7594

OBJECTIVE: Facilities Management

QUALIFICATIONS

Over 20 years of exceptional management experience. Proven ability to successfully complete projects cost effectively and on schedule. Received numerous awards for completion of high quality projects.

Implemented comprehensive programs that dramatically improved productivity and efficiency of personnel.

PROFESSIONAL EXPERIENCE

ENGINEERING MANAGEMENT - Eight years of demanding and successful "hands on" engineering management and plant management responsibilities. Coordinated hundreds of repair jobs conducted by both own work force and outside contractors. In one instance increased overall plant reliability by 300%. While providing repair support for 12 naval ships over a three-year period, reduced equipment downtime by 50%.

FACILITIES MANAGEMENT - As Chief Engineer and Material Manager, directly responsible for operation, maintenance, and repair of steam and diesel electric power plants. Associated equipment included heating, ventilation, and air conditioning systems; firefighting and sprinkler systems; and various emergency equipment. Charged also with infrastructure repair and modifications. Supported numerous office and work station relocations in minimal time and without loss of productivity.

CONTRACT ADMINISTRATION - Broad experience in working with prime and subcontractors in overseeing scheduled and emergency repairs. Represented the U.S. Government in the management of an $18 million resupply contract for 76 remote sites in the Pacific.

TROUBLESHOOTING - Volunteered to rebuild a faltering yet critical department of 95 personnel. Within 45 days identified all major problem areas and initiated a corrective action plan that included a comprehensive training program for 900 people. The revitalized training program improved morale and decreased absenteeism over 60%. Received a special commendation for the project.

EMPLOYMENT

United States Navy 6/83-1/03. Completed Naval service with rank of Commander.

EDUCATION

MA - Political Science, Naval Postgraduate School (1990)
BA - International Studies, University of Washington (1983)

IS A FUNCTIONAL RESUME FOR YOU?

Functional resumes do have drawbacks. While reviewing functional resumes, employers often wonder where the experience occurred since dates, job titles, and employers are not specified for each particular area of experience. Their eyes tend to dart up and down the page looking for the answers. They often become frustrated because the information in the resume is difficult to read and interpret—the applicant is making them work too hard. They may also suspect that something is being hidden.

Keeping these considerations in mind, you may still want to use a functional resume under the following circumstances: if 1) You are changing careers; 2) You are changing industries and you have related experience but no direct experience; 3) You have major gaps in employment; 4) A functional resume seems to be a perfect vehicle to showcase your strengths; 5) The Qualifications/Chronological employment format seems unsuitable for your background; 6) Your background can easily be listed in categories such as Management, Supervision, Coordinating, Troubleshooter, Motivator, or Training; 7) You've had your current job for many years and you want to highlight different aspects of it.

If you think a functional resume may be good for you, go ahead and write one. Test it out on friends or business associates to determine if it truly sells you and is easy to read. If you get positive feedback, you made the right decision.

Be sure to study the format of the qualifications/chronological resumes. I like the format because it has virtually all of the advantages of the functional resume *and* the chronological resume, with none of their individual drawbacks.

WRITING YOUR FUNCTIONAL RESUME

Once your job sketches have been completed, the first step in writing an effective functional resume is to list the points or experiences that you want to include. Write the points quickly, without being concerned for polished writing. Once you're through listing the points you'll begin to see that some just naturally fit together. At that point begin to select the category titles that you will use. Most functional resumes should contain three to six categories. For your highly specific or technical categories, you'll have to come up with those names on your own, but that should not be difficult. Some of the commonly used categories include: Management, Supervision, Training, Planning, Designing, Research, Coordination, Negotiating, Public Relations, Administration, Marketing, Public Speaking, Organization, Counseling, Writing and Editing, Design, and Teaching.

Next, put the categories on two pages so you'll have plenty of room to write in your points. Initially you wrote those points quickly; now rewrite them in a more polished form as you place them in their appropriate category. Once all the points have been placed in a category, determine the order the points should be in. Usually your strongest points would be listed first within each category. At that point you've done all you should for one day.

After one or two days, review what you've written. By having set the resume aside for some time, it will be fresh and you'll be better able to see ways to improve your writing. In your second draft look for ways to make each point clearer and more concise. Virtually all of the other instructions for writing a resume apply to the functional resume as well.

Writing Your Resume

GETTING STARTED ON YOUR RESUME

Having read through this section on resumes and having completed your job sketches, it's time to start writing your resume. I can't emphasize enough how valuable you will find your job sketches as you write your resume.

Once you have reviewed your job sketches, you're ready to start. Use a pencil and feel free to erase. If you compose well at a computer, by all means use one, but double space so you can write and edit between the lines. I always begin by writing the name, address and phone number at the top. Next, I write the objective. After that I then write in "Qualifications" and skip enough space to complete it after I've written the rest of the resume. Since the qualifications section is often the most difficult section to write, I leave it until last.

At that point I have spent only about three minutes writing, but psychologically I am totally involved with the resume. Three minutes earlier I had been looking for an excuse to postpone the writing, but now I'm *into* it. Next I tackle employment, the section which nearly always requires the most time and thought. Be prepared to spend three or more hours on your first draft. It may be frustrating at times, but keep plugging away. The effort will all be worth it in the end. Once you've completed a first and second draft of your employment section, you'll be ready to work on the qualifications section.

DON'T HESITATE

You should write your first draft relatively quickly without worrying about perfection. Concentrate on getting your thoughts on paper; you can polish the phrasing later. Once you write a phrase, read it out loud to get a feel for how it sounds. When reading, most people subvocalize; while they may not move their lips, their mind is actually saying each word almost audibly. In other words, the way a phrase sounds to you when you say it out loud is the same way it sounds when read by an employer. By the time I finish writing a resume I have read every phrase aloud four to ten times. While I don't worry about perfection on the first draft, I will rewrite some phrases and add or delete words as I go along.

Frequently I will finish the first draft of a resume late in the afternoon. While I may not be satisfied with it, I do know that all the main thoughts and descriptions are there. I will simply set it aside until the next morning. When I pick it up the next day, my thoughts are fresh and I'm able to look at it objectively. Improvements often come spontaneously.

Read over the resume and ask yourself if all the important points have been made. You might think of a point that could be covered in the employment section or an important idea you want to get across in qualifications. Make those changes on the original draft. Go through the draft sentence by sentence and phrase by phrase, rereading them out loud. Cross out extraneous phrases. Ask yourself if you can make the same point with fewer words. Use action words whenever possible. Once you've finished this process, retype or rewrite the resume, incorporating the changes you've made. You have completed your second draft. Set it aside for at least half a day.

SPIT AND POLISH

When you pick up the resume again, take care as you go through it; this may be your last draft. As you read your resume out loud, it should flow. Are there any phrases or words you have used more than twice? If so, look for alternatives. Are all of your sentences very long or all very short? A mixture of short, medium, and long sentences reads best. Too many short sentences makes the resume seem choppy and abrupt. Lots of long sentences cause a reader to forget the main point. Long sentences can often be made into two sentences. This adds clarity and punch.

Look for any troublesome phrases that sound awkward, unclear, or confusing. Your desire is to have employers read your resume completely and thoroughly. You don't want them to stop at any point and wonder what you mean. Just one awkwardly written, hard-to-understand sentence can reduce your perceived value by 10%. Don't let that happen.

Of course *you* know exactly what you mean by everything you've written, so unclear sentences may be hard for you to spot. Have others read your resume and ask if any sentences tripped them up. Ask for their overall impression.

Avoid big, unfamiliar words. The mark of a good writer is the ability to say exactly what is meant by using everyday words.

Spelling must be perfect. It is worth it to make one quick pass through your resume, dictionary in hand, looking up words you "know" are correct. You may be surprised to find that you have been misspelling a word for years. Do not depend solely on computerized spell checkers. If your misspelling is an actual word in the spell checker, it will go undetected. Ask someone to review it to make sure it is grammatically correct and that words are used correctly.

Type the final draft and review it one last time for phrasing, spelling, and punctuation. If you use a word processing service, presenting a typed draft will help reduce your cost and will ensure that everything is readable.

PUTTING IT ALL TOGETHER

Essentially, writing a resume consists of putting all of the pieces together. Most sections, such as education, training, special projects, and employment are independent of each other. So, if each section is well written, the entire resume will be effective when you pull them all together.

Rate Your Resume

Use this form to rate your own resume or to have others rate it. Ask others to make suggestions for improvement. Keep working on your resume until you can ultimately rate it excellent in all categories. It may take extra time but it will be worth the effort.

	Excellent	Good	Fair	Poor	Suggestions For Improvement
Is the resume easy to scan and pick up key information?					
Is there a good mix of longer, shorter, and medium length sentences?					
Have action words been used when appropriate?					
Is the writing clear and concise?					
Could words or phrases be eliminated?					
Is there any irrelevant information?					
Is the layout inviting to the eye?					
Do key points stand out?					
Have accomplishments, results, and contributions been stressed wherever possible?					
Do qualifications come out loud and clear?					
Are problem solving skills emphasized?					
Does it emphasize benefits to an employer?					
Does the resume support my job objective?					
Does it show me in the best light regarding experience and potential?					
Have negatives or liabilities been minimized or removed?					
Does the resume accurately convey my responsibilities?					

Ways To Personalize Your Resume

There are dozens of ways you can personalize your resume to make it uniquely yours in appearance. While most of the resumes included in *Resume Power* utilize the same basic layout, feel free to use a format that presents you in the best way possible. Regardless of the layout you choose, the following ideas will show you some of the ways you can personalize your resume.

1) **Headings**
   Name centered, bold, upper/lower case, 12-point, 158, 178
   Name centered, bold, upper/lower case, name 16-point, address/phone 13-point, 197
   Name centered, rest of address/phone far left and far right, 196
   Name centered on one line; address/city/city/state/phone all on one line, 195
   Everything bolded, 189
   Name using small caps, 187
   Heading right justified, 209
   Heading left justified, 186
   No bolding, 163, 177

2) **Category Titles** (like Qualifications, Education, Employment)
   Upper case, bold, 185
   Bold, small caps, 187, 191
   Category title centered, bolded, all caps, 195, 196
   No bolding, 183

3) **Job Titles**
   Bold and capitalized, 185
   Bold and upper/lower case, 180
   Bold with small caps, 186
   Upper case, not bolded, 178
   Job title listed on one line, a line skipped, followed by job description, 203
   Job title bold, above the name of employer, 196
   Job title and date on one line, with job description following on next line, 189

4) **Font Size For Text**
   13-point, 183, 206, 213
   12-point, 161, 188
   11-point, 157, 160, 165
   10-point, 163

5) **Fonts**
    Sans-serif
        Antique Olive, 197, 214
        Arial, 195
        Avant Garde, 177
        Century Gothic, 216
        Eras Medium, 190
        Helvetica, 160, 173, 179, 186
        Tahoma, 206
    Serif
        Benguiat, 165
        Bookman, 168, 169, 178
        New Century Schoolbook, 185, 213
        Palatino, 201
        Times New Roman (equivalent to Times Roman), 157, 158, 163, 170, 174, 187

6) **Bullets**
    Just within job description, 209, 213
    Qualifications and job descriptions, 206
    Just qualifications, 214
    Just accomplishments, 177, 197

7) **Key Accomplishments Within Job Descriptions**, 177

Part Two
The Electronic
Résumé Explosion

The Electronic Resume Explosion

EVERY DAY JOB SEEKERS ARE STARTING new positions that they discovered over the Internet. In the past seven years the value of the Internet for job seekers has exploded. There are hundreds of commercial sites where you can post your electronic resume, giving you the opportunity to be contacted by employers seeking someone with your background. From among tens of thousands of resumes within a resume databank, yours can be found in less than a minute.

There are now thousands of employers that have their own company web sites. Many of them list and describe open positions. When you discover a desirable position, you can send your resume to them by e-mail or via a form on their web site.

Because of all these technological developments, the electronic resume is having great impact on the way resumes are created and the way job seekers are finding jobs. Because the number of job seekers submitting their resumes electronically has grown so rapidly, and because so many employers are now using this technology, no solid job search would be complete without creating an electronic resume that will sell you. Keep in mind that the U.S. Department of Labor estimates that approximately 85% of all available jobs are never advertised, even on the web. While posting your electronic resume increases your chances of getting the job you want, do not rely on it as the answer to your job searching efforts.

In the following pages I will show you how to make plain-text and scannable resumes, as well as web portfolios, that can be used in your electronic job search.

TYPES OF RESUMES

For your job search you should have three types of resumes: formatted, plain-text, and scannable. You may want a fourth type, the web portfolio.

Formatted: The formatted resume is the resume you would create with MS Word, WordPerfect, or other word processors. Those programs allow you to use italics, bold type, bullets, columns, your choice of typefaces (fonts), and other features. These are the features that let you be creative and produce an attractive looking resume to print or to send as an e-mail attachment.

Plain-Text: Plain-text, also known as text format and ASCII format (pronounced as-kee), is a universal format that virtually all computers with all operating systems can interpret and use. ASCII stands for American Standard Code for Information Interchange. Your plain-text resume would be used whenever sending your resume as text within an e-mail message to an employer or storing it in a commercial resume databank.

Scannable: The scannable resume is the paper resume you send to employers who scan resumes into resume databanks. Virtually all formatting features are removed, making the resume less attractive. The point to keep in mind is that no one else's will look any more attractive than yours. It is important to create a resume in such a way that when it is scanned, all of your words will be properly interpreted by the optical character recognition (OCR) software.

Web Portfolio: A web portfolio is a web site that contains your resume as well as links to other documents, including samples of your written work, photographs, or audio and video clips. The use of web portfolios is growing, but still uncommon.Often an employer would look at your web portfolio after having found your resume in a resume databank and then typing in the web address (URL) that would be included in your resume.

HELPFUL HINTS AND DEFINITIONS FOR ELECTRONIC RESUMES

The Internet and the World Wide Web: The Internet is a worldwide network of computers that can pass information back and forth. Internet Service Providers (ISPs) and a network known as the backbone, with servers and routers, keep track of information and can reach the desired server to pull information from it. The World Wide Web (or "web") is the graphical portion of the Internet that permits you to obtain graphically presented text with drawings, photographs, video, and audio. The Internet also permits messages, known as electronic mail or e-mail, to be sent from one computer to another in a matter of seconds.

Resume Databank: A resume databank is any database that is designed to store resumes, with the ability to retrieve them through the use of key words. Resume databank and resume database are basically synonymous. There are commercial resume databanks that permit you to post your resume so that employers and recruiters can access the database and find people whose background fits what they are looking for. Most are free to the job seeker. Companies also have their own resume databanks, enabling you to submit your resume directly to them.

URL: A URL (Uniform Resource Locator) is also known as a web address. Each web site has a unique URL, enabling you to find and view that site. Most URLs are in lowercase and begin with http://www. followed by the domain name, such as cmr-mvp. This is followed by the extension, which indicates the type of organization it is. A commercial or business site uses .com. A school site uses .edu, while a nonprofit site uses .org, and a government entity uses .gov. Other extensions are used but these are the most common.

Text Editors: A text editor, such as Notepad in MS Word, allows you to edit your plain-text (ASCII) resume or any other type of plain-text document. From a text editor you can copy and paste your resume or document into an e-mail message you are sending to an employer.

Getting Connected: To get connected to an Internet Service Provider (ISP), you first need a computer with a 486 or Pentium processor (or equivalent). If you have a Macintosh you'll need a PowerPC or a 68000 processor or higher. A representative of an ISP or those who know computers can tell you if yours will be sufficient. Your computer also needs a modem. Your modem should provide speeds of at least 28.8 kb, meaning they can transfer data from a web site at up to 28,800 bytes per second. Most modems purchased in the last three years will be 56 kb, meaning they are twice as fast as the 28.8-kb modem. If you've heard about fast connections, you know the terms cable modem and DSL. Both types provide speeds five to twenty times faster than a 56-kb modem.

You may have received a CD-ROM from AOL, MSN (Microsoft Network), or others asking you to connect with them. They then give you 50-250 hours of free access for one month. This can get you started and then you can decide whether you like the service. After your free month you can get unlimited monthly service for $20 to $25. You can also get limited monthly service for anywhere from free to $5.00 and up. Be careful of these plans. If you use more than your monthly allotted hours, a significant charge will incur on your bill for each hour over your limit. Finally, there are many ISP's who will provide free Internet connections at unlimited or limited hourly service. A few of these are Juno at www.juno.com and Free I-Net at www.freeinet.com. Ask your friends and computer experts about their experience before signing on with an ISP. Try to stay away from an ISP that asks you to sign a three-year agreement. Three years in Internet time is a lifetime.

The CD-ROM will come with a web browser, probably either Microsoft Internet Explorer or Netscape Navigator, and everything you need to get started. If you have trouble installing the software, you can call your ISP and they will walk you through the process by phone.

Free E-Mail Services: Having an e-mail account is part of a successful online job search. It provides an easy means of sharing information with potential employers and job search contacts. See page 96 for a list of free e-mail services.

If You Don't Have A Computer: Many libraries now offer Internet access. You have to sign up for a session, usually no more than an hour at a time, but you can accomplish a lot. If you use one of the free e-mail programs you can obtain your messages from any computer that has Internet access. If you're unemployed you may have access to computers at your state Employment Security offices, often known as WorkSource Centers, One-Stop Centers, or Job Service Centers.

Attachments: Attachments are files that can be added to an e-mail message. During a job search this would typically be a resume or cover letter. People often send MS Word attachments and most people's computer systems can open them up and read them. Once opened, the resume can be saved as a Word document. People also attach plain-text resumes.

CREATE A KEY WORD RESUME

Creating a key word resume is the first step in producing a resume that can be submitted to resume databanks. First of all a resume must be searchable and retrievable. This is accomplished through the use of key words.

Searchable and Retrievable

Once a resume makes it into a resume databank, it will be found when a recruiter asks the databank to supply all of the resumes of those people who have a certain type of background. They do this by searching for resumes that contain their desired key words. If the employer wanted a highly skilled mechanical engineer the key words might be: mechanical engineer, BS, and PE. The resumes that become available to the recruiter will all be from people who have a BS in engineering, they will be practicing mechanical engineers, and they will have been doing it long enough to have gained the professional designation Professional Engineer. Your challenge is to determine the key words employers might use to find someone with your background and then to make sure your resume has them.

Put Key Words Into Your Resume

The best time to start identifying your key words is when you're writing your job sketches. Of course, if you've already created your resume, now is the time to see which key words are already in your resume and which should be added.

The most common way for resumes to be accessed is through key words. The term "key words" simply means that employers will determine the desired background of the ideal candidate, and then will determine which words and terms the ideal candidate would likely have in his or her resume.

Start the process by simply listing all of the words and terms that you think an employer might look for. Then seek ways to get those words into your resume. The best way is to place yourself in the position of an employer seeking someone with your background. In essence you are asking, "How would I find myself?" Key words are usually nouns such as marketing, Visual Basic, MS Windows, project management, graphic design, behavior modification. Key words can also be gerunds, noun-like verbs, like negotiating and analyzing.

There are several ways to identify key words:

1. Search the want ads in your field and notice what words they specify in the requirements and duties sections.

2. Talk to people in the field and ask what they believe the key words would be.

3. Read professional journals in your field to help identify the current hot terms.

Do all of these things, but then come back to considering how you would find yourself if you were looking for someone like you. Produce as extensive a list as possible and then determine the twenty most likely terms, and make sure they appear somewhere in your resume. If some of these words were not already present, look for ways to include them in existing sentences or create sentences that each use one or more of the key words.

It's helpful to understand how resumes are pulled out of resume databanks. I spent part of a day with a resume databank expert as we worked together on several searches. Typically, when we used five key words in our search, we found too few resumes; when we used only one or two words we sometimes got too many. After putting in the key words, the database would indicate how many matches had occurred. When there were too few we eliminated a term or tried other words to get the right number of matches. When we used five key words we got fewer resumes because only those with all five key words were selected. The person putting in the criteria can also ask for those that possess at least three of the five key words.

Once a resume came on screen it often took only five to ten seconds to see whether that person had the required experience. If not, with a simple mouse click we were instantly viewing the next resume. This might happen, for example, if we were looking for a computer programmer with three or more years of Visual Basic experience. If Visual Basic was our only key word, then every resume that used that term would come up on screen. Sometimes, however, the person had merely studied Visual Basic and had not developed any programs in Visual Basic for pay. If three years of job experience with Visual Basic was required, that person would be eliminated in less than ten seconds.

When doing a key word search, resumes will appear on a computer screen one by one, and the key words in the resume will be highlighted. A person will skim through each resume to determine which people appear to be good candidates. When a highly qualified candidate pops up on the screen, the person reviewing the resumes will print that one. Those not so qualified will simply remain in the database awaiting future openings for which they may be better qualified.

Observe what has happened. The inclusion of the right key words in the person's resume caused the resume to be selected from within the database. The resume was then reviewed by someone. At that point the actual experience the person had, and the quality of the presentation of that experience, determined whether the resume was printed out.

If your resume does not contain the right key words, it will not be selected from the database for viewing. And if it is not well written you will unlikely be called for an interview.

Buzz Words

To develop your list of key words, begin by including all of the buzz words in your field. This would include the jargon, technical terms, and nomenclature in your specialty. List the current hot terms, the standard terms that have been around for a long time, and the new terms that may soon be hot. Once you have your list, decide which ones are appropriate for you.

Synonyms. When you list a term, also list its synonyms. For example, if you list personnel administration as a key word, also list human resources management. If you list attorney, list lawyer also. For example, if you had the term human resource (singular) management, and the key word search by an organization is human resources (plural) but without the word management, there would still be a match on most search systems. A match would not occur on some systems; therefore you will want to use as many variations of the same key words as possible.

Acronyms. If registered nurse is one of your key words, make sure that it appears somewhere in the resume as RN. If you are going to use certified financial planner, make sure that CFP appears as well.

With the synonyms and acronyms you are trying to cover all of your bases. If the employer uses human resources management as a key phrase, while you used personnel administration throughout your resume, the computer may not see your resume as a match and the employer will never read it. If you only use the term certified financial planner but the employer searches only for CFP, you also risk not having your resume viewed.

When using acronyms realize that personnel clerks often perform the initial screening of the resume, and neither they nor a human resources manager will be familiar with all acronyms in all fields. In principle, the first time you use an acronym which you suspect not all people will recognize, spell out the acronym and then in parentheses, indicate the acronym. This is how it might appear in the qualifications section of an RN: Over ten years' experience as a Registered Nurse (RN), including five years experience in Emergency Room (ER) and Critical Care (CC). From that point on you can use the acronym without having to spell it out. You will also have ensured that the computer will be able to find both the term and the acronym.

Key words should not be inserted in a resume merely because you feel an employer might look for them. They must truly be somewhere in your background. For example, when computer people list programming languages, most list those they've used on the job, as well as those they've studied. That's perfectly acceptable. Once your resume shows up on the screen, however, it is up to the employer to determine if your experience and knowledge matches the need. In a telephone or face-to-face interview you must be prepared to present how extensive your experience actually is.

With more companies resorting to computerized resume databanks each year, it is in your best interest to ensure that your resume achieves maximum exposure.

Once the request goes in for resumes with certain key words, thousands of resumes in the databank can be searched in less than a minute. The computer will find all of your key words and highlight them on the screen. Where your key words appear makes no difference to the computer, but it may to a reader. For that reason many people prefer to use a key word section for resumes that will be scanned or sent electronically.

Some of the resume tracking systems used by companies will rank the resumes based on criteria that consider key words, education, and years of experience. Some give more weight to resumes that have key words early in the resume. So you may want to include your key word paragraph when you know or believe it is likely that your resume will go into a resume databank.

Many jobs request a bachelor's degree. If you have tons of experience, but never quite finished that degree, this could cause you a problem. If you believe you are qualified for a position, you will want to prevent yourself from being screened out merely because you're ten credits short. Of course, if you come up on an employer's screen, you'll have to have the goods or with a quick mouse click they'll be on to another resume. Here are some ways which can work:

BA (equivalent)

This would be used by a person who has significant college credits, a lot of seminars, and perhaps a certificate or two from recognized institutions.

Currently enrolled in BA program

Or

BA (to be completed in June 2003)

Either of these could be used if appropriate.

Using a Key Word Section

A key word section is frequently used by people who are e-mailing their resume to a commercial web site or a company web site, or when sending a paper copy to an organization that will likely scan it. If you have created a qualifications section, a key word section will fit right into that format. For a salesperson it might work like this.

OBJECTIVE: Sales Representative

QUALIFICATIONS

Strong sales background. Consistently exceed quota and always become a top producer. Effectively build long-term relationships with accounts. Excellent at cold calling and adding new accounts.

Areas of experience include: Calling on key accounts; territory management; sell to OEMs, retail chains, wholesalers, and distributors; experienced with co-op advertising; marketing; advertising agencies; market research; repeat and referral business; consultative selling; increase sales; increase market share; increase profits; cold calls; international sales; tradeshows; develop collateral material; number one West Coast rep; work effectively with buyers and merchandise managers; turn around problem territories.

In this example the first paragraph already exists and it contains some desirable key words. The second paragraph is the key word section. Some of the terms in the key word section appear elsewhere in the resume but most do not. This person has just increased the likelihood that her resume will show up on the employer's computer screen when initiating a key word search.

If you choose not to make one of your qualifications paragraphs a key word section, you can insert a key word section at the end of your resume. Simply label it: Key Words. Then under this new section, type in a paragraph of key words (nouns and buzz words) with each key word or each phrase separated by a comma or semicolon. The computer does not care where a key word appears, as long as they do appear. This key word section would look virtually identical to the example just above.

A key word section, while very helpful, is not absolutely essential. You probably have many of the key words already included in your job descriptions. However, adding this key word section allows you to easily view all of your key words or key word phrases at once, thereby ensuring that you have not missed any important ones. Since it can be quite difficult to make sure that all of your key words, and all of their variations, including synonyms and acronyms, have been included in a sentence somewhere in the resume, a key word section is highly recommended.

Some computer resume databanks rank your resume based on the number of times a key word appears in your resume. This ranking assumes that the more times a key word appears in a resume, the greater the likelihood that this person has more years of experience in this field. On the other hand, some databanks rank your resume not only on a key word, but on how recently you submitted your resume. This assumes that the more recently submitted resumes are from job seekers who are most likely still looking for work.

What all this means is that you should have the primary key words in your resume more than once (be appropriate, and don't overdo it) and that you should update your resume in any particular databank every couple months.

That's how you create a key word resume. Having taken care of the key word portion of your resume, it will be important to create your plain-text resume that can be sent to employers by e-mail and your scannable paper resume that can be sent to those employers who will electronically scan your resume into their databank.

CONVERT A WORD-PROCESSED RESUME TO AN ELECTRONIC RESUME

In order to create a resume which will look consistently good when e-mailed, scanned, or viewed within a text editor, you must use the simplest formatting possible. This means sacrificing the advanced formatting features of your favorite word processor, such as italics, columns, bolding, and custom fonts.

Follow these steps to create a resume that will look good no matter where you send it. These directions will work for MS Word 6.0 and up. Ignore any "lost formatting" warnings that may occur during this process.

IMPORTANT: Be sure to save a backup copy of your resume before converting it. Put a copy of your resume on a floppy disk just in case your hard drive crashes.

If you are using a word processing package other than MS Word, the steps will be the same, but some of the special techniques and methods that I suggest are unique to MS Word.

1. Open your formatted resume in your word processor. Make sure your desired key words are already in your resume. This should be your final version that says everything exactly the way you want it.

2. Go to the File menu and select Save As. (See Figure A) Choose Text Only in the Save As Type drop down menu at the bottom of the dialog box. (See Figure B) If you are using Word 2002 with Windows XP, choose Plain Text. Name the file something like *resume electronic* or *electronic resume* so you know immediately that this is your electronic version. After selecting Plain Text, a dialog box will appear and you should choose Windows Default. Click Save or press Enter

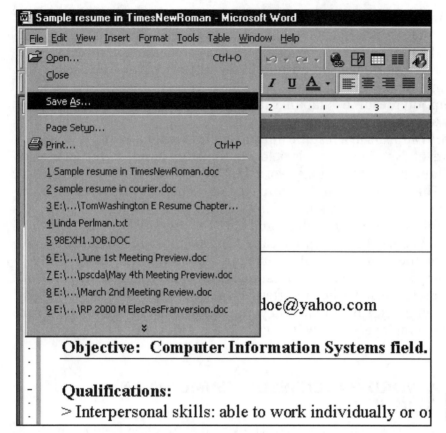

Figure A
Save As

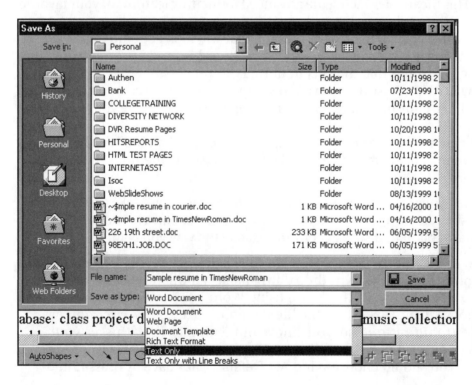

Figure B
Save As
Text

to save the file. Immediately a warning will come on screen that says "Document may contain features that are not compatible with Text Only format. Do you want to save the document in this format?" Go ahead and click Yes. Click Yes whenever that warning comes up in this process. Make note of which folder or location you have saved your resume in so you can find it later.

3. Close your resume document (not the word processor program), then immediately reopen it.

Quick tip: MS Word has a handy feature that allows you to quickly reopen the last 4-9 files you've been working on. Simply click on the File menu and scroll down to the document you want to open. In this example you can see that "resume electronic.txt" is the most recent file. (See Figure C)

Your new text resume should now be in the Courier or Courier New font. This automatic font change was done by your word processor when you selected Text Only as you used the Save As feature. The Courier font family is a fixed-width printer font that uses the same width for all characters. Most plain-text editing programs use Courier.

Note: Office 97 and the newer MS Word programs automatically convert your text settings to 10-point font size. A font size of 10-point is fine for your plain-text resume that you will e-mail or submit to resume databanks. If you convert this resume to 12-point, and Save As Text Only again, it will revert back to 10-point.

4. Go to the File menu to Page Setup. (See Figure D) Change your left and right margins to 1.7" each. (See Figure E) Click OK. Then save your resume. This should ensure that none of the lines in your resume will exceed 65 characters. This is important because on some systems, the most characters that can be seen on a screen is 65. This 1.7" rule will work if your word processor has converted your type to 10-point. If it is 12-point you should set your margins at 1.4" left and right.

Quick Tip: To confirm that none of your lines exceed 65 characters, highlight the longest line in your resume. Highlight by putting your cursor at the beginning of the line until it becomes an arrow, then "left" click your mouse and the line will be highlighted. Then go to the Tools menu and select Word Count, then look at Characters With Spaces. This will tell you how many characters (including the blank space between each word) are in your longest line. If your longest line has been indented from the left margin, add the number of spaces to the number you were just told, and make sure the combined total is less than 65.

5. Check to see if you've used any tabs. If so, remove them. Without removing the tabs your plain-text resume will not look the way you want it to. If you have just a few tabs the easiest way to remove them is to simply delete them. If you have over fifteen, utilize the Quick Tip which follows.

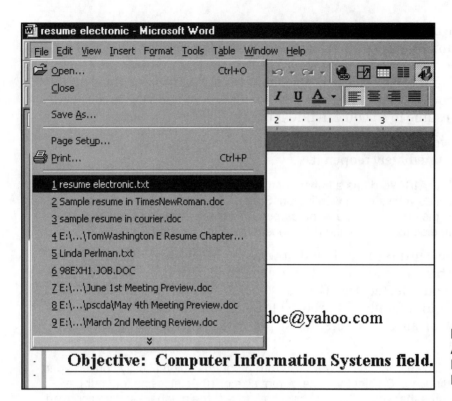

Figure C
Accessing
Recently Used
Files

Quick Tip: To remove tabs in seconds, click on Edit in the menu at the top left of the screen and then click on Replace. A small dialog box will appear on your screen. In the dialog box, you will see a line that says "Find What." Insert a caret (use Shift and enter the number 6 key on your keyboard) along with a small t. (It will look like: ^t) Move your cursor to the line in the same dialog box that says "Replace With" and insert a blank space simply by hitting the space bar on your keyboard. Now click the button on this same dialog box that says "Replace All." You should then get a message on your screen indicating how many tabs were found and replaced with blank spaces. Close both dialog boxes.

6. Save the resume by going to the File menu and selecting Save As. Select Text With Line Breaks. (See Figure F) Close the resume and then immediately reopen it again. There should be line breaks at the end of each line. You'll know there are line breaks if you see a paragraph sign (¶) at the end of each line. If you see no paragraph signs and no dots between words, it means that function has been turned off. To show those signs, hold down the shift and control keys, and press the number 8 key. You'll immediately see the line breaks.

7. Now is your opportunity to edit your resume so you can get it looking the way you want within the limitations of a plain-text resume. Now that all the tabs are gone, all text will probably be flush left.

If you want to indent some portions such as job descriptions you can do that with the space bar. To indent a line, put the cursor in

126

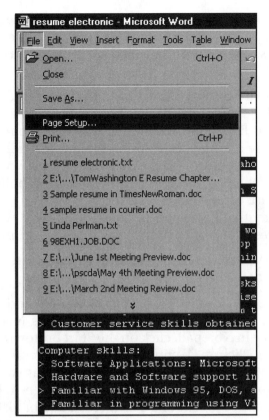

Figure D
Page Setup

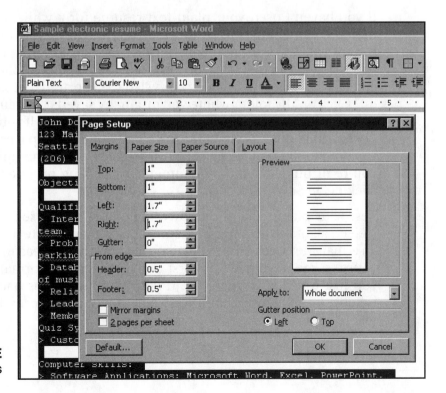

Figure E
Setting Margins

front of the first word in the line and press the space bar to create as many spaces as you desire. If you want to create spaces between words, simply use the space bar to create as many spaces as you want.

There are other editing functions you can do. You can capitalize words you want to emphasize, such as your name, the section titles such as Education and Employment, or job titles. This is necessary because saving your resume as plain-text will remove bolding and italics. If you want to create a bulleted list you can use the asterisk (*), hyphen (-), or plus sign (+) in place of bullets. This is necessary because when you convert to plain-text, any existing bullets will be automatically turned to asterisks. If you want to double space between categories or between paragraphs, this is the time to do it.

8. Once you have finished editing your plain-text resume, save it one more time.

To see your results, close your document and your word processor. Reopen it in a plain-text editor such as Notepad. To open your resume in Notepad, click on the Start button in the lower left of your screen. Click on Documents and then click on your resume. It should now appear in Notepad. Notepad ensures your resume is in plain-text format and ensures that when it is e-mailed to an employer databank or is sent to a commercial databank, it will have the same appearance to employers as you now see in Notepad (or the text editor you are using).

If you haven't used your plain-text resume for a while, the above method of opening your resume in Notepad may not work for you. In that case click on the Start button, click on Programs, click on Accessories, and then click on Notepad. (See Figure G) Click on File and click on Open. The Dialog box will have a portion that says "Look in:" Click on the folder where you originally saved it. When you find your text file click on it and it will come up in Notepad. If your resume doesn't look quite right, you can still add or delete spaces and you can double space between categories or between paragraphs. When you're through, save the document by clicking on File and then clicking on Save.

Test your plain-text resume by e-mailing it to yourself. Highlight (select) all of the text in your resume, copy it, and paste the text into an e-mail message you are e-mailing to yourself. The reason you send your resume to yourself the first time is to test the formatting that you just finished working on. If your resume comes back to you exactly the same way that it was sent, you have a successful plain-text resume.

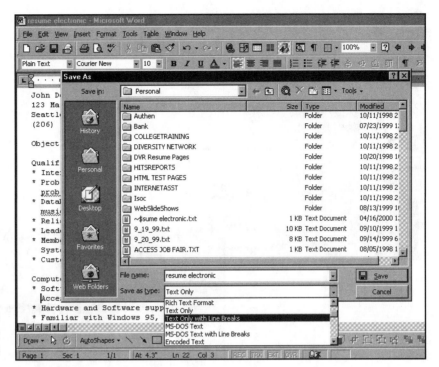

Figure F
Saving as Text
With Line Breaks

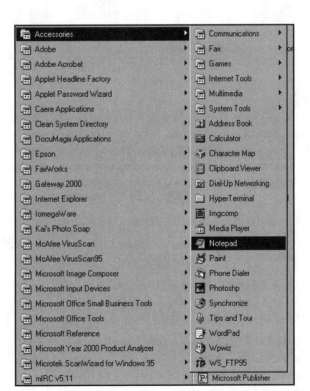

Figure G
Opening Notepad

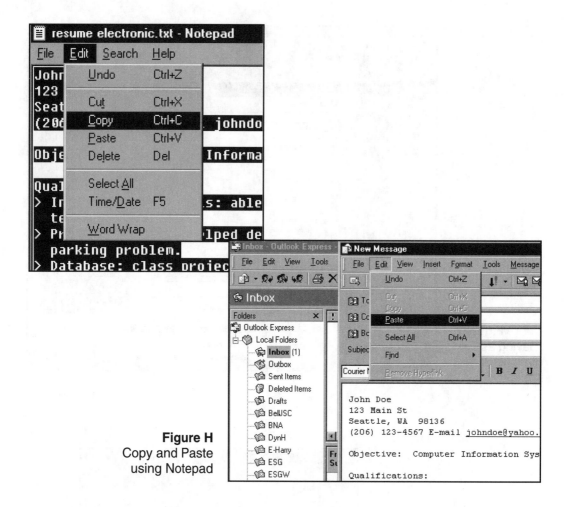

Figure H
Copy and Paste
using Notepad

Quick Tip: For those not familiar with copy and paste I'll walk you through the process. To copy the text in your resume, start by highlighting the entire resume. To do that click on Edit, then click on Select All. Then go back to the Edit menu and click on Copy. (See Figure H) Next, open up your e-mail software to start a new e-mail message. Put your cursor in the space for an e-mail message where the text will be pasted in. Go back to the Edit menu and click Paste. (See Figure H) Your entire resume will now be pasted in the space.

Once you have completed the pasting process in the e-mail, click Send. Then open up your e-mailed resume and print it out. If you're satisfied with the appearance, you're ready to send it to employers.

Having completed all of these steps you are ready to proceed to the process of actually sending your resume to employers or to commercial resume databanks.

WARNING: Do not send your resume as a file attachment to an e-mail message unless the employer specifically requests that you do. Pasting your resume directly into the e-mail will ensure that you are not transmitting a virus along with the message.

How Many Pages?

A computer does not care how long your resume is. It can store and retrieve a ten-page resume as easily as a one-page resume. The answer to the question regarding the best length of a resume remains: It should be long enough to adequately sell you and not so long that a person hesitates to read it. Most resumes are one or two pages in length, with a three-page resume being appropriate for some people.

Electronic resumes are often a little longer due to the short 65 character lines for plain-text. For this reason my advice is that one-, two-, and three-page resumes will work fine. Just make sure that everything in the resume is there because it helps sell you.

After They See Your Resume Will They Call?

Having your resume seen on a person's monitor will not necessarily result in an interview. You must have the right background and you must sell your background well. Creating an effective electronic resume is not difficult, but it will take additional time. Whether your resume is scanned into a corporate resume databank or sent by e-mail to a commercial resume databank, it will work for you only if it contains the right key words and if it is well written.

Some Systems Will Accept Only One Resume At A Time

The systems at some corporations, Boeing for example, will keep just one version of your resume in its databank. In such a system, if you have previously sent a generic resume, but now you are sending a targeted resume for a specific position, that new resume is the one that will stay on file. If you haven't been called in for an interview in about four weeks, resubmit your generic resume so that it becomes your resume on file.

In most databank systems it is relatively easy to update your resume. If you have moved, added a degree or certification, or completed a successful project, update your resume and resubmit it. Just remember to keep track of your user name and password for each resume databank. A good routine to keep is to write down your user name and password immediately as you create it.

USING YOUR ELECTRONIC RESUME FOR YOUR JOB SEARCH

Sending your electronic resume to potential employers can be well worth the small amount of effort it takes. Resume web sites have been successfully used by people in high-tech careers for several years, and their use by those in more traditional occupations is growing rapidly. If you have never used a resume web site, take time to browse them. See page 281 for the web addresses of some of the major sites where you can post your resume. Most of them have a lot in common, including clear instructions and ease of use. Getting familiar with them can guide your choice of which to use.

Submitting Your Resume to Resume Databanks

Two major types of resume databanks or web sites exist. Most are databanks that store your resume text (but not its formatting or layout) and make it available to employers who search for people with specific skills and experience. These are easy to use and free for job seekers. Sites include Monster.com, Hotjobs.com, and many others.

How It's Done

First, let's look at the databank-style resume web sites. See page 281 for a list of the major sites and their web addresses. Follow the site's links to register with the site. Each site will want to get some basic information about you. Rather than refer to it as registering, some will indicate they want you to "create a new account" or "store your resume." You'll generally have to select a user name and a password, although some sites assign these to you. Many people use their own name or a nickname for a password. In any case, record this information. Keep track of the user name and password you use at each site.

You could try to use the same user name and password with each site, but if a user name or password has already been used, you'll be told to select another.

The resume you're going to give the web sites will be your plain-text resume. The text isn't pretty, but it is functional.

Once you've created a text-only resume, the basic procedure for most web sites is similar. Fill out the forms on your screen (with your name, address, and other vital pieces of information), and then paste your entire resume into a larger window provided for that purpose. That's about all there is to it.

Some sites also prompt you to supply a cover letter in another window. Create a short cover letter that hits your key skills and experience. In the world of electronic resumes, cover letters are often ignored, so if you want yours to have impact, keep it short and to the point.

Privacy

If you're concerned about your employer discovering you're job hunting, or concerned that your name and e-mail address are being made available to marketers, follow the link to the site's privacy policy statement and read it. Some sites don't have one available. Those that do usually state that they will not disclose specific or personal information to outside parties without your permission. But the organization behind the resume web site may "offer third-party services and products to you based on the preferences that you identify in your registration and at any time thereafter" (in other words, send you junk mail), as in the case of Monster.com. If you are employed you may want to post your resume only at the safest sites. The safest sites require the organization interested in you to e-mail you and tell you who they are. You can then respond by e-mail indicating you are interested. With other sites, the resume databank will contact you by e-mail and ask you to reply if you are interested in the organization, which will be revealed to you at that time.

If your concern is that your present employer may see your resume on the web and find out that you are looking for a new job, look for options in each site that allow you to make your resume nonsearchable. This means the web site will contact you for permission to show your resume to interested employers instead of including it in the results of any search conducted by any employer. Not all resume web sites offer this option.

Another option to control the privacy of your posted resume is to remove the names of your last two employers, and instead of your name and address at the top, just list your e-mail address. Also at the top would be a request that interested organizations e-mail you and indicate who they are and a little more about the position. Such a technique could cause some employers to skip you, but those really interested would not be deterred. For maximum privacy, obtain a new e-mail account that you will use just for the job search. Create an e-mail address that does not contain your first or last name or your initials.

Like other web sites, many career and resume sites use cookies. These are files placed on your computer by web sites you visit in order to recognize you when you return and to target online ads to your demographic. (Preferences can be set within your computer to refuse to accept some or all cookies, but this setting will stop you from visiting some sites.)

Useful features often included in resume web sites:

- Clear instructions, including information on how many characters will fit on each line (so that you can put in manual line breaks accordingly)

- A window where you can paste the entire resume

- An option for a confidential resume, which means that the web site will contact you for permission to show the resume to interested employers; this can prevent your current employer from stumbling across it

- A statement of the web site's privacy policy

- A preview button that allows you to view the resume after pasting it into the window

Tips to keep in mind when building and submitting your resume:

- Record your user name and password for each site. In some cases you will select these; in others they will be assigned to you.

- Start with a finished resume. Save it as a text (.txt) file. It will lose any special formatting such as centering, bold and italic type, and bullets. You can then copy and paste this version into the "paste your resume here" windows provided by the web sites.

- Check on how long the site will keep your resume.

A SCANNABLE RESUME

Although more and more companies are preferring that resumes be sent to them electronically by e-mail, many companies are still scanning resumes into their resume databank. When a paper resume comes in, someone in HR will scan the resume and use the optical character recognition (OCR) software to submit it to the resume databank. At that time it becomes available to a manager who can then find it through a key word search.

Scanners, and the OCR software that translates the images into words, have limitations. Many cannot properly interpret italics and if the print is too small, the OCR software will not recognize the letters, creating typos throughout the resume. In the next five years scanners and OCR software may reach a level of sophistication where they can even read the handwriting of physicians. Until that time arrives, it is best to follow the rules that virtually ensure a one-hundred-percent accurately scanned resume.

Take the time to insert your key words so employers can find you. Personnel file drawers containing resumes have for years been referred to as black holes. Once a resume got in a file drawer, it never seemed to see the light of day again. At least now, if you understand the following rules for creating a scannable resume, your resume will pop up on many computer screens and you'll have the opportunity to sell yourself.

Paper resumes sent to employers, who then scan them into their resume databank, must be formatted in such a way that all the words you've used to describe yourself go into the databank exactly as you composed them. If done incorrectly, your scanned resume could enter the databank filled with typographical errors. Resumes with such errors rarely result in interviews.

Tips On Using Your Resume

Whenever possible, resumes should be sent to a specific person. If the organization is identified in the ad, call and ask for the best person to address your cover letter to. Make sure you ask how their name is spelled and if it is female or male. Mr. Chris Smith is a lot different than Ms. Kris Smith. Although not every organization will give you a name, many will. Then address your cover letter to that person with the correct title. While you have a person from that organization on the phone, also ask if they scan resumes. If they don't, send only one version of your resume, the one that visually looks the best. If you simply don't know whether your resume will be scanned, and the organization has over one hundred employees, send both versions. Few companies under one hundred employees scan resumes.

Creating A Scannable Resume

Many organizations with one hundred or more employees will scan your paper resume into their resume database. When a resume arrives at an organization which scans and stores resumes, it first passes through an electronic scanner which in essence takes a picture of the page. It then must be analyzed by the OCR software to change it from an image to a plain-text file that can then be stored in a database and accessed. Problems can occur in both the scanning and analyzing stages. If there is not a good contrast between the paper and letters, the scanner may not take a good picture of the page. This could occur when a resume with black ink on dark blue paper is scanned. If the letters are too small or if an unusual font has been used, the OCR software simply cannot recognize the letters and the resume will be unreadable.

Scanners and OCR software are constantly improving so that the newest high-end hardware and software may have little trouble with typical resumes. The problem is that many organizations are still using older hardware and software, and you have no way of knowing who is state of the art and who is not. What this means is that the great-looking resumes that people create with their computers and laser printers will need to be modified.

Although it seems like extra work to create a scannable resume, it will take little extra time if you follow a few simple suggestions. Following these instructions should lead to a resume which is scanned and stored with one hundred percent accuracy.

Since many companies are still scanning paper resumes into their resume databanks, it's important to send a resume that will scan properly. Keep in mind that many scanning systems have no trouble with some of the items I'll mention, but it is better to be safe than sorry. Since many scanning systems have trouble with underlining, it is simply better to eliminate underlining. Underlining and using too small a font can cause typographical errors to occur. At some companies, if errors are detected, they may be willing to correct four or five errors. They do this by comparing the paper resume with the ASCII version now in the resume databank. Words that the OCR software had trouble with will use a tilde character, which looks like ~. The clerk will look for tilde marks (~) and then use the paper resume as a guide to make corrections. If ten or more are found they may correct a few or none at all. Some organizations will merely ensure that your name, address, phone number, and objective are correct. Errors in other portions of the resume may be left as they are. The following sentence appeared in the resume of one of my clients:

Placed over 100 people with disabilities into competitive jobs, a rate 30-40% above the norm.

After it was scanned into the databank the sentence became:

Placed ove~ 100 people with disabilities into competitive jobs, a rate 3040~ above the nomm.

You can see why it is important to create a scannable resume. The ~ symbol is placed there by the OCR software, acknowledging that a letter or symbol is there but it cannot properly decipher it. In the case of the 30-40% portion, the OCR did not detect the hyphen and it could not decipher the percent sign. The word norm became nomm. In this case part of the scanning problem was due to using a 10-point font. I do not recommend using a font smaller than 11-point for resumes that will be scanned, and 12-point is preferred.

THE KEYS TO CREATING A SCANNABLE RESUME

Below are 19 points that, if followed, will result in your resume being scanned with virtually total accuracy.

Use a 12-point font

I have long recommended a 12-point font size because it is the most readable. It also happens to be what scanners and OCR software prefer. When I tested different font sizes and typefaces (such as Arial and Times Roman), they all did better with 12-point type than with 10-point. For your name at the top of the first page, 14- or 16-point font sizes are fine.

Use a sans-serif typeface

I like serif fonts like Times Roman for resumes, but for your scannable resume you should stick with a sans-serif font like Helvetica or Arial. Letters with serifs have the little stroke in parts of each letter.

This is Times Roman. It has serifs.

This is Arial. It does not have serifs. It is a sans-serif typeface.

Resumes using a sans-serif typeface scan slightly better than those with serifs. In those typefaces which use serifs, the letters sometimes touch, and this can give fits to a scanner. Typefaces come in many names, and often there are only slight differences between them. Some sans-serif typefaces that will scan well include Arial, Helvetica, Univers, and Century Gothic. Most sans-serif typefaces will scan well. Sans-serif typefaces from Word 2000 that will scan well include:

This is Albertus Medium
This is Antique Olive
This is Arial, the most commonly sans-serif typeface used in resumes
   (It is almost identical to Helvetica, another popular font)
This is Century Gothic
This is Franklin Gothic Book
This is Lucida Sans
This is Tahoma
This is Univers
This is Verdana

Keep your lines to 75 characters or less

Some systems permit no more than 75 characters per line on the screen. If your resume has more than 75 characters per line, your resume on screen and on paper may look like this:

```
    Eastside Employment Services, Renton, WA 1984-1993
    EMPLOYMENT COORDINATOR - Met with clients with
disabilities and assessed
    their mental and physical skills. Matched clients
with prospective
    employers and sold those employers on the
benefits of hiring each client.
    Successfully placed over 100 people with
developmental disabilities in
```

Most firms will simply not take the time to improve its looks. A word wrap problem has occurred because not all the words could fit on the line. It doesn't look pretty.

A basic rule is that if you use a 12-point font and have margins of 1.4 inches on both sides you should be safe. To be sure, count the characters (count the space between words as a character) in your longest line. Remember, to count your characters in one line automatically: Highlight one entire line, go to Tools, then click on Word Count. Look at Characters with Spaces. If your line has been indented, you need to add the number of characters to the left as is shown in the example:

Data Systems, 1973-Present

SENIOR PROJECT MANAGER, Little Rock, Arkansas, 1989-Present. Negotiate contracts, schedule deliveries, and troubleshoot all phases of computer installations. Work closely with customers to determine their needs, then gain contractual commitments from manufacturing and field engineering.

In this case you would count the characters in the line starting with "needs." That line has 69 characters. Since that sentence was indented two spaces in from the company name, you would have to count it as 71, still well within the 75-character rule. This job description would not create a word wrap problem as was demonstrated above.

Use white or light-colored 8.5" x 11" paper and print on only one side

Scanners need maximum contrast between letters and the background. They also do best with standard 8.5" x 11" paper. When I scanned a resume with black ink on dark blue paper, the errors immediately went from zero to about 15. A few people print their resumes on 11" x 17" paper to create a presentation folder. It is folded in half, with printing on all four pages, the first page acting as a cover. The style is not well accepted, and it causes major problems for scanners.

Avoid the use of underlining

Some systems handle underlining just fine, but problems can occur when the underline touches the lower part of letters such as "g" or "p."

Avoid the use of bolding

Although most systems handle bold letters without any problems, some do not. Avoid bold type.

Avoid fancy fonts

Some of the unusual fonts that are available are very difficult for scanners to read. I gave one system a resume using a script typeface *which looked like this*. To the scanner it was total gibberish. Such a resume would have been tossed out by virtually any employer. Other fancy fonts that would not work well include: **Bauhaus**, Papyrus, *Forte*, ALGERIAN, Footlight, matura, Tempus, *Lucida Calligraphy*, and Bradley Hand.

Don't use bullets or hollow bullets

The bullets will be stripped off when the resume is scanned so you might as well not even use them. Hollow bullets on a paper resume can be interpreted as zeroes or as the small letter o when it is scanned, so avoid using them.

Print your resume on a high-quality laser printer

Although ink jet printers have improved a lot in the last few years, they still do not produce the sharpness of letters that are achieved with laser printers. Ink jet printers are fine for cover letters and other correspondence with employers, but when you want your resume scanned with one hundred percent accuracy, stick with laser printers. Recent, top-of-the-line ink jet printers, however, are approaching the sharpness of laser printers and should work fine.

If you don't have a computer or have access to one, look in the Yellow Pages under "Word Processing," or "Secretarial." Such services will have top of the line computers and laser printers and will know how to create a good looking resume. Expect to pay $40 to $70. At copy shops such as Kinko's, you can rent a computer. If you don't already know how to use it, however, you're better off with a word processing service.

At Kinko's and other copy shops with computers, you can also take in your disk and, for about fifty cents per page, can have your resume printed on a laser printer. If you have your own laser printer I would suggest mailing only originals.

Put your name on the top line and use one line for each telephone number listed and one for e-mail

Many scanning systems assume that the first line of a resume contains your name. Therefore, for your scannable resume, have only your name on the top line. It will also increase accuracy if you give one line for your home phone and another line for a work number. Your e-mail address would also be on a separate line. If you have a web resume, put your web address (URL) on a separate line as well. Although it is considered best to have a single line for each item on the scannable resume, you could put both phone numbers on one line as long as you put at least six spaces between them. Typically you would write Work after your work number and Home after your home number. Another common approach is to put (w) or (W) after your work number, (h) or (H) after your home number and (c) or (C) for cell phone. Put parentheses around your area code: (425) 879-0098.

Use caps to give emphasis to key areas

Since you've been advised to eliminate some of the nice word processing touches that make a resume attractive, about the only design option you have left is to capitalize certain words for emphasis. Your job titles and you headings like Education and Employment could be capitalized. Your use of capitalization will be maintained in the text version.

Send a resume unfolded, unstapled, and flat in a 9" x 12" manila envelope

A crease through letters can cause a scanner to misread words in that line. Although there is an extra cost to sending it unfolded (for 2003 that cost is 60¢ for up to two ounces), it will scan better. Besides, even if the firm does not scan resumes, it will have a nicer appearance. The resume will be taken apart before scanning, so leave it unstapled. Use a paperclip instead.

Avoid the use of italics

Many scanners do just fine with italics, but italics can cause problems for others. In part this is because with italics the characters come so close to merging with each other that the OCR software cannot discern what the letter should be.

Avoid the use of shading

There's really no reason to use shading, but some people use it on resumes just because it's available. Scanners need clear contrast between the letters and background. Shading destroys that contrast. Shading like this will really make a scanner go bonkers.

Avoid the use of columns

Many scanners handle columns just fine, but for some scanners each column is assumed to be a separate page.

Avoid the use of boxes or vertical lines

Vertical lines can fool a scanner, which may read them as the letter I. Vertical and horizontal lines and borders add nothing to a resume, so just leave them off.

Avoid compressing space between letters and between lines

Today's word processing packages enable one to compress the space between letters and between lines. It enables more words to get on a page, but can cause problems for scanners. Stick to using the standard spacing between letters and lines and paragraphs.

Print only on one side of the page

Print on just one side of the page. Printing on both sides of a page gives scanners real problems.

Never send a resume by fax unless requested

The quality of a fax so degrades the sharpness of the letters that errors are virtually guaranteed. If requested to fax a resume for the sake of speed, send your scannable resume by mail the same day so they will have your high-quality resume as well. Or, consider sending only your scannable resume, but sending it by next day air or second day air. If you fax your resume, try to fax it directly from your computer since this will create a higher quality document when they receive it.

Pulling It All Together

Although I have given you a number of points to follow, they are really quite simple to apply. These rules do diminish some of the nice visual touches that are possible with today's word processing programs and laser printers, but once a resume is scanned and goes into the database, all of those things are stripped off anyway. When a resume is printed out after being stored, there will be no bolding, underlining, italics, shading, or any other special little things that people like to do with their resumes. So, if there is a chance the resume will be scanned, you might as well remove those things at the beginning and ensure that the scanner will read it with total accuracy. As scanning systems improve, some of the advice provided above will change, but for now, this is what you must do to ensure that your resume is accurately scanned and stored in a database.

If you decide to send two copies of your resume—one for scanning and one that visually looks the best—you could attach a note to the scanning resume that says, "Resume version intended for scanning purposes."

Although not all cover letters are scanned into computer databases, you should still take the time to create a strong cover letter because many employers use cover letters to learn a lot about you. It too should utilize a 12-point, sans-serif font.

On the next page is an example of a resume which should scan perfectly on virtually any scanning system. It uses 12-point Arial type and its longest line does not exceed 75 characters.

ADRIAN MASTERS
2199 Roxanne Avenue
Long Beach, California 90815
(213) 645-0968

OBJECTIVE: Import Manager

QUALIFICATIONS

Strong import and transportation experience with knowledge
of customs regulations and procedures. Consistently establish
procedures that cut costs and provide timely delivery of product.

EDUCATION

B.A. - International Business, UCLA (1992)

EMPLOYMENT

Raha Sportswear, Long Beach, California 10/97-Present

ASSISTANT IMPORT MANAGER—Manage a staff of five who
monitor $95 million in wearing apparel imports and a $44 million
letter of credit line. Proposed, developed, and implemented an
ocean freight consolidation program which has reduced ocean
freight costs by 30% and provides better tracking control. Planned
and developed a manual tracking system which for the first time
has enabled the company to analyze the performance of vendors.

Breslin Inc., Los Angeles, California 5/93-8/97

IMPORT SPECIALIST—Coordinated the transportation of all
retail purchase orders through communication with brokers,
agents, and product managers. Recommended the establishment
of a specific footwear rate, saving an estimated $30,000 in ocean
freight rates.

Appara, Los Angeles, California 4/90-5/93

IMPORT CLERK/ALLOCATION CLERK—As Allocation Clerk,
adjusted inventories and future shipments to meet store orders.
As Import Clerk, tracked all imported product to assure consistent
flow of goods by communicating with brokers, truckers, and
foreign agents.

THE BENEFITS OF CREATING A WEB PORTFOLIO

Research shows that job seekers who use several jobhunting techniques consistently find jobs more quickly than those who rely on just one or two. That's why I suggest that you seriously consider using a web portfolio. This tool can improve the impression you make on prospective employers and can communicate much more than a resume alone. Today's technology makes it possible to create a useful web portfolio for an investment of several hours and $100 to $450. Despite its capabilities, less than one-tenth of one percent of all job seekers use a web portfolio. But though the use of web portfolios is still rare, people in virtually all occupations are using them. Photographers, artists, graphic designers, architects, web designers, and others with work samples that are primarily visual have been among the first to utilize web portfolios. If your type of work doesn't seem to lend itself to online viewing, you can still benefit from a web portfolio. (I'll give you some specific ideas later in this chapter.)

A web portfolio is very much like an artist's portfolio in electronic form. The electronic version, however, can accomplish far more than any physical portfolio. For one thing, your web portfolio is out there working for you 24/7. A web portfolio is intended to get you interviews, while a physical version is used almost exclusively during interviews.

In essence, a web portfolio is your own website (with its own URL, or web address), designed specifically to sell you to employers. Your web portfolio is like a buffet of links to your work samples and other information. Each viewer can select just the links that interest him and suit his needs, rather than visiting all of your linked pages.

Because the viewer goes only where he or she chooses to go, you can pack a lot of material in your web portfolio, putting each piece on its own page to avoid clutter. An effective web portfolio may have as few as four links or as many as 20, with the average being six to twelve. There are no laws, only principles.

Your home page directs employers to your resume and to other linked pages that provide samples of your work, such as a marketing plan you created. Linked pages could also include other material that promotes you and your achievements, such as a photograph of you receiving an award, or expanded descriptions of your top work accomplishments. Well-written accomplishments of 50 to 400 words can reveal a tremendous amount about you and make the viewer want to meet you. Other links could lead to a research report you wrote or samples of logos you created. If you want to emphasize your speaking ability, you might provide sound clips. (See page 148 for many more ideas.)

Employers find your web portfolio by obtaining its URL, usually from your resume. The URL should appear at the top of your print and online resumes, along with your telephone number and your email address, so that prospective employers can quickly survey your web portfolio. The portfolio must be attractive and useful to cause them to linger.

Having a web portfolio doesn't diminish the importance of having a top-quality resume. If your resume is poorly written or does not sell you effectively, few employers will visit your web portfolio. On the other hand, if you pique their interest, many will invest at least a few moments to learn more about your accomplishments.

BUILDING YOUR PORTFOLIO WEBSITE

There are basically two ways to create a web portfolio. You can build your own website from scratch or you can use one of several sites that walk you through the process of creating a web portfolio. Building a site from scratch requires you to purchase a domain name and subscribe to a hosting service for a fee (more about that later). It will require you to learn some HTML (hypertext markup language) or to use specialized software such as Microsoft FrontPage to create the site. If that seems a bit intimidating, you can hire a web designer to produce the site for you. See page 147 for more ideas on how to approach the building of your own site.

If cost or time are limiting factors, you'll want to use one of the services that provide templates and that walk you through the process. The primary services are Tripod (a Lycos service), GeoCities (a Yahoo service), and Workfolio, a specialized web service designed to create web portfolios. Although Tripod and GeoCities give you the option to create a web portfolio for free, your portfolio will contain intrusive banner and popup ads unless you choose their inexpensive fee-based services. Because you will want to have complete control over the content of your web portfolio, which is intended for employers and recruiters, I strongly suggest that you not allow ads to appear on it.

Building A Website With Tripod Or GeoCities

Tripod (www.tripod.com) and GeoCities (www.geocities.com) provide many templates to help you build a website (in this case, your web portfolio). When you've chosen a template, you'll see what your site's home page looks like with generic placeholder text. You'll replace this text with your own. Depending on the service you're using, you'll add your own text either by typing over the placeholder text or by filling in the blanks in a web form.

Like many online services and software packages, Tripod and GeoCities utilize "wizards" to walk you through the building of your site, one simple step at a time. They even provide examples of how to modify its design, depending on the template you selected. The first page you'll build is your home page, which introduces the site as your portfolio site. Follow instructions to add photos or graphics as needed. Then add more pages to the site, and a link to each from the home page, by using Windows-style menus. Each page should contain a sample of your work or other material that promotes your accomplishments. Again, you'll type your text into a placeholder or a web form, and you'll upload and add photos and graphics as needed.

Building a website with wizards and templates utilizes concepts and tools that are not complicated, but nevertheless it's a slow process. It involves making many detailed choices, and requires patience with interfaces and instructions that can be confusing. Don't be discouraged. Be persistent and you can benefit from having a quality web portfolio.

Take the time to find and use a template you like and try to avoid modifying its design. Even though the services offer this capability, it's easy to get bogged down in the process and to create a design that doesn't look as good as you thought it would. Ask a more web-savvy friend for help, or hire a designer, if you get stuck.

To eliminate ads from Tripod or GeoCities, you'll pay $5 to $10 per month. That monthly fee also buys more storage space. The free plans offer around 10 megabytes of storage space, while with the small monthly fee, you get 25 megabytes. If you want to place many photos or audio/video files on your site, you can quickly outgrow the free space. Each one of the mentioned services adds numerous other benefits that come only with the monthly fee. For these reasons, and for the ability to get rid of ads, make the decision to invest in yourself and pay the low subscription fee.

There's much more to learn about building a website. The useful book *Creating GeoCities Websites*, by Ben Sawyer and Dave Greely (1999), takes the approach that "knowledge of HTML is helpful but not absolutely necessary." It can show you how to keep the process as simple and low-cost as possible, and assumes that rather than writing HTML, you'll use a website-building tool such as Microsoft FrontPage. One section of the book shows samples of the best GeoCities sites along with discussion of what makes them so good. These visual examples can help steer you in the right direction as you design your site.

Building A Web Portfolio Using Workfolio

The Workfolio website (www.workfolio.com), will walk you through creation of a web portfolio, called a Workfolio, for a fee that is in line with the other services mentioned. The fee is $95 for the first year, and $25 per year after that to cover the web hosting. The service provides enough storage space and bandwidth to host photographs and audio and video files. The added value of this web portfolio lies in its organization of your online resources into a logical format for a potential employer.

The Workfolio contains six sections: Career Vision, Career Highlights, Professional Links, References, Activities and Interests, and Resume and Work Samples. Each section consists of a title and a link to the relevant work sample. You'll build the sections one at a time with easy-to-use web forms. To add more links, follow the instructions to add more sections. You can add an image to act as an icon for each section, and several dozen images are provided (or use one of your own). In the Career Highlights section, a writing-tips page titled "Accomplishment Builder" is helpful when you're stumped for pithy accomplishments or need inspiration to re-tool some of your experience. A multiple-choice questionnaire helps you think and write creatively about your accomplishments.

When you've finished, you have a compact, crisp portfolio overview page. The icon images add a touch of color within a consistent format, which sacrifices design flexibility for the benefit of clarity—and prevents bad design decisions. This is a good feature for job seekers who want a web portfolio but are not experienced designers. And the links you've added in some or all of the portfolio sections allow you to show off as much of your work as you can put online. Once you've created your Workfolio, it appears on a web page with a URL like this: www.workfolio.com/stars/yourname

Building A Portfolio Website Using Your Own Domain Name

Building your web portfolio from scratch on your own website provides the most flexibility and stability. (Think of it as owning a home that you can improve, remodel, and decorate in any way you wish, as opposed to renting a room from someone else.) Start by purchasing your own domain name and paying for hosting on a web server. This allows you to avoid ads, to have complete control over what appears on your site, and to have a concise, memorable web address that you choose (such as www.johnsmith.com). You'll have to handle more technical details without the step-by-step instructions and wizards offered by Tripod or GeoCities. That means you'll have to use website building software such as Microsoft FrontPage ($110) or hire someone to build the site for you. If you use a web designer, expect to pay $25 to $60 per hour for five to ten hours.

To learn more about purchasing your own domain name and subscribing to a paid hosting service, search the Internet for "domain name" and/or "website hosting service." The cost of purchasing a domain name for a year is $20-25. A hosting service for your website could cost about $120 a year and up, depending on options such as how much server space and bandwidth. Bandwidth refers to the amount of downloading your ISP will permit per month. A website that is visited by only 40 people per month would probably require less than 100 megabytes per month of downloading to your visitors. Your basic fee would more than take care of the necessary bandwidth. You can often pay by the month or the quarter for website hosting.

If you want to learn more about building a website without learning a lot of technical jargon, one useful book is *Poor Richard's Web Site*, by Peter Kent (2000). Kent provides insight on the benefits of keeping your site simple, on finding a professional designer you can afford, and on the many types of files and scripts that make websites interactive and useful. "Geek-free" and "common sense" are the refrains throughout the book.

Another book, *The Complete Idiot's Guide to Creating a Web Page*, by Paul McFedries (2002), presents everything you need to know to create your first website, including basic HTML and how to create links and add photos. Also explained: choosing a website hosting service and using FTP to put your site on the host server. Once you're comfortable with working on your site, McFedries teaches you how to enhance it with style sheets, forms, and other web tools. They're all explained in clear terms with examples and screen shots.

Additional Reading And Help

For help with building your website, try searching the web for phrases such as "help building website." You'll retrieve many sites, some helpful, some confusing, and some outdated. In general, the Internet is a better source for up-to-date help with technology that changes faster than book publishers can revise their books. A few of the more extensive web-development sites that have sections for beginners are:

- www.webstyleguide.com
- www.w3schools.com
- www.webmonkey.com (click your choice from the How-to Library list)

- www.wdvl.com (click Beginners Guide)

- www.builder.com (click Web Site Authoring)

The first two sites above are specifically designed for beginners. The rest have beginners' sections linked from their home page, though you may have to scroll down and/or look closely to find them. Don't be put off by the advanced offerings that are featured more prominently on some of the above sites.

If you'd rather hold the information in your hand, here are a few books (mentioned above) that emphasize general principles of website content and design for beginners. Remember, books are updated less frequently than high-quality websites. All three of these books provide more details about how to be found by search engines; basic HTML, scripts, and other code concepts; and basic design dos and don'ts. None of the books are specifically about creating web portfolios; instead they give you the basic knowledge you need in order to create any type of website. If you have the time to build your own site, these books can help you do it without being intimidated by the technology and the details.

Creating GeoCities Websites. Ben Sawyer and Dave Greely, Muska & Lipman, 1999.

Poor Richard's Web Site: Geek-Free, Commonsense Advice on Building a Low Cost Web Site. Peter Kent, Top Floor Publishing, 2000.

The Complete Idiot's Guide to Creating a Web Page, Paul McFedries, Alpha Books, 2002.

Because the process of creating a web portfolio is challenging, you may want professional assistance. For a referral to an experienced, qualified web portfolio consultant with reasonable fees, send email to tomw@cmr-mvp.com with your name, email address, city, and state. Our web portfolio consultant will send you information about these services and fees. If you wish to follow up, you can then contact the consultant directly.

Visit our website at www.cmr-mvp.com to learn more details on creating a web portfolio. Because the technology is changing quickly it is best to present the latest information through the website. You can visit the following web portfolios and more via links from the Career Management Resources website (click Web Portfolios) or by typing the below URLs into your browser. Take a look at some of them to get a sense of what can be done.

www.geocities.com/portfoliosample/webportfoliosuccess
www.geocities.com/jasonjobseeker/hireme
www.workfolio.com/stars/twashington
www.workfolio.com/stars/bgregory
http://judyjobfinder.tripod.com/jerrywelskop

At the CMR website you can also find insight into how each portfolio was constructed and how the decisions were made.

What to Include in Your Web Portfolio

Scan the list below to get a sense of the types of material people have included in their web portfolios. If you haven't already, visit the portfolio sites we've suggested above.

A web portfolio can contain files created in such programs as Word, WordPerfect, Excel, Access, Flash, and others, as well as graphics, sound, and video files. If you have a paper document such as a certificate or letter of appreciation, you can scan the document or have it scanned at a full-service copy shop. Scanning creates a digital file that can be uploaded to your web portfolio. Digital and scanned photos are easy to place in your web portfolio. See Photos in the list below to get an idea of how to use photos effectively.

Audio and video links can be very useful. You could include a recorded interview or a video of a seminar you gave. See below for more ideas. GeoCities, Tripod, and Workfolio can walk you through the process of uploading audio and video files. A digital video camcorder makes the process easier and eliminates the cost of digital conversion. See the Career Management Resources website (www.cmr-mvp.com) for more ideas and help with audio and video files.

Keep this in mind when building your web portfolio: Even though web technology allows you to include links to any website there is, think carefully about whether each link accomplishes its specific purpose, which is to promote your abilities. For example, some web portfolios provide links to the person's college. I don't see value in that. I would rather have an employer spend time looking at pages within ~~my~~ the job seeker's site than send him to another site. If there is relevant information about you within the college's website, your link should take the viewer directly to that spot, not to the home page.

Some web portfolios include links to past employers' websites. Again, before you provide a link to a company's site, ask yourself how it will it help an employer decide whether she wants to meet you. In most cases it won't—unless the company website contains samples of or information about projects you worked on. In that case, link directly to that page, rather than to the organization's home page.

A "functional" section can be very useful in a web portfolio. If you've read pages 99 to 108 regarding the use of functional resumes, you'll know that for most people I recommend a qualifications/chronological resume. You may want to consider creating a functional page with a link to it. Your page would include the functional portion as seen in the functional resumes on pages 101, 105, and 107. You would include the functional section because it provides useful information about you. Your link could indicate the categories you've selected and might be entitled "Areas of Experience."

What To Include: Specific Ideas

Writing Samples
Brochure
Newsletter
Published article (in a company newsletter, a professional association newsletter, a newspaper, or virtually anything with a readership of 50 or more
Book excerpt (chapter or partial chapter, table of contents, photo of cover), reviews
Poem
Music lyrics
Short story
Play
Published letter to the editor
Press release
Documentation of new or revised process
Software documentation
Technical writing or instructions (include sample drawings)
White paper
Research report
Marketing plan
Grant writing (the proposal, indicate if successful, possibly the amount)
Documents on how to assemble something (include drawings)
Sample of edited material (scan the document with your editing notations and include the final draft, showing the impact of your editing)
Translation (show the document in its original language and your translation)
Course handout
Sample of recommendations made to a boss or group (shows persuasiveness and logic)
Business or work-related document
Interoffice memos or emails expressing plans or recommendations

Work samples
Projects
Timelines, schedules, PERT charts used in project management
Patents
Inventions

Accomplishments (longer descriptions than what appears in resume)
Photo(s) with captions
Each accomplishment could have a link to a relevant sample, if available

Education/training
List degrees, diplomas, certificates
List courses completed (link to summary or course syllabus if available and relevant)
Describe class projects and include results
Transcripts (scan in)

Awards/Commendations/Publicity
Dean's list
Cum laude
With honors
History student of the year
Employee of the month
Rookie of the year
Letter of commendation
Bonuses awarded
Trips won
Team/Department award
Letters of thanks/praise from customers, clients, coworkers
Articles written about you (including In-house company newsletter, school paper, local newspaper, professional organization newsletter, magazine)
Articles in which you are quoted

Computer literacy/expertise
Application software (can rate each on a 1-5 scale for level of experience)
Operating systems
Programming languages
IT experience (installing software and peripherals)
Digital equipment and software (scanners, digital cameras, digital video recorders)

Work samples done on computers
Design or chart
CAD drafting, three-dimensional drawing, or design sample
Computer-generated graphics using Flash and other such programs
Program code you wrote
PowerPoint slides
Reports created with spreadsheets, database managers, accounting software, inventory management software, enterprise software, etc.

Community service
Work samples
Letters of recognition
Photos of projects, programs
Brochures

Professional memberships
Offices held, include years
Committee chair or cochair
Describe activities and results
Citations
Letters from people describing the
successes of your projects or events
Article about you in a newsletter
Summary article of a talk you gave to the
membership

Captioned photos
People you worked with
You receiving an award
Things designed, built
Point of sale display
Trade show booth
Toy
Game
Invention
Book cover
Logo
Team with team project
Equipment you can operate
Photo of you using the equipment
Equipment sold
Happy customer with product in hand

Art/graphics/music
Graphics created
Charts, flow charts, graphs hand drawn or
with graphics software
Drawings, sketches, paintings, sculptures,
photographs
Photos of art work
Music (include lyrics when appropriate)
Reviews of art, graphics, music

Video/audio
Acting performances
Talk, speech
Course taught
Teaching in a classroom
Sample job interview
Demonstration of how to do something
People praising you or describing you
Speaking a language or interpreting
You interviewing or counseling someone

Teaching/workshop presenter
List of classes, workshops, courses taught
(could include how many times given)
Include descriptions, course syllabus
Summarize reviews from students/
attendees (90% rated workshop good or
excellent)
Quote from some of the reviews ("Jan's
talk brought this complex subject alive
in a very understandable way.")
Overheads, PowerPoint slides, photos
Audio or video clips

Biographies
Provide short biographies of people who
appear in your portfolio

References
Evaluations or portions of evaluations from
supervisors (see page 136)
Letters of reference from bosses,
coworkers, customers, clients,
professional colleagues, teachers,
people who can vouch for your
character and skills

Part Three
Sample Résumés
To Use As Guides

Sample Resumes To Help You

USE THE FOLLOWING SAMPLE RESUMES to get ideas and to get a sense of how an entire resume fits together. Over 50 sample resumes have been used to help you. Various fonts (typefaces) have been used so you can determine which you like best. The name of the font appears at the top right of each resume. Times Roman and Helvetica are the typefaces people most commonly use for their resumes. When you see Times, it means Times Roman. Microsoft Word calls its version of Helvetica, Arial.

Because this book presents the basic principles of writing an effective resume, it does not provide examples of resumes for all job titles. The principles given here can be applied or adapted to fit any job title. Feel free to borrow a phrase here and there, but make your resume your own. Instill it with your own flavor and character. Make it personal. And sell yourself.

As you read the resumes, notice that the people being described seem like real, living, highly capable people, a quality rarely found in resumes. Strive to make your resume as interesting as theirs. Do everything possible to bring results into your resume.

Essentially all occupations and people fall into 18 categories. Those 18 categories include:

Note Before You Read The Sample Resumes

Many of these resumes were originally two pages. They were reduced in length to enable you to concentrate on key areas.

Resume Samples

GRADUATING COLLEGE STUDENTS

Although you may not have a lot of work experience, make the most of what you have, especially any experience related to what you want to do. Bookkeeping, for example, is valuable experience for an accounting major. It's not the same as accounting, but it is excellent, practical experience and is recognized as such by employers. A forestry major would emphasize any work with a timber company, even if it was only menial summer work.

As a recent or soon-to-be graduate, you have four things to sell: your education, your personality and character, related work experience, and work experience in general. If you have little or no related work experience, most of your resume will be devoted to revealing your personality, character, and work ethic. Employers need to sense the type of employee you will be. College graduates typically remain with their first employers for less than two years, so it's fair for employers to seek those who will quickly contribute to the organization.

Make the most out of whatever work experience you have. Internships and jobs where you've had a high level of responsibility, are particularly valuable. In John Etter's sample resume on page 157, only one job was actually described because its value was so much greater than the other summer jobs. You, on the other hand, may want to describe each of your summer jobs. Do your best to identify a result in each one. It doesn't have to be big, after all, it was a part-time or temporary job.

Look for ways to reveal your personal qualities. Citing offices held in high school and college reveals leadership and responsibility. Lettering in sports indicates learning the value of teamwork and cooperation. Excellent grades indicate discipline and intellectual capacity. Participation in debate and theater can reveal speaking ability, quick thinking, and willingness to take risks. Participating in school committees and organizations reveals responsibility, willingness to put out a little extra, and loyalty.

The qualifications section of a resume is an excellent place to describe and call attention to some of the qualities you want an employer to know about, as the example below demonstrates.

OBJECTIVE: Mathematics/Statistics

QUALIFICATIONS

Excellent training in math and statistics.

Maintain excellent relations with supervisors. Always a valued employee.
Loyal, cooperative, and easy to work with.

Work well under pressure, learn quickly, hard working.

You may have noticed that none of these statements was backed up with facts. The student who wrote this statement picked qualities which she knows to be true about herself; she is more than ready to give details or examples during an interview. Carefully select the qualities you mention. Be sure they are accurate—don't pick them just because they sound good. You may get an interview as a result, but you'll never get the job unless the "you" in person matches the "you" on paper.

Most graduates should expect to write a one-page resume, but a two page resume is certainly acceptable. Students who earn more than 50% of their total college and living expenses or who are willing to relocate, should consider stating it in the resume. These items may be stated in the following way:

PERSONAL

Earned 60% of college expenses
Willing to relocate

Offices held while in college should nearly always be mentioned. If you're proud of some of your results, describe those results rather than merely listing the offices you held.

Class projects are often worth mentioning in a special projects or education section. Perhaps you were in a group with business students who developed a marketing plan for a small company or in a group of industrial engineering students who solved an actual manufacturing problem. Below is a special projects section by a student who was very active on campus:

Planned and organized the University of Puget Sound 1999 Spring Parents Weekend and set a new record for attendance. Arranged programs and activities, obtained speakers, made hotel arrangements, ordered food, and headed up a four-person committee. Increased attendance 20% over the previous year. Evaluations by parents indicated it was the best organized program since its inception in 1977.

Published the first Parents Association Newsletter which was sent to 3,500 parents of UPS students. The first two editions were well-received and the newsletter has become an official school publication, published three times each year.

JOHN ETTER

Current Address   Permanent Address
426 Harris Hall   1227 Pineway N.W.
Burlington, Vermont 05401   Ascutney, Vermont 05030
(802) 795-2631   (802) 683-2796

OBJECTIVE: Entry-Level Training and Development Position

QUALIFICATIONS

Excellent program development skills. Developed new intramural programs and increased participation by women 220%.

Strong research and writing ability. Published an article in the *Vermont Historical Society Quarterly*.

Speak well before the public. Won numerous debate tournaments and placed fifth in the 2002 national tournament.

Cooperate well with supervisors; reliable and responsible; work hard and complete projects on schedule.

EDUCATION

B.A. - History, University of Vermont, will graduate June 20003 (3.6 GPA)

Business Courses: History of 20th Century Business, Macroeconomics, Microeconomics

PUBLICATIONS

"Effects of the Abolition Movement in Burlington, Vermont 1826 to 1866" *Vermont Historical Society Quarterly*, January 2003 edition

AWARDS

"Outstanding History Senior" selected by the History Faculty (2003)
Fifth place, national debate tournament, extemporaneous speaking (2002)

EMPLOYMENT

University of Vermont, Burlington, Vermont 9/00 to Present

Director of Intramural Sports - Planned, staffed, and organized the intramural sports program. Working with a tight budget, assessed equipment needs, received bids from sporting goods suppliers, and purchased sports equipment. Supervised two assistants and recruited and supervised dozens of volunteers. Developed a new concept in women's athletics and actively promoted the program. Participation by women grew from 20% in previous years to 76%. Maintained the high participation rate in the men's program and organized a successful basketball refereeing clinic.

Summer Employment:

Records Clerk, Stephenson Steel, Ascutney, Vermont 6/02 to 9/02
Mail Sorter, U.S. Postal Service, Ascutney, Vermont 6/01 to 9/01
Laborer, Isaacson Contracting, Ascutney, Vermont 6/00 to 9/00
Farm Worker, John Tyler, Ascutney, Vermont 6/99 to 9/99

POLLY GLADSON
275 S. Pine Blvd.
Henniker, New Hampshire
(603) 971-2653

OBJECTIVE: Entry level accounting position with a CPA firm.

QUALIFICATIONS

Excellent college training and on-the-job experience. Have worked closely with a CPA firm and helped prepare taxes. Prepared documents for an IRS audit. Have practical business experience handling all bookkeeping functions at a busy restaurant.

EDUCATION

B.A. - Accounting, New England College, 3.21 GPA (June, 2003)

EXPERIENCE

Gulliver's Restaurant, Henniker, New Hampshire (1/98 to Present, full time)

Waitress (2/02 to Present). Provide outstanding service and consistently receive the highest tips among the restaurant staff. Highly professional.

Bookkeeper (4/99 to 2/02). Responsible for accounts receivable, reconciling charge slips, payroll, balancing five registers, recovering on bad checks, reconciling petty cash and inventorying bar supplies monthly. Monitored costs by preparing monthly reports comparing gross sales to labor costs for each department.

Worked closely with accountant and prepared figures as requested. Each year helped auditor track and reconcile all financial transactions. A 1995 IRS audit stated the books were very complete and accurate. Highly respected and trusted - had full access to safe and every part of restaurant.

Podium Hostess (1/98 to 4/99). Redesigned the reservation system which significantly improved service to customers. Developed excellent relations with customers and helped create a loyal clientele. Trained seating hostesses in all facets of the job.

Village Inn, Henniker, New Hampshire (6/96 to 1/98, full time)

Hostess/Waitress - Greeted and seated customers, opened and closed the restaurant, and prepared the registers each day.

ACTIVITIES

Member, American Society of Women Accountants

Active in jazz dancing and dog obedience training

WOMEN RETURNING TO THE WORK FORCE

The biggest problems women face when returning to the work force are a lack of self-esteem and a belief that what they've done for the last several years is not valued in the workplace. To overcome these twin problems you must first recognize that you possess numerous transferable skills that are valued in many types of positions.

If you lack confidence in your marketability or your job finding ability, begin looking for a career planning and job finding program at a community college, or consider obtaining help from a career counselor. Also look for a support group made up of women who are returning to work or look for a broader-based support group that the local YWCA or some similar organization may have. If you are divorced or widowed, or must become the primary wage earner, you will probably qualify for a "displaced homemakers" program. Such programs are often available at low cost through community colleges and can really help women get through an emotionally trying period. They typically provide career exploration assistance, job finding guidance, and emotional support.

Even though you have not worked for several years, make the most out of whatever paid work experience you do have. Scour each job to find whatever results and contributions you may have had, even if it was 20 years ago. Establishing the fact that you have been a good employee in the past, even 20 years ago, will effectively convince employers that you have a strong work ethic.

Those who have been out of the work force for many years must often emphasize their volunteer experience. In actuality, volunteer activities are merely jobs you didn't get paid to do. They can be as mundane as licking stamps or as interesting and challenging as organizing a blood donor drive, or handling public relations for a small nonprofit organization. If you consistently spent ten or more hours weekly on a volunteer position, treat it as a job with a job title and a job description, with results included. In the resume there is no need to state the number of hours spent weekly. If an employer is curious you can explain in the interview. If most of your volunteer activities were of short duration, you could treat them as projects (see Special Projects page 43). Concentrate on results, but also describe duties.

Make the most out of each activity. If you held an office, say so. If you obtained excellent results, describe them. *Don't be modest.*

How good a position you get depends on the quality of your resume and how well focused you are. There is probably no need to return to school for a degree, but you may need to study your preferred field on your own or take a few classes at your local community college. Study enough to know the terms, history, and trends in your field.

I've included Sharron's resume because it is so strong in the volunteer area. Don't be intimidated by it. You may not have been as active or may not have had such quantifiable results, but it shows what can be done.

SHARRON COSGRAVE
526 South State Street
Wilmington, Delaware 19803
(302) 543-9161

(objective unstated, but basically looking to become an administrative assistant
  to a director of a nonprofit agency)

QUALIFICATIONS

Strong experience in developing effective new programs, motivating and
coordinating large numbers of volunteers, and making office systems more
efficient.

Excellent fund-raiser. Have written three successful grant proposals, one
of which was funded for $20,000. Through PTA fund-raising activities,
increased revenue 18% above the previous record.

EDUCATION

University of Delaware, Liberal Arts, 96 credits, 1980 to 1983

PROJECTS/ACTIVITIES

PTA President, Robert Frost Elementary, 2000/02. Increased attendance
at monthly meetings from 51 to an average of 92. Worked with principal
and teachers to develop five new volunteer programs for parents. Participation in programs increased from 26% of parents to 58%. Because of active parent involvement, vandalism at the school decreased to almost zero.

Fund-raising Chairperson, Robert Frost PTA, 2000/01. Coordinated the
efforts of over 400 children and 95 adults in six fund-raising activities.
Exceeded the previous record by 18%.

Board Member, Wilmington Crisis Clinic, 1995 to Present. Analyze and
approve annual budgets, interview and select new directors, and study
proposed program changes. President of the board 1992 and 1993. Wrote
grant proposal which obtained $20,000 in federal funds.

President, Wilmington Chapter, MADD (Mothers Against Drunk Drivers),
1991 to 1994. Organized the local chapter and tripled dues-paying membership each year. Testified as an expert witness before the Delaware Legislature. Coordinated statewide lobbying efforts and helped pass legislation
which significantly strengthened laws against drunk driving.

EMPLOYMENT

McClinton, Brandeis & Nelson, Wilmington, Delaware 1983 to 1986

Office Manager - Handled bookkeeping, payroll, bank statements, accounts payable, and accounts receivable. Purchased office equipment and
supplies. Greeted clients, answered phones, scheduled court reporters for
depositions, and developed an improved appointment and court scheduling
system for 8 attorneys.

The next resume is perhaps more typical of a woman returning to work. Janice has had two part-time jobs since she got married. In 1999 she decided to return to work on a full-time basis. From her experience at Debbie's Designs (four years, part-time) she knows she would like to own her own shop someday. Her plan is to get a full-time retail sales job at a small but classy store and eventually become the manager or assistant manager. While working there she intends to learn the business inside and out so she'll be ready when she opens her own shop.

JANICE STEVENS
4060 W. Warwick
Chicago, IL 60626
(312) 476-2917

OBJECTIVE: Retail sales

QUALIFICATIONS

Excellent retail experience. Work very effectively with customers - able to identify needs, tactfully answer questions, sell products, and solve problems.

EDUCATION

Northeastern Illinois University, Psychology, 20 credits 1987 to 1990

Bates Community College, Liberal Arts, 42 credits 1974 to 1976

WORKSHOPS

Window Dressing, Retail Merchants Association, 12 class hours (2001)
Retail Bookkeeping, Retail Merchants Association, 24 class hours (2000)
Retail Selling/Know Your Customer, Retail Merchants Association,
  20 class hours (1999)

EMPLOYMENT

Debbie's Designs, Chicago, IL 2/99 to 4/02

RETAIL SALES - Consulted with customers in the selection and coordination of furniture, fabrics, carpeting, wallpaper, draperies, and gift items. Purchased and priced products and developed attractive displays. Functioned as store manager for extended periods when the store owner was on vacation.

Illinois Arts & Crafts Association, Chicago, IL 9/82 to 8/87

GALLERY ASSISTANT - Assisted customers in the purchase of art objects, explained the processes used by each artist, and trained and supervised other volunteers. Handled numerous details for the annual arts and crafts fair, including registering artists, judging art work, and overseeing sales and bookkeeping.

THOSE OVER 50

The greatest concern of people over fifty years of age is usually age discrimination. While federal law prohibits discrimination on the basis of age, we know that it persists in both overt and subtle ways. With this in mind, you must decide whether you will reveal your age, since employers by law cannot ask your age or birthdate. Your resume should contain only information you choose to reveal to an employer.

Make the most of your experience and maturity. Some people unnecessarily worry that youth always has the edge. In your resume and during interviews, reveal yourself to be an energetic and youthful person, but one who has the maturity and sound judgment that comes only with age and experience. If you have planned your career carefully, you will probably be at a level where only those with similar age, experience, and results will even be considered as qualified. If that is not your case, then simply recognize that your age is another barrier that must and can be overcome.

Trenton is a 59 year old insurance executive. In his resume education was not included because he does not have a degree. Showing his one year of college was deemed unnecessary because he has so much experience. Two early jobs were left off which accounted for five years. Using a prior employment section was an effective way to concentrate on his higher level jobs.

TRENTON McGRATH
2215 Broadway North
Houston, TX 77012
(713) 785-2761

OBJECTIVE: Sales/Marketing Management

QUALIFICATIONS

Complete knowledge of Mortgage Lending/Mortgage Finance/Secondary Markets.

Recognized as an outstanding trainer and motivator of sales staffs. Substantially increased market share in each position held.

Broad marketing experience. Developed and marketed new products and services which have consistently been accepted in the financial community.

EMPLOYMENT

Diversified Mortgage Insurance Company, Minneapolis, MN 1/82 to Present

Regional Vice President 1/94 to Present, Houston. Moved into a troubled 16-state zone and have increased market share 61% from 3.2% to 5.2%. Have aggressively marketed new services and became active with the Bond Business, Pension Funds, Swaps, and assisting lenders with Portfolio Sales. Travel extensively and work closely with 4 district sales managers and 20 salespeople.

Senior Vice President, Sales and Marketing 12/87 to 1/94, Minneapolis. Developed and implemented a reorganization of the national sales force, moving from 12 divisions to 4 zones. Reorganization has been credited with strengthening DMI's national market share. Took part in the development of the Mortgage Finance Unit which has successfully moved DMI into new markets. Developed strategies for participation in Mortgage Revenue Bonds, Pass Through Certificates, Pension Funds Issues, Builder Buy-downs and Pay-through Bonds.

Vice President, Northwest Division Manager 9/85 to 12/87, Portland. Covering 9 western states, trained and supervised a staff of 9 account executives, 3 underwriters and 2 secondary market managers. Increased market share in the territory by 88%. Traveled extensively throughout the territory and made calls on CEOs.

Product Manager 1/82 to 9/85, Minneapolis. Developed and implemented marketing plans for specialized insurance products for mortgage lending financial institutions: Error/Omission Coverage, Special Hazard Coverage, and Officers/Employees Liability Coverage. Responsible for national marketing of the products. Sales volume for these products increased an average of 22% per year.

American Insurance Company, Atlanta, GA 6/78 to 1/82

Director of Field Operations 6/80 to 1/82, Atlanta. Had total responsibility for sales production of 6 regional and 21 state managers. Introduced new mortgage life and disability insurance programs and created a highly effective sales training program.

Regional Manager 6/78 to 6/80, St. Louis. Supervised operations of 4 state managers and personally generated new business in metropolitan St. Louis.

Niagara Home Life Assurance Company, Palo Alto, CA 8/72 to 6/78

Assistant Vice President - Negotiated exclusive contracts with S&Ls for the sale of Niagara Home Life's Mortgage Life Plan and Disability Plan. Designed and implemented a specialized Insured Savings Plan for Savings and Loan depositors which had an excellent effect on insurance sales. Recruited and trained sales agents.

Prior Employment

Sales Agent/Trainer, Home Owners Security, Inc. 2/68 to 8/72
Sales Agent, Home Security Associates 2/66 to 2/68

PEOPLE WITH PORTFOLIOS

Architects, drafters, artists, designers, photographers, models, and writers, use portfolios to help sell themselves. They often make the mistake of placing too little emphasis on a top-quality resume, assuming the portfolio alone will sell them.

As important as your portfolio is, don't shortchange yourself. There are lots of talented people out there with outstanding portfolios. Taking the time to develop an effective resume will make an important difference to your job hunting success. Your resume can reveal qualities and background that won't come across in your portfolio. A portfolio can express your technical or creative ability, but a resume reveals where you've been and how you developed your ability. In fact, without an effective resume you'll rarely get the opportunity to show that fantastic portfolio you so painstakingly assembled.

Artistic people are stereotyped as temperamental. In your resume do everything possible to demonstrate that you are flexible and easy to work with.

Consider reproducing two or three samples of your work on 8½" x 11" paper. Then, either enclose it with your resume, or give it to employers when you meet them face to face. When reviewing the samples a week or two after meeting you, the employer will be helped to remember both you and your portfolio better. Writers should attach clippings or short pieces for a similar effect. Graphic artists and designers should feel free to come up with creative formats for their resumes.

The most important thing to note in Bobbie's resume, is simply that employers will know much more about her than if they only saw a portfolio. Quantifying results is harder for artistic people than for many others, but do your best. In Bobbie's resume, there are no quantifiable results. Still, you get a sense that she is dedicated and very capable. If employers liked her portfolio, the resume will help them remember her more easily.

BOBBIE BLANE
1127 Mariposa Drive
Santa Barbara, California 93110
(805) 651-2720

OBJECTIVE: Graphics/Illustration Artist

QUALIFICATIONS

Develop excellent relations with clients and have satisfied even the most demanding. Specialty is personality portraiture used in advertising.

Excellent graphics and illustration training and experience. Skilled in design, layout, paste-up, lettering, story boards, and the use of darkrooms and stat cameras. Knowledgeable of printing procedures and experienced in preparing work for printing. Have operated printing presses and other printing-related equipment. Prepared work for black-and-white and full-color reproduction, as well as two- and three-color.

EDUCATION

Bachelor of Fine Arts, Illustration, Seymour Art Center (1997)

EMPLOYMENT

Freelance Work 1998 to Present

ARTIST - Painted and sold over 45 portraits and scenes using water color, graphite, pen and ink, egg tempura, and oil.

Provided graphics and illustration for numerous projects: notebook cover, Advancetec (2002); brochure cover, Barr & Associates (2001); map and tour guide, Santa Barbara Museum of Natural History (2000); catalog and advertising design, Briton Engineering (2000); work order design, Armor Advertising (2000); logo and menu design, Silk Oyster Restaurant (2000); logo, business card design, Donner Electronics, Inc. (1999); magazine illustration, *Psychology Today* (1999); catalog design, Sunstra Inc. (1999); scratchboard portrait of DeVinci for ad appearing in *Smithsonian* (1998); layout, design, illustration, *Infoworld* (1998).

Jonathan Edwards Galleries, Santa Barbara, California 1996 to Present

ART DEALER - Assist customers in purchasing art works for both personal viewing and as investments. Help customers in understanding the artist and the art piece. Have developed an excellent reputation with customers for knowledge, helpfulness, and tact.

Redecorate the gallery as new works are shown and touch up damaged pieces. Commissioned through the gallery to do portraits. Currently showing several personal works of children and scenes including "Cool Mist," "High Noon," "Children in the Sun." Help design the monthly newsletter and provide calligraphy and design expertise for gallery signs.

MILITARY PERSONNEL

To write a successful resume, the person with 6–30 years in the military needs to have confidence that the abilities he or she possesses are marketable. Without that assurance the resume will probably come out bland and next to useless. Feel good about yourself. Regardless of your function in the military, you developed skills there which are valuable in the civilian job market. If you plan well, analyze your strengths, and are clear on what you want to do in civilian life, you should have no more difficulties than anyone else finding the job you want.

Use Your Strengths

Analyze your background carefully and emphasize the experience that will help sell you into a civilian job. There may be functions you performed in the military that are so unique to the military that they should be mentioned briefly or not at all. You've done plenty of things which civilian managers are looking for so emphasize those things.

If you have been involved in any phase of electronics, computers, mechanics, or other technical fields, you are highly marketable. The U.S. government has invested thousands of dollars training you, and there are employers who seek your expertise and experience.

Many ex-pilots have gone to work for airlines and defense contractors. Don't feel limited to seeking jobs that are directly related to your military functions, however. As an officer you were assigned various command positions. Describe them properly, and you can sell yourself into a midmanagement or executive position. Whatever your background, sell your experience.

Things to Avoid

As you write your resume, scrupulously avoid military jargon, also known as militarese. Let a civilian read your resume to determine if your descriptions are understandable.

Be careful about mentioning the supervision of large numbers of people. In the military, to have responsibility for 500 people is not unusual, but most presidents of companies never have 500 people under their control. Seeing such large numbers can seem threatening. Generally you would only list the number of direct reports.

Avoid phrases like "Responsible for overseeing a $95 million budget." In the military overseeing large budgets is common, but in the private sector, only executives with large companies could make such statements. Again, it can seem threatening.

The same principle would apply if you were a pilot or ship's captain: "Responsible for a $21 million piece of equipment" (pilot) or, "Had total responsibility for operating and maintaining a $260 million piece of equipment" (captain of a destroyer). The statements may sound impressive, but they are actually counterproductive.

166

Using Evaluations And Letters Of Commendation

As a military person you have undoubtedly saved your fitness reports, evaluations, and letters of commendation. Selected short quotations can be included in your resume to make positive statements about yourself. Praise coming from an objective third party, especially from a superior, will carry more weight than if you made the same statement about yourself. Rarely should anyone include more than one or two quotes in the resume, so choose them wisely. See page 170 for an example of a retired military person who used extensive quotes from evaluations as an addendum to his resume. In places where the evaluation would have said "Captain Handle," it simply states "Handle," in order to remove as much military terminology as possible. These quotes were heavily edited, with only small portions of each evaluation included. When skipping portions of the evaluations there was no attempt to use ellipses (...) to signify a gap. Instead, it was all woven together to make a strong statement about Handle and allowing commanding officers to say things he couldn't say about himself.

Generally you should take your addendum (label it "Portions of Annual Evaluations") with you on interviews so that if it seems appropriate you could give a copy to your interviewer. Occasionally you might include it with your resume when you send it in the mail, but our research indicates that people with professional or technical experience are usually better off not including letters of recommendations or evaluations with their resumes.

For some military people a functional resume works best because no matter how they describe their jobs, those jobs don't sound like anything that goes on in the civilian world. See page 107 for an example.

In the first sample resume, Sanders does an excellent job of convincing the reader that he is totally dedicated to safety. It is clear that the record he set for the most consecutive months without a major accident, came by his dedication and the development of a comprehensive safety program.

In the second and third sample resumes, Tolson and Handle clearly sell their technical ability.

PETE SANDERS
237 Durham Way
Durham, California 95938
(213) 628-9714

OBJECTIVE: Safety Administrator

QUALIFICATIONS

Developed a comprehensive safety program which resulted in six years
without a serious accident to any of the 800 personnel.

Proven ability to set up effective, low-cost, industrial safety programs which
rely heavily on instilling a safety consciousness in all employees.

Totally familiar with OSHA regulations and compliance procedures and have
worked closely with OSHA inspectors.

WORK EXPERIENCE

U. S. Army 1973 to 2003

Safety Officer - 1979 to 2003
While Safety Officer at Ft. Bradley for ten years, was responsible for the
safety of 800 air field personnel ranging from mechanics, machine operators,
and vehicle operators to supervisors and management staff. Developed a
comprehensive safety program which set a Ft. Bradley record for safety.
Awarded a six-year safety award for 72 consecutive months without a major
accident (over $5,000 property damage or loss of life).

Directly supervised three safety technicians and coordinated the efforts of 20
officers responsible for safety in their immediate areas. Held monthly safety
seminars to promote and enhance safety awareness within each specialized
group.

Made daily and weekly inspections of offices, maintenance facilities, and
mechanical, paint, electrical, and machine shops, to ensure compliance with
safety regulations and performed on-the-spot corrections for minor
infractions. Identified potentially hazardous practices and recommended
changes.

Formulated and administered safety policies and procedures to ensure
compliance with federal and state safety acts. Worked closely with OSHA
inspectors and developed excellent knowledge of OSHA regulations.

Airfield Safety Officer/Pilot, Ft. Bradley, California 1989 to 2003
Airfield Safety Officer/Pilot, Munsun-ni, Korea 1983 to 1989
Airfield Safety Officer/Pilot, Ft. Lewis, Washington 1979 to 1983
Pilot, Ft. Benning, Georgia 1973 to 1979

EDUCATION

Business - California State University, 85 credits (1989-1992)

SAFETY EDUCATION

Accident Prevention, U. S. Army Agency for Aviation Safety, 640 class hours
(1979).
U. S. Air Force Crash Investigators School, 320 class hours (1979).
Aviation Safety Officers Course, University of Southern California Safety
Center, 960 class hours (1976). Course covered reconstructing accidents,
investigative procedures, evidence acquisition, analysis of causation factors,
methods of accident prevention, and gaining employee cooperation.

RICK TOLSON
PreComUnit USS Antrim
1102 S W Massachusetts Avenue
Seattle, Washington 98134
(206) 641-2737

QUALIFICATIONS

During seven years in Naval Communications gained broad experience
in troubleshooting electronic systems. Specialty is recognizing system
or circuit deterioration, isolating the fault, and restoring the system
or circuit to normal operation through corrective procedures or by an
alternate route. Personally construct, operate, and maintain all types
of communication systems.

AREAS OF EXPERTISE

Constructing Communications Systems

Satellite Systems, High Speed Data Systems, Voice Systems, Teletype
Systems, Continuous Wave.

Maintaining Communications Systems

Perform quality control and performance monitoring on audio and
DC circuits.

Electronic Communications Equipment

Transmitters, transceivers, receivers, modems, multiplexers,
demultiplexers, cryptogear, microwave, couplers, antennas, high
level black patch panels, high and low level red patch panels, and
numerous types of test equipment.

EDUCATION

Graduated Pisgah High School, Pisgah, Iowa (1993)

Navy Schools - Technical Control, Satellite Communications,
Management, Communications Supervision, Maintenance and Material
Management, High Frequency Transmitters, Antenna Maintenance.

WORK HISTORY

U.S. Navy August 1993 to Present

Tech Controller, 1st Class Radioman Assignments have included Naval
Communications Stations, Naval Telecommunications Centers and three
Navy ships. Since 1997 have supervised numerous groups of technicians
and trained them to use sophisticated communications equipment. While
involved with the construction of an FFG-7 class ship, developed an
extensive set of lesson plans to explain the construction of the circuits
and also diagrammed all of the wiring and block schematics for this new
class of ship. These two projects will save hundreds of training hours.
Participated in the quality control tests of the USS Antrim.

Top Secret Security Clearance

PAUL HANDLE
3715 Pearl Ave. N.
Everett, Washington 98206
(425) 954-3721

OBJECTIVE: Electrical, Electronic, Mechanical Maintenance

QUALIFICATIONS

Consistently rated superior in both technical expertise and supervisory ability. Constantly finding more effective methods of making repairs and reducing downtime of equipment.

EDUCATION

Graduated - Sheppton High School, Sheppton, Pennsylvania (1969)

EMPLOYMENT

US Navy, 10/69 to 12/02

Electronics Instructor 2/93 to 12/02. Provided comprehensive instruction to maintenance technicians and pilots covering aircraft electrical and electronic systems. Courses ranged from basic electricity and electronics to advanced solid state theory and repair. Taught 13 separate courses averaging 80 classroom hours each. Course Manager for 5 of the 13 courses. Took difficult courses and made them more practical and easier to understand. Wrote numerous manuals and lesson guides which simplified previous courses. Students consistently outscored the students of other instructors.

Senior Supervisor 7/79 to 2/93. Supervised 2 shift supervisors and up to 35 technicians. Developed work schedules for personnel, scheduled maintenance, and provided overall management of a large maintenance shop. Trained new technicians and personally performed many repairs on state of the art aircraft electrical systems, automatic flight control systems, and navigational systems.

Took over one command position where outdated maintenance and record keeping procedures had created serious maintenance problems. Reorganized the reporting and maintenance procedures and streamlined the operation. In 36 months the unit moved from "poor" to "excellent" in readiness reports.

Electronic Maintenance Supervisor 6/73 to 7/79. Supervised up to 20 technicians in the repair of electrical and electronic aircraft systems.

Aviation Electrician 10/69 to 6/73. Maintenance and service technician on aircraft electrical and navigational systems.

TRAINING - Navy Schools (completed over 75 courses with a total of 2,400 classroom hours)

Advanced Electronics Courses (1974 - 1999)
    Polyphase power and control systems (200 hours)
    Advanced magnetic devices (240 hours)
    Digital, analog, solid-state, and T.T.L. devices (400 hours)
    Advanced syncro/analog/solid state control and indicating systems (400 hours)
    Hybrid solid-state inertial navigation systems (200 hours)
    High resolution hydraulic/electronic T.T.L. control systems (160 hours)
    Component/miniature component repair, including P.C.B (160 hours)

Aviation Electrician Course, 1969 (320 hours)

Paul Handle
PORTIONS OF SEMIANNUAL EVALUATIONS

Handle's broad qualifications and maintenance know how on A6A electrical systems have enabled him to become a particularly valuable instructor. He is always striving to make difficult courses easier for the students to comprehend by ensuring that proper maintenance procedures are included in his lessons. His willingness to work at any task, no matter how large or small, has contributed materially to the mission of NAMTD. His conduct sets an example worthy of emulation by other officers. He has amply demonstrated a fair and unbiased attitude, readily accepting each and every person as an individual. Handle is industrious, thorough, and accurate in this work and extremely conscientious in all duties and endeavors. He is alert and stable, displaying a creative mind. He shows great ability to develop effective procedural methods and to prepare excellently written and easily understood lesson guides. He secures the attention and respect of his students whom he guides and directs with understanding and tact. He is frequently called upon by other rate groups of this detachment to help solve technical problems in the writing of lesson guides. He attacks these problems with a cheerful and aggressive nature, seeing any problems through to a successful conclusion. Success in his work is shown by the students' final grades and their comment sheets. January 2002

Handle is intelligent, exceptionally quick to learn, with the ability to grasp pertinent details rapidly. Given broad guidelines, he accomplishes assigned tasks in an enthusiastic and exemplary manner. Handle is a conscientious and concerned instructor who demonstrates a sincere feeling of responsibility towards his students and works very hard to ensure they receive maximum benefit from his instruction. He is equally at ease before a group of juniors or seniors. He is very effective in conveying his thoughts clearly and fluently, both in casual conversation or when presenting a formal lesson. During this reporting period, he has been assigned the task of writing the avionics portion of AZF under the individualized instruction format. He willingly assisted other instructors with this new format and readily assumed the responsibility of insuring that uniformity was met by all rate groups. He spent many hours researching instructions. Acting as liaison between rate groups, he arranged and conducted meetings to achieve this goal. January 2000

Handle has been extremely instrumental in the training of the less experienced men assigned to the branch. He can be counted on to do any assigned task correctly, efficiently and safely. January 1998

Handle is a dedicated, knowledgeable First Class Electrician who strives to ensure work is completed safely and that the proper maintenance procedures are utilized. He keeps his superiors informed of all potential trouble areas and draws on his vast experience to propose viable solutions. He leads with an easygoing, unobtrusive manner, never interfering with the personal initiative of those he supervises. He plans the work load efficiently and utilizes a smooth rapport with the men to carry out the work. January 1996

Handle has demonstrated a high proficiency in his field and is very adept at putting his knowledge and experience to good use. He has an ability to quietly evaluate difficult situations and to arrive at practical solutions while working under trying conditions. He is a very thoughtful and sincere person who has the ability to communicate with the younger technicians and to define some of their problems. January 1994

Handle is a calm and reserved supervisor who receives the full support of his subordinates without haranguing or berating them. His assigned tasks are never too insignificant to warrant his total attention. The capable manner in which he plans and assigns work to his technicians is further enhanced by his cheerful and pleasing personality. These traits, coupled with his willingness to work with others, make for a smooth running crew on his shift. January 1992

COMPUTER SPECIALISTS

The computer business is a unique field and requires a special type of resume. This is especially true for programmers. Since the average programmer stays only 18 months with an organization, managers usually look for someone who can step right in and do the job, based on past experience with the computer, language, and operating system used in that organization. This is a source of great frustration for programmers because many feel that in two to three weeks they can master any new system—all they need is an opportunity to prove it. Your task is to make the most out of the experience you have and to demonstrate your adaptability.

It is generally best to list all languages you know, as well as all hardware, operating systems, and applications software you've been exposed to. Usually they would be listed in your order of expertise. The interview is the place to discuss your level of expertise. Listing everything you have exposure to can make the difference in whether you will get an interview because so many companies are using key words when they search their own resume databank, as well as commercial resume databanks.

The data processing resume is actually fairly simple to write because it consists of several distinct sections that practically write themselves. Start with Areas of Experience. Typically, it will consist of Languages, Systems, Special Programs, Computers, Conversions, and Applications. Applications can be further divided into New Applications and Maintenance. It should be easy, almost like filling in the blanks.

Because programming and other computer jobs are so project-oriented, it is often better to place more emphasis on projects than on job descriptions. A special projects section will work great. Provide just enough information in each project description to give an employer a feel for what you did, then concentrate on results. This section is very important and will probably require three drafts. Start by listing the projects you feel would be most impressive. Since employers usually use resumes as a basis for interviews, be sure to choose projects that you would want to explain and describe in more detail in an interview.

For the first draft of your projects section, don't worry about length, just get your thoughts down on paper. In the second draft look for unnecessary words or phrases. The employer does not require a complete understanding of all the details, just enough information to indicate the degree of complexity and what was required to complete the project. Finish the project by describing the result. Your third draft will simply be a finer tuning of the second.

By emphasizing your areas of experience and special projects sections, your job descriptions will probably be quite short.

172

KEN WANDER
902 McKenzie Dr. SE
Calgary, Alberta T2Z1T2
(204) 563-2412

QUALIFICATIONS

Six years of database programming experience involving SQL Server, interface design, and multimedia systems, and office automation. Recognized for ability to learn new technology and complete projects on schedule, utilizing unique design concepts.

EDUCATION

B.S.—Computer Science, University of Calgary (1997)

AREAS OF EXPERIENCE

Languages: Visual Basic, C/C++, Java Script, Active X, HTML
Applications: Access, Excel, SQL Server
Operating Systems: NT 4.0, Windows 3.1/95/98, MS DOS, UNIX

EXPERIENCE

Randal & Associates, Calgary, Alberta 6/00-Present

Software Developer—For this major real estate development company, develop databases and Visual Basic applications to improve office productivity. Designed the SQL Server integration for the firm's building inventory using RDO and Visual Basic Enterprise. Developed an Access data structuring and reporting system to manage the server financial database of the firm's tenants, properties, land acquisitions, and construction projects.

Major project has involved developing MS Word Wizards to produce all company contracts. Defined business requirements to build strong technical designs for the creation of legal contracts. Contracts are now produced in half the time and they have a more consistent look and feel and are easier to read.

Crandal Industries, Calgary, Alberta 6/97-6/00

Software Developer—As developer for this conveyor systems manufacturer, developed complete business information systems in Access, Excel, and C++ from concept to coding to error proofing. Using RDBMS database design concepts, designed a C++ front end to an existing network reports database using DBRascal for live previewing and editing of data. Sales forecasts are now produced three days after month-end instead of five days and a single C++ procedure replaces the tedious editing of over 30 monthly sales reports. Now 96% of the sales reps access this system weekly, versus 65% in the past.

Aamad Jamaala

250 Templeton   Omaha, NE 68154   (402) 454-0987

QUALIFICATIONS

Strong background in the planning, installation, and maintenance of microcomputer systems, including LANs and WANs. Broad experience in connectivity and group processing. Work effectively as programmer and analyst to customize systems. Strong knowledge of PC-based operating systems including Windows XP, Windows 2000, NT 4.0, NT 3.51, Windows 98/95, MS-DOS, Unix, and Novell.

Broad experience in building database, spreadsheet, and desktop publishing systems that enhance and expand current capabilities. Extensive experience with dBase, Access, FoxPro, Clipper, Paradox, Lotus 123, Excel, Pagemaker, and Ventura Publisher. Provide excellent training for users. Experienced with C/C++, Visual Basic, COBOL, and FORTRAN.

EDUCATION/CERTIFICATIONS

A.A. - Computer Science/Accounting, Belmont Community College (1989)
Novell Certified Network Engineer (CNE) (1995)
Qualified Instructor, PageMaker, Ventura Publisher (1994)

PROFESSIONAL HISTORY

Cyrus Computer, Omaha, NE 1999 to Present

PC Specialist - Install LANs, WANs, and PC systems. Select appropriate software and install on all PCs at each site. Train users and provide support. Create custom software and modify off the shelf software. Special projects include:

Wrote a database listing product in C/C++ for a major bank that works on an intelligent 3270 work station with proprietary BIOS. Developed an Access file update program giving users ability to update DBF formatted lists using pull-down menus. Product was completed on schedule, exceeds all requirements, and is liked by users.

Complex data conversions to a Windows-based environment include: Large customer data list from a DEC PDP-11 using MDAC code. 120MB of data from IBM IMS database to SQL database using COM/DCOM and MDAC code.

Wrote a claims tracking system in FoxPro. System has been in use for two years with no bugs. It has streamlined the claims process and permitted greater accessibility to claims data.

Developed a Lotus spreadsheet interface to the Great Plains Payroll program, permitting a greatly simplified entry process to produce payrolls. Interface was written in Paradox to allow greater flexibility during data entry and better report generation capability.

Micro Accounting Consultants, Omaha, NE 1989-1999

Technical Support - Produced a variety of custom programs for small businesses in the greater Omaha area.

SALESPEOPLE

Salespeople typically hate to write. That fact is generally quite evident in their resumes, most of which are poorly written, poorly designed, and reveal very little of substance. Taking just four to five hours of your time to write a quality resume could net you an extra $100,000 in your lifetime earnings.

The sales resume is usually one of the easiest to write because it is so results oriented. Sales resumes rarely require extensive details about duties because sales managers already know what you do. What they care about is the bottom line. Don't tell a sales manager how hard you worked or how many phone calls you made or how many sales calls you went on. Did you sell? That's all that counts.

There are a number of ways to show results:

1) sales awards,

2) your ranking within your sales organization,

3) improving the position of your territory compared to other territories in the company,

4) increasing sales,

5) increasing profits on sales,

6) increasing market share.

Use whatever is most appropriate. If you know your market share or can estimate it pretty closely, use that figure. Market share is effective because it provides an excellent means of comparison. During an economic boom with high inflation, the gross sales of even a mediocre salesperson will increase 5–8% annually. To increase market share, however, means you have taken business away from competitors and increased your share of the pie. It means you're doing something right. Employers won't know if you've done it on the basis of your great personality, your outstanding closing techniques, your strong product knowledge, your hard work, or your excellent time management, but it won't matter. Sales managers care only about results.

Showing increases in market share is great, but most companies simply don't do the research to know what those figures are, territory by territory. Use whatever figures will work best for you. During the last recession even many outstanding salespeople were not able to say that they increased sales. In some industries just holding steady was the mark of a great salesperson.

To show yourself in the best light you might use a combination. Let's say from 1988 through 1991 you sold office machines. Those were recession years in some parts of the country. You took over an established territory and only increased gross sales 14% in three years, slightly less than inflation. You obviously won't brag about your sales increases. Out of a sales staff of 18, you were second in sales, since no one else sold well either. That would be the result you would use. From 1992 to 1994 you sold photocopiers. You were in the right place at the right time and sales really took off and increased 20% each year for an actual increase of 44% over two years. Assuming you didn't know what market share was, nor how you did compared to the rest of the sales staff, you would certainly want to use the sales increases.

From 1994 through 1996 you decided to sell cars. You did well and each year won an award from the manufacturer. You were also Salesperson of the Month eight times during your 34 months with the dealership. You were competing with 12 other salespeople. For that job you would mention the awards and the number of times you were Salesperson of the Month. In 1996 you went to work for a tractor manufacturer which paid a research firm to determine the market share in each territory. In five years the market share in your territory increased from 15% to 20%, a 33% increase in market share. In 2000 you joined a heavy equipment distributor and moved the territory from seventh to second. The resume might look something like this:

B & N Machinery, Tempe, Arizona 6/00 to Present

Marketing Representative - Developed and implemented marketing strategies to increase heavy equipment sales to the construction industry in Arizona. Took the territory from 7th (out of 8) in the company to 2nd during the first 36 months.

John Deere, Phoenix, Arizona 10/96 to 6/00

District Representative - Assisted 26 dealers in Arizona and New Mexico in marketing John Deere products. Set up five new dealers and developed their sales, parts and service departments. Moved seven dealers from near bankruptcy to very strong financial positions. Increased market share 33%.

Gerald Lincoln Mercury, Phoenix, Arizona 1/94 to 10/96

Salesman - Each year won the Professional Sales Counselor award for sales excellence. Out of a sales force of 12, was salesperson of the month 8 times in 34 months.

Canon Corporation, Trenton, New Jersey 1/92 to 1/94

Sales Representative - Sold a full line of photocopiers to end users. In two years increased territorial sales 44%.

Olivetti Corporation, Trenton, New Jersey 1/88 to 12/91

Sales Representative - Sold typewriters, calculators and dictating equipment to office equipment stores throughout metropolitan Trenton. Worked closely with store managers and sales staffs and provided excellent training in selling Olivetti products. Ranked 2nd in sales in 1991 out of a regional sales force of 18.

If you haven't been doing so up to this time, begin collecting and saving all the sales data you can. Whenever you start a new position, get data on what the territory was doing prior to your taking over. In the absence of cold, hard figures, rely on your memory and your knowledge of the territory. Estimate and guesstimate when you must, but do come up with some figures which you feel are accurate, and be sure you can explain how they were derived.

PAUL KIRSTEN
525 Bates S.W.
Beaverton, Oregon 97006
(503) 962-0013

OBJECTIVE: Sales Representative

EMPLOYMENT

Prescal & Hemsted Wire Rope Company, Beaverton, Oregon 3/89-Present

Sales Representative (2/94-Present). Sell wire rope through 18 distributors and through direct sales to OEM accounts, covering Oregon, Washington, and Alaska.

Key Accomplishments
- Between 1994 and 2000, built sales from $652,000 to $1,404,000.
- Have trained all inside sales staff in effective sales techniques.

Inside Sales Manager/Office Manager (3/89-2/94). Handled all inside sales, purchasing, inventory control, and traffic. Supervised the warehouse and shipping/receiving operations.

Key Accomplishments
- Reorganized the office and warehousing procedures which increased on-time deliveries and customer satisfaction.
- Coordinated a switch from a manual to a computerized inventory control and billing system. Increased productivity 32% and decreased errors 21%.
- Regional sales manager attributed most of the 43% sales increase between 1989 and 1993 to the new level of professionalism at the order desk.

Peterson Manufacturing Company, Coos Bay, Oregon 2/83-3/89

Sales Representative (3/87-3/89). Sold replacement parts for the barkers and chippers manufactured by Peterson, covering Oregon, Washington, Idaho, and Montana.

Key Accomplishment
- Increased sales of replacement parts 16%.

Inside Sales (2/85-3/87). Called on customers of Peterson products and sold replacement parts. Worked closely with purchasers of new machines to ensure an adequate inventory of the parts most likely to need replacing.

Key Accomplishment
- Increased sales of replacement parts to existing customers by 18%.

Expediter (2/83-2/85). Responsible for expediting, scheduling, and inventory control in the manufacturing of custom-made wood barkers and chippers.

Key Accomplishment
- Significantly increased total production and on-time deliveries.

EDUCATION

B.S. - History, University of Oregon (1983)

GAIL SHUMWAY
2928 Sunset Blvd.
Phoenix, AZ 85004
(602) 755-2428

QUALIFICATIONS

As Division Manager and Area Marketing Manager, increased market share each year by effectively identifying new markets, recruiting and developing successful sales teams, and obtaining quantifiable results through Total Quality programs.

EDUCATION

MBA - Marketing, University of Colorado (1982)
BS - Electrical Engineering, University of Colorado (1978)

EMPLOYMENT HISTORY

Dyatech Inc. 11/90 to Present

DIVISION MANAGER - Phoenix Division, 7/95 to Present. Responsible for the total operation and profits for this distributor of electronic components and systems, with sales to industrial users, original equipment manufacturers, and federal and state agencies. Supervise 45 employees. Introduced an effective Total Quality program into an organization with low morale and loose controls. As a result, market share has increased from 10% to 14%, while customer retention has been increased 65%.

AREA MARKETING MANAGER - Denver Division, 11/90 to 7/95. Managed the 22-employee Colorado Area in the four-state Denver Division. Created and implemented a new concept in technical marketing which doubled sales and increased market share from 12% to 22%.

Insofen Corporation 5/85 to 11/90

FIELD ENGINEER - Denver, CO. Covering Colorado and Utah, sold high technology semiconductor products to major manufacturers of electronic equipment. Worked closely with engineers to get proprietary devices designed into new products. Increased sales from $60,000 to $210,000 per month.

Xytex Corporation 7/78 to 5/85

ENGINEER - Boulder, CO. Designed power systems and interfaces for data processing peripheral equipment.

WARREN DRISCOL
927 Honeycut Drive
Atlanta, Georgia 30032
(404) 527-6819

OBJECTIVE: Sales/Marketing Management

QUALIFICATIONS

Strong Sales and Marketing background. Significantly increased territorial market share in each position held, with increases ranging from 45-330%.

EDUCATION

B.S. - Forest Engineering, University of Georgia (1977)

EMPLOYMENT

Ubasco Machinery Company, Atlanta, Georgia 8/94 to Present

FOREST PRODUCTS SALES MANAGER - As Ubasco's first Forest Products Sales Manager, responsible for selling to key accounts and for training the sales staff in methods of increasing sales of earth moving equipment to forestry related companies. Perform extensive market research to target sales and identify sales potential. Gross profit has been increased from 14% to 18% and unit sales have increased an average of 16% per year.

John Deere Tractor Company 7/77 to 8/94

FOREST PRODUCTS SALES REPRESENTATIVE, Atlanta, Georgia 8/89 to 8/94. Developed and implemented marketing strategies to increase sales to the forest industry through 24 Southeastern John Deere dealers. Worked closely with the dealers and trained their sales people to sell earth moving equipment to the forest industry. Created a special training program which covered sales techniques and forestry applications of John Deere equipment. Unit sales were increased 148% and market share was increased from 6% to 26% between 1989 and 1993.

DISTRICT REPRESENTATIVE, Bangkok, Thailand 11/86 to 8/89. Responsible for increasing sales and service levels among all dealers in India, Sri Lanka, Bangladesh, Thailand, Taiwan, South Korea and the Philippines. Identified new market areas, developed marketing strategies for dealers, and trained sales forces in effective sales techniques. Increased John Deere's market share from 14% to 21%.

PRODUCT/MARKET REP, Hong Kong 2/80 to 11/86. Conducted market studies and consulted with dealers on applications and modifications of John Deere equipment. Developed an extensive market study on the uses of wheel loaders in Asia and concluded a huge untapped market existed for wheel loaders to replace track-driven loaders. Made sales calls with dealers throughout Asia as they visited customers. Businesses immediately switched to wheel loaders. Sales of wheel loaders increased an average of 76% each year between 1982 and 1988 and captured over 60% of that market.

MARKET REP, Spokane, Washington 7/77 to 2/80. Acted as machinery application consultant to dealers. Studied mill and mining operations and made recommendations for the most appropriate John Deere equipment.

PRISCILLA BEACHMAN
2820 232nd Place SE
Renton, WA 98055
(206) 765-2321

OBJECTIVE: Marketing and Sales

QUALIFICATIONS

Effectively market products and services and substantially increase sales. Create strong working relations with wholesalers and retailers. Excellent reputation and high credibility with buyers from all grocery and drug chains in Washington, Oregon, and Idaho.

Quickly promoted by Modern Circulation because of high sales and increased circulation. Opened up magazine sales in chains that had never before sold magazines. Cultivated excellent relations with those buyers and demonstrated how a carefully monitored magazine sales program could increase profits.

Developed new marketing techniques and tools which are now used throughout the industry.

EDUCATION

Riverside Community College, Business, 72 credits (1984-1986)

EMPLOYMENT

Modern Circulation 6/88 to Present

Marketing and Promotion Manager, Renton, WA 9/96 to Present. For the largest circulation company in the U.S., responsible for increasing the circulation of 750 magazines within Washington, Oregon, and Idaho. Supervise seven District Managers with a total volume of $40 million. Work closely with buyers from chain stores to obtain rack space for publications and to help increase the chain's profits through magazine sales. Handle publicity and special promotions for various magazines and promote magazines through national and regional trade shows.

Developed a marketing strategy for Rite Aid Drugs and introduced a magazine sales checkout program into 148 stores on the West Coast. Rated second in productivity among fifteen Marketing Managers nationwide in 2001 and 2002.

District Sales Manager, Portland, OR 3/92 to 9/96. Worked directly with five magazine wholesalers and dozens of retail accounts to increase circulation of publications. Solved serious problems with one major wholesaler and enabled it to move from 14th largest on the West Coast to 6th. Increased the Modern Circulation line 30% on $6 million of annual sales.

Sales Representative, Seattle, WA 6/88 to 3/92. Significantly increased magazine sales to independent retailers and was quickly promoted to District Sales Manager to work with larger accounts.

Colgate Palmolive, Seattle, WA 10/86 to 6/88

Merchandiser. Called on drug and grocery accounts, taking orders, creating displays, and stocking as needed. Opened up Skaggs for the first time to the full line of Colgate Palmolive products.

CAREER CHANGERS

And the day came when the risk to remain tight in a bud was more painful than the risk it took to blossom. —Unknown

I applaud people making career changes. Career changers can find greater job satisfaction and a lifestyle more in tune with their current values. Career changers, however, have the most difficult and frustrating experiences with resumes. When they use the traditional approach of mailing out 100 or more resumes, career changers experience very little success. While having an effective resume is still necessary for career changers, the resume *must* be used in a way that takes advantage of the hidden job market.

If you are a career changer, the first thing you must do is determine the type of position you'll be seeking. Then pick out every experience even remotely related to that line of work and insert it in some form into the resume. The qualifications section is often an excellent place to do this.

When you start describing your employment, you have two main goals: 1) show you were successful at what you did; and 2) emphasize any parts of your jobs which are related to your current objective. Your successes are important. Employers are dubious enough about hiring a career changer; they certainly want a person with a proven record of success. Essentially you'll be saying through your resume, "I've been successful in the past, and I'll be successful for you, also." Emphasizing related experience in each job is important. In most cases you should provide an adequate and accurate overview of your entire job, but that can usually be covered in one or two sentences. The remaining space should cover those functions which are related to your objective. In other words, duties which took up only 10% of your time may get 90% of the space.

Career changers tend to have longer qualifications sections than those who have years of experience in the same field. Career changers sometimes do better with a functional resume. Read pages 99 to 108 for a full explanation and several examples. Rosalyn used a lengthy qualifications section very effectively. The points made in qualifications could not have been adequately made in the employment section. Notice how she emphasized everything she had ever done that was related to training and development in any way.

Paula does everything possible to show she is sales oriented and that her efforts have consistently increased revenue. Although she has never held a job labeled "Sales Representative," it is very easy to picture her being successful in sales.

I also recommend that you join appropriate associations and volunteer to head up committees or special projects. Associations are usually begging for people to spend time on projects and you don't need to have been a member for five years. It is an excellent way to get recognized and to meet the top people in your field. Those projects or committee assignments could then go in a special projects section.

ROSALYN RODRIQUEZ
2315 Dixie Avenue
Charleston, South Carolina 29406
(803) 976-4204

OBJECTIVE: Position in Training and Development

QUALIFICATIONS

Broad background in planning and developing programs. Skilled in determining program needs through task analysis. Planned and organized numerous programs, including the Council for Exceptional Children 2001 State Conference.

Extensive knowledge and experience in determining needs, setting behavioral and learning objectives, and developing assessment tools. M.A. in Curriculum and Program Development.

Expertise in selecting appropriate teaching techniques to match the audience. Quickly establish rapport with groups.

Outstanding record in education. Received ratings of excellent to outstanding in all evaluations.

Evaluated and selected speakers and consultants for educational topics and conventions.

Extensive budgetary and purchasing experience with instructional materials.

Excellent writer. Wrote three successful grant proposals and published two articles on curriculum development for the *Journal of Education.*

Extensive knowledge of statistics and research methodologies for determining effectiveness of programs.

Strong abilities in performing and graphics arts. Directed, stage-managed, and designed sets and costumes for numerous theatrical productions.

Designed and produced newsletters, manuals, and brochures using desktop publishing.

Extensive experience writing, producing, and editing video programs.

EDUCATION

M.A. - Curriculum and Instruction, University of South Carolina (1985)
B.A. - Art, Arkansas State Teachers College (1980)

EMPLOYMENT

Teacher, Charleston Public Schools, Charleston, South Carolina 9/87 to Present
Teacher, Greenville Public Schools, Greenville, South Carolina 9/80 to 9/87

ASSOCIATIONS

Member - American Society for Training and Development
Member - Council for Exceptional Children; State Bylaws Chairperson 1995 to Present;
    Chapter President 1995; Chapter Vice President 1994

PAULA PROJASKA
1247 Morton Drive
Ottawa, Ontario K1Z1A6
(613) 743-1726

JOB OBJECTIVE: Sales

QUALIFICATIONS

Proven ability to sell products and services. Quickly develop product knowledge and relate very well to people at all levels.

EDUCATION

B.A. - Public Relations, Trent University (1989)

EMPLOYMENT

Four Winds Hotel, Ottawa, Ontario 1990-Present

Executive Assistant (1997-Present). Implemented numerous training and staff development programs which have raised guest service to the highest level found in Ottawa. Increased communication and cooperation between departments and implemented an effective cross training program. Since 1997 hotel revenue has increased an average of 14% per year. Work closely with the Chamber of Commerce and perform PR functions with other local businesses and organizations.

Food Services Coordinator (1992-1997). Introduced new food and room services which increased room revenue 11% per year and food/beverage revenue 12% per year. Supervised a staff of sixty.

Assistant Food Services Coordinator (1990-1992). Coordinated all food services including room service, coffee shop, dining room, lounge, and meeting rooms. Supervised a staff of 20. Designed a new training program which instilled more professionalism in the staff. Annual turnover was cut from 20% to 5%. As service improved, room revenue and food and beverage revenue each increased 40% in two years.

MANAGERS/SUPERVISORS

Providing results in a resume is important for everyone, but is especially critical for managers. Being a manager is unique in that most of the work you accomplish is through the efforts of others. As a manager, however, you get to take credit for any results of your department or work unit. While others did most of the actual work, you guided and oversaw the efforts, approved the actions taken, and of course, had responsibility for the success of your department as well as any projects or programs.

The resume is the place to describe your results and the interview is the place to provide the details as to how those results were achieved, who they were achieved through, and what your role was. The resume is definitely not the place to try to give credit to your staff, and it is unnecessary since everyone reading your resume will know that others assisted you.

In the resume and in interviews get rid of any tendencies toward false modesty. You must come across as confident, dynamic, and decisive.

If you have not done so already, start a habit of quantifying your results at the time they occur. As you begin a project do your best to quantify what the current situation is. If you are trying to decrease rejects you need to know the current level of rejects and the level of rejects after you have implemented your new process. If you are trying to improve customer satisfaction, you need to know the current level, probably through some type of a survey. In this way the numbers you report in your resume will be "harder" and thus more impressive. For results from the past, you'll have to be satisfied with your best estimates and whatever figures you have.

It often helps to indicate the size of your department, the number of direct reports, and the dollar value of your department's budget, but include it only if you feel it will help sell you.

See pages 34 to 46 for more on results. Sometimes it is best to show the before and after raw figures, other times it is preferable to use percentages or dollar figures. Do not get caught in the trap that your results must be super impressive. If rejects are reduced from 6.5% to 6%, that is still an 8% decrease and is very significant. Use your results to show that wherever you are, you constantly look for ways to improve your operations.

DOROTHY MICKULIN
9103 Union
Kansas City, MO 64133
(816) 276-4217

OBJECTIVE: Operations Management

QUALIFICATIONS

Strong background in branch operations management. As a branch operations troubleshooter, have turned around operations at eleven branches. At each branch have strengthened training, and reduced operations charge-offs, absenteeism, and turnover. Through extensive cross-training, have increased productivity and reduced overtime. Very effective in training staff to sell banking services and maintain customer loyalty.

EMPLOYMENT

Kansas City Trust & Savings 10/81-Present

BRANCH OPERATIONS MANAGER 9/97-Present. Responsible for the smooth functioning of branch operations, while supervising 20 employees. Produce many weekly, monthly and annual reports, including Charge-off, Dormant Control, Expense Accounts, Full Time Equivalent, Methods and Analysis Branch Study, Suspense, Internal Certification on Branch Accounts, and Budget and Profit Plan.

As Branch Operations Manager of two branches, have overcome morale problems and increased productivity. Worked closely with each staff and significantly improved morale through better training and supervision. At each branch absenteeism, turnover and operations charge-offs have been significantly reduced. The customer service rating has been increased at each branch at least 35%.

RELIEF SUPERVISOR 9/92-9/97. Functioned as temporary Branch Operations Manager at nine branches. Supervised 8 to 20 employees. Given a mandate at each branch to resolve operational, procedural, and employee problems. Turned around the situation at each branch to the satisfaction of the Executive V.P. of Operations.

Prior positions with Kansas City Trust & Savings:

Operations Supervisor 8/84-9/92
Management Trainee 8/83-8/84
Note Teller 10/81-8/83

DON ABRAHMS
6317 Avery Road
Fairfax, Virginia 22033
(703) 282-1971

QUALIFICATIONS

Broad experience in all phases of Property Management and Building Management. Able to keep occupancy rates high and tenants satisfied.

Strong ability in negotiating new and renewal leases.

Creative problem solver. Able to negotiate solutions to the satisfaction of all parties.

Effectively identify new methods for cutting operating costs while increasing tenant services.

EDUCATION

A.A. - General Studies, Whipple Community College (1990)

EMPLOYMENT

Bridgeport Property Management, Fairfax, Virginia 6/90 to Present

PROPERTY MANAGER 8/99 to Present. Property Manager for Southfield Office Park and other commercial/industrial properties in Fairfax County. Negotiate new and renewal leases, resolve tenant problems, and oversee the maintenance of the buildings and grounds.

As General Contractor, completed a major renovation of 10,560 square feet of office space at 18% under the estimated cost. Increased square footage rates 22% during the last year and a half and increased the occupancy rate from 92% to 97%. Using a long term, no interest federal government loan, initiated an energy management system which reduced energy costs 20%. Actively involved with budget planning and instituting cost controls.

BUILDING MANAGER 5/92 to 8/99. Managed all maintenance functions at Southfield Office Park and acted as General Contractor for tenant alterations and improvements. Worked effectively with subcontractors and consistently completed projects on schedule and within the budget. Planned and initiated an in-house HVAC mechanical department which reduced maintenance costs and increased tenant satisfaction. Obtained excellent results from janitorial and security services. Personally performed many repairs.

FIELD SUPERVISOR 6/90 to 5/92. Supervised grounds crews of up to 22 employees while constructing the Southfield Office Park. Operated cranes, cats, and other heavy equipment while supervising the land reclamation, and the construction of building sites, streets, parking lots, and utility systems.

JON ARNETT
19112 Edgecliff Drive
Cleveland, OH 44119
(216) 726-3982

OBJECTIVE: Manufacturing Management

QUALIFICATIONS

Strong background in all aspects of production supervision in the electronics industry including job scheduling, quality assurance, inventory control, purchasing, and customer relations. Consistently increase quality, productivity, and on-time deliveries.

EDUCATION

Business, Dennison Community College, 66 credits (1984-1987)

EMPLOYMENT

Advanced Circuits, Cleveland, OH 7/00-Present

Production Manager - Supervise 16 shop personnel in the production of prototype circuit boards. Handle cost estimating, job scheduling, production control, and inventory control. Reduced turnaround time on orders from three weeks to one without adding staff or increasing overtime. Established a Total Quality program which has reduced rejects 65%. Significantly reduced purchasing costs through a more effective inventory control program.

Digital Systems, Ashtabula, OH 5/96-7/00.

Drilling and Fabrication Supervisor - Supervised 12 production workers operating computer numerically controlled drilling and fabrication machines. Developed a new job scheduling system which reduced late deliveries by 30%. Researched inventory needs for raw materials and supplies and determined lead times. Data enabled company to reduce inventory on numerous items and also reduced work stoppages due to lack of parts approximately 40%. Increased production of printed circuit boards 22% with no additional employees.

Hudson Manufacturing, Akron, OH 3/86-5/96

Lead Production Supervisor - 6/90-5/96. Supervised two supervisors, four leads, and 35 production personnel. Implemented a job scheduling system which increased on time deliveries 44% with an average of 150 shipments monthly. Heavily involved in the design of a new facility and planned the actual move.

Shop Lead - 4/87-6/90. Assigned jobs to 18 production workers in drilling, screening, plating, fabricating, and camera work. Developed a maintenance program which reduced production losses due to breakdowns 70%.

Silkscreener - 3/86-4/87. Hand screened circuitry, bakeable and UV curable solder mask, and sheet metal front panels.

KYLE BAUMGARTNER
814 Horgen Avenue
Orlando, Florida 32807
(305) 981-4660

OBJECTIVE: Physical Distribution/Traffic Management

QUALIFICATIONS

Experienced in all phases of traffic management. Developed two traffic departments into smooth functioning, money saving organizations.

EDUCATION

A.A. - Transportation Management, Saltwater Community College (1994)

WORK HISTORY

Webber Industries, Orlando, Florida 8/01 to Present

Traffic Manager - Manage the Traffic Department of this $25 million appliance parts manufacturer. Annual freight costs total $2.3 million. Set policies for freight handling, route all orders, negotiate rates and contracts with carriers, maintain compliance with transportation laws, file freight claims, mediate customer problems and complaints, and audit freight bills for payment.

Negotiated freight rates with a major carrier, cutting the rate by 20% and saving $75,000 per year.

Introduced a routing and consolidation program, saving $80,000 per year through multi-bill consolidations, utilizing carrier discounts, consolidating orders, and carrier selection.

Negotiated a product classification change for California freight, saving $12,000 annually.

Custer Distributors, Orlando, Florida 6/94 to 8/01

Traffic and Distribution Manager - Managed the Shipping and Receiving and Distribution departments for this $28 million distributor of retail products. Annual freight costs totaled $1.9 million. Set up and managed a private trucking operation, saving $65,000 annually and significantly improving customer service. Introduced new procedures which increased productivity and created annual cost savings of over $85,000.

WILLIAM SAXTON
641 Arastradero
Palo Alto, California 94306
(415) 881-9595

OBJECTIVE: Purchasing Management

QUALIFICATIONS

Strong background in purchasing management. Consistently develop systems which cut costs and provide the timely delivery of products.

EDUCATION

B.A. - Geography, San Jose State University (1976)

EMPLOYMENT

Rhapsody Clothing, Palo Alto, California   7/93-Present

DIRECTOR OF PURCHASING
For this $20 million clothing manufacturer, supervise a staff of four and have responsibility for the purchasing of all nontextile items.

Developed an inventory control system which has eliminated duplication of supplies.

Increased the level of buying with key suppliers and developed stronger relationships as well as larger discounts, resulting in a reduced cost of 15-35% on items purchased.

Save $20,000 annually on continuous data processing forms and have increased copying efficiency 50%.

Developed and implemented a departmental charge back system for supplies. System has increased accuracy and equity in calculating actual departmental costs.

Administer all aspects of national and local trade shows, including planning, purchasing new exhibits, contracting with trade people, obtaining sites and floor spaces, purchasing materials, and handling transportation.

Trade show costs have been reduced $75,000 annually over the last three years.

Ryans Department Stores, Los Angeles, California   7/76-7/93

DIRECTOR OF PURCHASING - 9/87-7/93
Negotiated, awarded, and administered contracts with vendors for the procurement of over 500 items.

Personally redesigned gift boxes and saved $150,000 annually in production and storage costs.

Developed a unique automated packing material system which reduced labor and handling costs and saved $20,000 annually.

Planned and managed an increased volume of purchasing from $1.1 million to $3.2 million as the chain increased from 6 to 14 stores in four years.

Managed the paper stock warehouse and in-plant print shop.

Prior positions within Ryans: Assistant Director of Purchasing 3/82-9/87; Purchasing Agent 10/79-3/82; Purchasing Assistant 7/76-10/79.

Terry Prohaska
4047 Westavia Drive
Raleigh, North Carolina 27612
(919) 971-3242

QUALIFICATIONS

Strong experience in implementing cost saving purchasing programs. Extensive background in developing and introducing data processing systems to aid in cost reductions. Established reputation as an excellent negotiator.

EDUCATION

B.A. - Business Administration, Oakwood College, Huntsville, Alabama (1980)

EMPLOYMENT

Conway Inc., Raleigh, North Carolina 10/90 to Present

Manager, Facilities Purchasing - 6/96 to Present. Manage a staff of twelve buyers and four clerical personnel. Department annually purchases $80 million of supplies, parts, and equipment for the maintenance, repair, and operation of Conway facilities. Review and approve all purchases over $40,000 and resolve discrepancy reports.

- Developed and implemented a major program to reduce inventory and operating costs. Since 1997 inventory has been reduced from $5.4 million to $2.9 million, with documented savings of $1.1 million. Continuing to implement additional cost savings measures.

Supervisor, Corporate Procurement - 10/90 to 6/96. Negotiated, awarded, and administered contracts with vendors for the procurement of over 20,000 different standard parts. Worked closely with company plants throughout the country to calculate future needs for stocked parts. Improved coordination led to larger orders and decreased costs.

- Aggressively sought out new vendors desiring Conway business in order to take advantage of innovative equipment and methods they possessed. Full procurement program led to $15 million in documented savings in four years on purchases of $70 million.

Nova Co., Valdez, Alaska 8/86 to 10/90

Procurement Administrator - Installed a catalog list purchasing system and purchased all electrical equipment and hardware for this electrical contractor on the Hunt Oil Refinery.

- Developed procurement policies and procedures which led to significant savings and introduced volume procurement. The previous small order system resulted in parts delays and higher prices. Worked closely with the architect on this design-build project to predict future needs, then purchased the materials necessary to complete entire sections of the project.

Bronka Industries, Birmingham, Alabama 8/80 to 8/86

Materiel Administrator – Responsible for all facets of material management. Developed a solid foundation in the principles of purchasing. In 1981, with a task force of four people, designed and implemented a Stockless Purchasing System which is still used throughout Bronka.

- System reduced PO's by 75%, enabled the reduction of the buying group from sixty to twenty-five, and reduced administration costs 22%. Oversaw the system and continued to handle purchasing duties.

MARSHALL TREVES
924 Durhamtree Place
Louisville, Kentucky 40229
(502) 666-2413

QUALIFICATIONS

Coordinate well with contractors and subcontractors. Resolve problems effectively and maintain excellent relations.

Extremely analytical and inventive. Develop unique solutions to construction problems.

Proven ability to get projects completed ahead of schedule and under budget. Produce highly accurate estimates.

Experienced in all phases of construction.

EMPLOYMENT

Blouton Ceiling Installation, Louisville, Kentucky 7/901 to Present

Job Superintendent - Manage projects for this ceiling subcontractor. Projects have included the First National Building, the remodeling of eighteen Louisville schools, and the Westgate Mall.

As Job Superintendent for the First National office building, supervised a crew of four and coordinated with the contractor and subcontractors to handle the many changes in the smoothest way possible.

While functioning as foreman of a crew remodeling schools in Louisville, developed a system which speeded up the work and allowed the project to be completed under budget and ahead of schedule.

As Job Superintendent on the sixty-five shop Westgate Mall, took a project that was over budget and ten weeks behind schedule and turned it around. Developed an excellent working relationship with the general contractor, organized the work more effectively, and created a highly motivated crew. Project was completed under budget and ahead of schedule.

Treves Construction, Louisville, Kentucky 2/91 to 7/01

Owner/Manager - Provided subcontracting work in framing, finishing, dry wall, insulation, metal stud framing, aluminum siding, and soffits. Gained expertise in estimating, bidding, and purchasing. Developed a reputation for high quality work.

Prior Experience: Carpenter 6/80 to 2/91

EDUCATION

Electrical Engineering, Kentucky State University (1980-1982) 105 Credits

OFFICE/CLERICAL WORKERS

As an office worker your primary responsibility is to demonstrate that you possess strong office skills, that you are hard working and efficient, that you are easy to work with, that you are reliable and resourceful, that you can take on greater responsibility, and that you look for ways to improve office operations.

Either in the qualifications section of the resume or in a section called Office Skills, you can list the types of computers you have used, knowledge of operating systems such as Windows, and experience with various applications software such as Word, WordPerfect, Excel, Lotus 1-2-3, and others. If you are really an expert in one or more applications, you can state that in qualifications, or you can divide the applications software into two categories under office skills, and label them "Expert In" and "Experienced In." If a term like "expert in" is a little too strong, try "Highly Experienced In."

Demonstrating that you are a hard worker, efficient, and easy to work with, is usually best covered in the qualifications section and in the cover letter. If you really feel you have these qualities, simply tell the reader through the resume and cover letter. Another excellent way to sell these qualities is to show that you are a results oriented person. By selling your results you will sell the fact that you are efficient and easy to work with.

Do not feel that you must list every single duty that you had on each job. I've seen clerical resumes that were virtually unreadable because they simply consisted of a long list of duties. You may have had a duty which you carried out in each of your last six jobs, but in the resume you may choose to include that duty only in your first three jobs just to show that you have experience in that area. Of course with a key skill, you would list it in any job where you used it.

Some duties do not need to be mentioned at all. Since virtually every office person types and answers the phone, those two duties do not need to be mentioned unless you want to.

Sometimes a person is responsible for producing 10-15 different reports each month. Generally the names of those reports will have no meaning to a reader. If you are going to mention them at all, give them generic names such as "expense report" or "inventory report." You could say, "Produced 15 reports each month including the expense report, inventory report, and sales report."

As with any resume, your key task is to show your results. Initially many office workers tell me they don't have any results, but invariably we come up with several. The main question to ask yourself is whether you have improved processes or created systems which made something better, easier, or faster.

People frequently believe their improvement is not big enough to mention in a resume. Nearly any improvement is worthy of putting on a resume, but of course you would emphasize the most important ones. If a process saved you or your organization over ten hours per year, or if a system saved over $300 in expense or time, it may be worth mentioning. Even if you decide not to include some of your smaller results in the resume, you may still want to mention them in interviews.

Remember, to mention a result, it does not have to be big or to have saved thousands of dollars. Look at it this way, if *everyone* found ways to save a few hours here and a few dollars there, organizations would be much more profitable.

JANICE TENSLEY
13617 Moccasin Bay
Winnipeg, Manitoba R2Y1B5
(204) 727-5133

OBJECTIVE: Office Administration position utilizing computer skills

QUALIFICATIONS

Strong office administration background. Implement systems that significantly increase office productivity. Quickly learn word processing, database, and spreadsheet software. Excellent supervisor. Flexible, creative, and work well under pressure.

EMPLOYMENT HISTORY

BTC Computers, Winnipeg, Manitoba 5/01-Present

Operations Support - For this manufacturer and distributor of computers, created and implemented a computerized inventory control system. Introduced the system throughout the company and within three company-owned retail stores. System has enabled BTC to continue its rapid expansion with excellent control of its growing inventory. Instructed all staff in the use of the system and act as troubleshooter when problems or questions occur. System provides excellent controls and saves over 20 hours per week in staff research time.

Introduced a computerized accounting system utilizing Great Plains and a Novell network. Oversee the maintenance of the inventory, purchase order, posting, and order entry modules. Also involved with the input and mainte-nance of the accounts payable and general ledger modules. Provide technical software support and problem solving within the organization.

L & M Investing, Winnipeg, Manitoba 4/95-5/01

Office Manager - Supervised and trained five employees and coordinated all work flow in the office of this investment counselor and financial planner. Maintained all office information systems. Maintained files and computer databases on several hundred clients, as well as documentation dealing with securities, mutual funds, limited partnerships, and insurance. Tracked all purchases by clients and calculated commissions. Handled accounts receivable and processed buy or sell orders by clients. Produced and edited a monthly newsletter and created all graphics. Developed databases and spreadsheets which owner stated increased office productivity by 30%. Considered a key person in the growth of the firm.

COMPUTER KNOWLEDGE

Excellent knowledge of Word, WordPerfect, Excel, Lotus 1-2-3, Access, Great Plains Accounting, Windows, Q&A, Client Manager, Newsroom, PC Paint, Personal Publisher, Novell networking.

EDUCATION

A.A. - General Studies, Caribou Community College (1995)

GOVERNMENT EMPLOYEES

As with any resume, demonstrating results will help you get more interviews and more job offers. Your goal should be to demonstrate that you design and implement successful, cost-effective programs, or that you are highly skilled at your work. Quantify your results whenever possible. Do your best to show the before and after. If you were head of a program to improve air quality in a metropolitan region you should be able to provide accurate figures. If you worked with a summer youth program you might be able to indicate that you obtained more private sector jobs for youths than in previous years.

In addition to specific results, you should look for ways to demonstrate that you work well with the public. Show that you have a real feel for public relations, that you can sense in advance when there will be a public outcry over a new policy, and that you can defuse tense situations.

If your job will involve you with elected officials or citizen boards, demonstrate that you know how to deal with them. Show that you make persuasive recommendations and that your recommendations are usually approved. Show that you work well with community groups to gain their support for your programs, but that you are not afraid to stand up to them when necessary.

If your work is more in the planning area, describe your overall responsibilities and then mention key projects you were involved with. Provide the names of the projects or programs since some of your readers may be familiar with them, and in any case, it makes the project or program something they can better identify with. Also, provide key information so the reader will understand the size and scope of the project/program, as well as the complexity.

If you or your department has been particularly effective in obtaining grants, mention that. You may want to list the number of grants and their average amount, or you may want to merely list the amount of the largest grant obtained.

_____LAURA DONOHUE_____

401 Eastman West   Arlington Heights, Illinois 60015   (312) 871-2652

QUALIFICATIONS

Excellent organizational ability. Develop new systems that increase productivity and quality of work.

Broad speaking experience. Frequently speak to groups of 100-500 people. Received a standing ovation at an annual convention for making a difficult subject easily understood.

Excellent public relations ability. Work effectively with organizations and individuals while solving problems and explaining policies. Quickly gain the respect of all parties.

EDUCATION

Graduated - Colville High School, Colville, Washington (1985)

EMPLOYMENT

United States Railroad Retirement Board, Chicago, Illinois 11/91-Present

Contract Representative - 11/99-Present. Explain and interpret complex laws and regulations related to retirement, disability, and unemployment benefits. Interview claimants and obtain necessary documents. Substantiate evidence and determine eligibility and amount of benefits.

Provide training sessions for union and management groups to explain changes in regulations. Successfully introduced a group interview procedure for explaining unemployment compensation when claims rose from 250 to 2,100 per month. Developed numerous systems which decreased backlog and increased staff morale.

Unemployment Claims Examiner - 11/91-11/99. Interviewed claimants and former employers to determine eligibility for benefits. Monitored job finding efforts of claimants and assisted in their obtaining new positions. Developed a new system for coding claims and won the Region Accuracy Award in 1995.

Social Security Administration, Chicago, Illinois 6/85-11/91

Service Representative - 4/89-11/91 Provided assistance and technical information about Social Security, Medicare, and Supplemental Security Income to beneficiaries and the general public. Resolved problems, untangled red tape, and helped make the system work. Received a cash bonus award for suggesting improvements in Social Security forms.

Secretary - 6/85-4/89. Ran the office efficiently, answered correspondence, and compiled statistical reports.

CHARLES PARSONS

1226 3rd Avenue N.W.   Minnetonka, Minnesota 55343
(612) 378-5162   e-mail: cparsons@byte.com

QUALIFICATIONS

Over twenty years of progressively responsible experience in all areas of Human
Resources Management. Highly successful in planning, organizing, and coordinating
a wide variety of Human Resources Development programs.

EDUCATION

M.P.A. - Public Administration, Tufts University (1983)
B.A. - History, Western Kentucky University (1980)

EMPLOYMENT HISTORY

Personnel Management Advisor

U.S. Office of Personnel Management, Minneapolis, Minnesota   7/00 to Present

Responsible for promoting Human Resources Management practices with State and
Local governmental organizations in Minnesota, Iowa, and Wisconsin. Plan, design,
and implement Human Resources systems including policies, procedures, job
evaluation, compensation, benefits, recruitment, selection, employee relations,
employee development, management information systems, organizational
development, and safety.

As project manager, develop and adhere to budgets, supervise and train staff, and
coordinate activities with client agencies. Most recommendations have been adopted,
with agencies experiencing improved quality of service, increased morale, and greater
productivity.

Classification And Pay Manager

Hennepin County, Minneapolis, Minnesota   9/93 to 7/00

Developed, implemented, and directed the classification and pay function for a
totally new, comprehensive personnel management system. Unit became a highly
respected part of the County Office of Personnel. Designed and developed the
County's first uniform pay system. Promoted, planned, and coordinated a Personnel
Management Information System which significantly increased the amount of
personnel data available for management decisions. Improved service delivery 35%
by instituting a personnel generalist approach.

Supervisor Of Classification And Pay

State of Minnesota Merit Employment, St. Paul, Minnesota   7/90 to 9/93

Selected, trained, and supervised the professional staff which maintained and
improved the State classification and pay systems. Developed improved
classification and pay policies.

Administrative Consultant

Public Administration Service, Chicago, Illinois   8/83 to 7/90

Provided administrative, organizational, and personnel management consultative
services to state and local governments nationwide for this highly respected,
nonprofit consulting organization established in 1933.

Doreen Caffey
13206 127th N.E.
Kirkland, Washington 98034
(425) 821-4454

OBJECTIVE: Contract Administrator

QUALIFICATIONS

Broad Contract Administration experience, covering solicitation preparation and advertisement, contract awards, claim settlements, negotiation of changes, and terminations.

Strong ability to recognize potential problems, research the problem, and propose solutions or alternatives.

EDUCATION

B.S. - Sociology, Oral Roberts University (1993)

EMPLOYMENT

U.S. Forest Service, Seattle, Washington, 7/93 to Present

Contract Administrator - 6/00 to Present
Responsible for preparation of solicitations for bid, advertising solicitation, and opening and awarding contracts. Handle complete contract administration including negotiation of changes, settlement of claims, suspension of contracts, ensuring timely contract completion, and termination of contracts for default and convenience of the Government.

- Developed procedures which have reduced the time necessary to let a contract from 90 to 72 days.
- Work with corporate sureties in take-over agreements and claims against bid, performance, and payment bonds.
- Research previous contract law interpretations and work closely with the Office of General Counsel when contract appears or bid protests have been docketed.

Voucher Examiner - 7/93 to 6/00
Made payment to vendors for supplies and services. Prepared monthly report of obligations (accounts payable).

- As Property Accounting Clerk for the forest, converted a massive manual property accounting system to a computer system thereby increasing accuracy and substantially reducing maintenance costs.
- Worked with accountant and budget analyst in preparation of the General Administration budget for the forest.

TEACHERS

Teachers have a problem with their resumes because teachers all tend to look alike, after all, they all have the same duties. Using your nonclassroom activities can be one good way to set you apart from your competitors. Mention it if you were department chair, heavily involved in advising, active in after-school activities, or actively involved in school committees. Mention any awards you've received or any improvements in standardized test scores in your classroom. Your cover letter could be the place to quote a few snippets from your reviews, or perhaps even from parents who have made comments to you or sent letters to you.

It is critical that the reader realize that you are an energetic, enthusiastic, effective teacher. Your resume and cover letter are your tools to accomplish that. Your cover letter can be an excellent place to state a concise version of your teaching philosophy. Also, use your cover letter to express what it is that makes you a highly effective educator. Typically cover letters are fairly short documents, but you may want to write an expanded cover letter in order to reveal things about you which are difficult to get across in the resume alone.

BRENDA BERKELEY
5693 Smugglers Cove Road
Portland, ME 04017
(207) 876-3562

OBJECTIVE: Educator

QUALIFICATIONS

Strong teaching background. During nine years of teaching have obtained excellent results with children and have instilled a desire to learn. Thoroughly enjoy working with kids and seeing their personal growth.

EDUCATION

MA - Curriculum Development, Boston College (1997)
BA - Education/Speech Therapy, University of Maine, Farmington (1994)

PROFESSIONAL EXPERIENCE

Portland School District, Portland, ME 1994-Present

Educator - 2001-Present. Teach first through third grade to high risk students. As chairperson of the Staff Training and Development Committee, completed a needs assessment and identified numerous training needs among teachers and teacher's aides. Sold the teaching staff on the need for training and developed a training program which has met all of its objectives.

Program Coordinator/Educator - 1996-2001. Coordinated all aspects of the Early Childhood Special Education Program, including hiring and training of staff and support professionals, and the design and implementation of curriculum. Marketed the program throughout the community and in six months tripled the size of the program to 190. Persuaded parents to participate in special events with their children, resulting in a 70% increase in parent involvement. Spoke to business, community, and physician groups which gained community support for the program and enabled professionals to make appropriate referrals.

Communication Disorders Specialist - 1994-1996. Provided therapy to students with communication disorders. Participated in all aspects of Project Redi, a screening program for kindergartners, including the selection of assessment procedures, training staff, and analyzing statistical reports. Presented information on the process to other schools which resulted in their adopting similar procedures.

ENGINEERS/SCIENTISTS

By all means keep your resume interesting. Although it is perfectly acceptable, and often necessary, to have a resume filled with technical terms and jargon, be careful of overdoing the technical terminology. Listing key buzz words, however, will certainly help because human resources people and hiring managers will be looking for evidence of experience in certain areas.

When you write your resume, use both broad terms and specific terms. If you have spent your last two years working in a highly specialized area, it is unlikely that another employer will hire you to do *only* that type of work, unless it just happens to be a very hot specialty. In qualifications, for example, you might say, "Ten years experience in _____, with specialties in ____, _____, _____, and _____. In the job description portion of the resume you might say "Responsible for all areas of _____, including _____, _____, _____, and _____." In this way the broad term gets embedded in the mind of the employer, as well as the specific areas.

Although experience with certain technologies is important, it is just as important to reveal that you are good at what you do. When you can truly claim it, indicate that you virtually always complete projects on schedule and within budget. If you designed a product that became a hot seller, mention it. Do not worry that people will think you are claiming you did it all by yourself. Everyone will know that you did it as part of a team. Do your best to bring results into your resume.

Organizations today are looking for team players who can also work well independently. Show that you have worked as a team member on projects. Then take credit for your individual achievements as well as for the team achievements.

Quantify results whenever you can. In your job sketches list the objectives or specifications of the product, or research project. Then determine if you met the specifications or goals. Once you've determined that you met the specifications, try to quantify some aspect. If you've got hard figures, by all means use them, but don't hesitate to use numbers even if you have to do some estimating.

Engineering and scientific fields are typically very project oriented. Therefore, in the first paragraph of your job description you would typically begin with an overall description of your duties. Often the remainder of that job description will consist of describing three or four key projects. Most projects will require 2–4 lines to adequately describe them. Don't try to give all the details of the project. Instead, give just enough information so that the reader will have a reasonably good idea of what the project was about, and then concentrate on results.

200

JOHN MYERSBY
9023 York Street
New Westminster, BC V3L453
(604) 271-3157

OBJECTIVE: Electronics Engineer

QUALIFICATIONS

Excellent engineering background including experience with microprocessing design.

EDUCATION

B.S. - Electrical and Computer Engineering, Simon Fraser University (1995)

EMPLOYMENT

Ransey Systems, Vancouver, BC 6/01 to Present

Senior Engineer - As part of a team of Software Quality Assurance Engineers, evaluate CAD/CAM software and make recommendations for improvements before software is made available to users within the company. Review functional specifications to ensure all portions are testable and fully meet user needs. Analyze test results, identify problem areas, and make final recommendations.

Performed a cost improvement study which documented savings through the Software Quality Assurance Program of $400,000 annually. Program has eliminated duplication of testing, produced a more organized software development process, and resolved problems at earlier stages.

Mutual Signals, Vancouver, BC 7/95 to 6/01

Manager of Engineering Services - 4/96 to 6/01. For this firm which designs, sells, and installs industrial and municipal signaling and alarm systems, designed systems and oversaw installations. Analyzed job specifications to determine necessary equipment, did takeoffs from blueprints for bids, modified or designed/built equipment, and provided technical support on sales calls. Oversaw installations and tested large systems upon completion. Played a key role in enabling the firm to grow an average of 18% per year.

Electronics Technician 7/95 to 4/96. Installed and tested systems and did takeoffs from blueprints, as well as supervised technicians at installation sites.

PROFESSIONALS

With this category I am referring to those in the "professions" such as medical doctor, attorney, professor, accountant, psychologist, and counselor, as well as all other professions, those occupations in the sciences and liberal arts which typically require degrees.

Professionals often find resumes hard to write because it can be difficult to quantify results. Despite the difficulty, virtually everyone can come up with results and find ways to sell those results in the resume.

Before beginning your resume, first determine how you know you are good at what you do. You can certainly include that your boss, your colleagues, and your clients all tell you that you are good, but don't stop there. Ask yourself why they feel you are good. Write down those points regardless of whether you can quantify any of them. When you are through, determine which of them you can use in your resume, and which would be best used in your cover letter. Some points will be best left for an interview. Remember that your goal is to cause people to want to meet you.

Although you may have done many things in your career, emphasize those things that you would like to do more of in the future. Devote more space and detail to those things.

Use your nomenclature where appropriate but don't overdo it. You will want to include key buzz words and hot terms, but only when appropriate.

Professionals often do well by including special projects in their job descriptions, or even having a separate "projects" section if many of the projects have occurred off the job or as part of a professional society.

MARIAN OSTEGAARD
4006 Walton Avenue
Ypsilanti, MI 48197
(313) 264-2372

OBJECTIVE: Director of a Social Service Agency

QUALIFICATIONS

Strong social service administration background gained during 24 years with one of the most respected agencies in Michigan.

EDUCATION

M.A. - Social Work, University of Michigan (1981)
B.A. - Sociology, Psychology, University of Michigan (1978)

PROFESSIONAL EXPERIENCE

Counseling Services of Detroit, Detroit, MI 7/78 to Present

Assistant Executive Director 6/00 to Present

Direct the agency's counseling program, including ten branch offices and 30 employees. Manage the salary budget which represents 85% of the total budget. Created and implemented a new middle-management structure which has increased accountability of branch operations. Counseling productivity has been increased 24% through improved training and time management.

Unit Administrator 9/94 to 6/00

Managed five branch offices, and supervised 15 professional employees and eight volunteers. Taught Family Life Education classes, and acted as Field Instruction Supervisor for counseling interns. Provided consultation and training to other organizations, and spoke before numerous business and public groups. Organized a Citizen's Advisory Committee.

Senior Counselor/Branch Manager 7/86 to 9/94

Opened and managed several branch offices. Responsible for counseling services, Family Life Education, Field Instruction, volunteer supervision, and public speaking.

Counselor 7/78 to 7/86

Provided counseling services to a wide variety of clients on individual, family, and marital issues.

DEBRA SLAWSON
1503 Adrian
Minneapolis, Minnesota 55102
(612) 281-6964

QUALIFICATIONS

Broad experience in designing, teaching, and supervising training programs in a large training department.

Develop effective teams and establish a strong sense of commitment.

EDUCATION

M.S. - Curriculum Design Administration, University of Minnesota (1981)
B.S. - Education, Moorhead State University, Minneapolis, Minnesota (1978)

EMPLOYMENT HISTORY

Prodigital, Inc., Minneapolis, Minnesota 10/94 to Present

Medical Training Administrator 10/00 to Present. Responsible for designing and implementing workshops nationwide which train medical professionals in the uses and benefits of digital radiography. Consult with Prodigital subsidiaries to assess training needs and help them establish training departments.

Developed a comprehensive program to train the fifteen-member technical training staff in effective teaching techniques. Ratings from customers after equipment installations have improved 40% since the program was implemented.

Clinical Application Training Supervisor 6/97 to 10/00. Administered and monitored week-long training workshops for domestic and international customers. These workshops have firmly established Prodigital's reputation for providing excellent service and training after the sale. Developed programs for introducing new product lines to the national sales force. Hired, trained, and supervised a staff of three medical trainers.

Training Specialist 10/94 to 6/97. Designed and created one-week product orientation courses for customers. Due to the success of the courses, the format and procedures were adopted for all training courses.

Thompson Manufacturing Co., St. Paul, Minnesota 9/88 to 10/94

Training Support Manager 8/92 to 10/94. Developed sales training courses and materials for new and experienced salespeople. Took highly technical data and constructed practical, understandable courses.

Technical Training Specialist 5/90 to 8/92. Identified needs and designed a five-week technical training program for domestic and international specialists. The program became the model for other workshops within Thompson.

Administrative Assistant To Product Planning Manager 9/88 to 5/90. Researched market trends and studied products and marketing plans of competitors.

Prior Employment: Teacher 9/78 to 6/88

MANUFACTURING/LABOR

This category includes machine operators, assemblers, machinists, tool and die makers, technicians, laborers, warehouse workers, and carpenters, as well as any people who work with their hands.

The main goals for your resume should be to show the breadth of your experience, the tools and equipment you can use, and the fact that you are very good at what you do.

It may be appropriate for you to use a section called "Tools," "Equipment," or "Processes." In other words, if you have special knowledge or experience, you may want to use a special category to showcase it. You'll need to come up with the most appropriate term.

As with all resumes, identifying results will help set you apart from the competition. Try to recall any improvements you have brought about. Perhaps you discovered ways to produce a product with fewer steps. For example, perhaps you found a way to produce a part using only three different machines instead of four. Perhaps you discovered that a hole was specified at plus or minus .001, but you determined that for the product's purpose, .005 was actually quite acceptable, and as a result fewer parts were rejected. Perhaps you discovered a faster way to assemble a component and thus increased productivity by 15%. Perhaps you found a way to maintain equipment more effectively and thereby reduced downtime. The possibilities are nearly endless.

Use your cover letter and resume to demonstrate that you learn new pieces of equipment easily and that you are the type of person who is always looking for a better way to do things.

PAUL YOKIHANA
13097 Mona N.E.
Honolulu, Hawaii 96821
(808) 292-3724

OBJECTIVE: Machine Operator

QUALIFICATIONS
- Strong mechanical, tool, and woodworking ability.
- Excellent knowledge of the working characteristics of a variety of hardwoods.
- Easy to get along with. Cooperative. Flexible.

EDUCATION

Wood working, Kauai Community College, 60 credits (1995)

EMPLOYMENT

Exotic Woods Inc., Honolulu, Hawaii 6/95 - Present

Machine Operator
- Responsible for production of domestic and exotic hardwood molding for this small picture frame manufacturer.
- Handle all operations including selecting wood, ripping, rabbeting, shaping, rough sanding, finish sanding, staining and oiling.
- Set up and operate jointer, table saws, wide belt sander, molder-planer, radial arm saw, and wood shaper.
- Duties include operation of hand sanders and chopsaws.
- Occasionally finish and assemble frames.
- Train new employees and ensure smooth operations in the shop.
- Produce a very high quality product which has helped the firm to double its business since 1995.

Previous Employment

Maintenance, CST Inc., Honolulu, Hawaii 5/91-6/95
Waiter, Spring Winds Resort Hotel, Kapaa, Hawaii 4/89-5/91

RITA SAWYER
1202 Guthrie Avenue South
Tulsa, Oklahoma 74119
(918) 693-4217

OBJECTIVE: Quality Control Inspection

QUALIFICATIONS

Excellent training and experience in all phases of quality control inspection. Work hard and produce excellent results. Work well with engineers, production supervisors, production workers, and vendors.

Broad experience with many measuring devices, including Vernier calipers and scales, micrometers, sineplates, air gauging equipment, durometer and Rockwell hardness testing, XYZ coordinate measuring machines, optical comparators, roughness measurement equipment, and height gauges. Experienced in surface plate inspection.

EDUCATION

Graduated - Keota High School, Keota, Oklahoma (1988)

TRAINING

Advancetech, Certificates in: D.C. Electronics, A.C. Electronics, Semiconductor Devices, Digital Technology, Geometric Tolerancing

EMPLOYMENT

Advancetech, Inc., Tulsa, Oklahoma 10/96-Present

Quality Control Inspector - Responsible for all first article inspections and final inspections for this sheet metal fabricator. Using blueprints, calculate dimensions and bend factors to check and approve flat pattern layouts. Verify proper sequencing of production plans. Receive and log incoming sheet metal and other products. When parts do not meet customer's specifications, work closely with engineers to discover if the fault was in the original design or in the fabrication process. With discovery of fault, work with engineers to correct it. Through improved processes reduced rejects by customers by over 20%.

Electrotech Laboratories, Oklahoma City, Oklahoma 3/92-10/96

Quality Control Inspector - Inspected incoming vendor-supplied sheet metal and small precision parts. Used hand measuring devices as well as XYZ measuring machines and optical comparators. Inspected for conformance to geometric tolerances. Inspected and tested electrical components and electrical subassemblies.

K & I Industries, Muskogee, Oklahoma 8/88-3/92

Machine Operator - Set up, operated, and maintained six Brown & Sharp and two Traub single spindle screw machines. Inspected manufactured parts. Recorded set-up procedures for ease of manufacturing the part in the future, saving approximately 100 hours per year among five machine operators.

HEALTH PROFESSIONALS

In your resume you will want to make the most out of your experience, demonstrate that you seek opportunities to further your knowledge, show that you are good at what you do, and prove that you are a dedicated professional.

Health professionals often have a hard time because it can be difficult to quantify results. You should, however, look for every opportunity to identify your results, and if possible, quantify them.

Results will most often be found in a special project you worked on. Perhaps you were part of a committee that examined a process and recommended that it be done differently. If the new procedure was found to be superior, you could mention the result on your resume and would make every effort to quantify it.

List any awards you may have received such as employee of the month or of the year. You would mention the award whether it was for the whole facility or just your department. Awards demonstrate that people think highly of you. Indicate on the resume the reasons for receiving the award rather than merely listing it.

You will likely want to mention seminars you have attended, as well as significant in-services. The information would probably be listed under "Special Training." If you intend to list more than ten, the category should appear at the end of the resume on the second page, or you should consider an addendum page which would be labeled "Training" or "Special Training."

You may want to showcase your areas of experience. That can easily be done by using a paragraph under qualifications which would read, "Broad experience in _____, _____, _____, _____, and _____." If you have numerous items you want to mention you could have a separate category below the qualifications section which would be called "Areas of Experience."

If you know yourself to be a highly qualified health professional, please do not be satisfied with merely listing your duties and showing your years of experience.

ELEANOR SIEVERS
3116 Indale Avenue
Athens, Georgia 30606
(404) 643-8014

OBJECTIVE: Director of Nursing/Administrator for Nursing Services

EDUCATION

M.A. - Hospital Administration, University of Houston (1981)
B.S. - Nursing, University of Texas (1975)

PROFESSIONAL EXPERIENCE

University Hospital, Athens, Georgia 4/89 to Present

Associate Administrator For Nursing Services 4/97 to Present.
Direct the activities of a 520 FTE nursing staff with a $40 million budget in a 380 bed medical center. Responsible for all inpatient units including medical, surgical, and cardiac intensive care units, an eight room operating suite, and a level one trauma/emergency department.
- Work directly with four Division Directors and twelve Nursing Supervisors.
- Developed new standards for care and set up daily mechanisms which ensure compliance.
- Established more effective budgetary and staffing monitoring systems which save over $400,000 per year.
- Opened six critical care beds and added a head nurse.

Division Director, Acute Care 1/93 to 4/97.
Responsible for this eight unit division with a 205 FTE nursing staff—190 beds, $16 million budget. Established workable and effective budgetary controls.
- Installed and coordinated a capital equipment purchasing system which saved $85,000.
- Implemented two medical services.
- Established, trained, and supported a service for ventilator dependent quadriplegics in the Rehabilitation unit.
- Trained staff in troubleshooting ventilators and working with patients.

Nursing Administrative Supervisor, Medical/Surgical 4/89 to 1/93.
Had responsibility for two 24-bed units with a 69 FTE staff.
- Established a six bed telemetry unit and a cardiac patient teaching program.
- Developed a primary nursing care model and upgraded the staff from mostly aides to mostly RNs.
- Increased the role of head nurses by giving them greater budgetary and administrative responsibilities.
- Established preoperative standards.

The Methodist Hospital, Houston, Texas 5/75 to 4/89

Nursing Administrative Supervisor, Acute Medicine 3/85 to 4/89.
Administered two medical units with 62 beds and a 65 FTE staff.
- Trained new staff as the units moved from mostly aides to a staff of RNs.
- Worked with head nurses as they were given more managerial responsibility.

Inservice Instructor 3/81 to 3/85.

Head Nurse, Cardiac Unit 2/79 to 3/81

Staff Nurse, Intensive Care, Intensive Care Unit, Cardiac Unit 5/75 to 2/79

PETER SIMMONS
1527 Broadway #217
Irvine, CA 92713
(714) 523-7615

OBJECTIVE: Emergency Room Nursing

QUALIFICATIONS

Highly trained and experienced. Considered by supervisors to be an excellent emergency room nurse. Strongly motivated, provide quick, accurate assessments, and work effectively with doctors and other ER staff. Develop excellent rapport with patients.

EDUCATION

Diploma, School of Professional Nursing, St. Luke's Methodist Hospital, Cedar Rapids, Iowa (1989)

Certificate - Emergency Medical Technician (1988)

EMPLOYMENT

University of California, Irvine Medical Center, Orange, CA 10/96-Present

Staff R.N. - Emergency Room - In this busy, twenty-two bed emergency room, work with up to sixty patients per shift. As the triage nurse on the seven nurse staff, stabilize patients, make critical decisions, and handle the flow of patients. Receive a high number of trauma patients.

Scripps Memorial Hospital, San Diego, CA 6/93-10/96

Staff R.N. - Emergency Room - Night shift charge nurse for this eight-bed emergency room. Worked with many cardiac, respiratory, and psychiatric emergencies. Independently assessed patients and initiated diagnostic procedures. Ordered x-rays and lab tests. Consulted with patients by telephone and determined appropriate actions.

Las Cruces Memorial Hospital, Las Cruces, NM 5/91-4/93

Staff R.N. - Emergency Room - Performed all emergency room functions at this sixteen-bed emergency facility. Trained nursing students and supervised the outpatient methadone treatment program. Also assisted in the minor surgery department and the bronchoscopy department.

Mercy Medical Center, Roseburg, OR 6/89-4/91

Staff R.N. - Emergency Room - Treated many motor vehicle and sawmill accident trauma patients at this twelve-bed emergency room. Charge nurse last ten months. Also functioned as mobile intensive care nurse working by ambulance with an EMT and respiratory therapist. Taught IV therapy, CPR, and assessment skills to EMT's as part of an extensive training program.

BARRY KOCH
1706 5th N.E.
Ryersly, Pennsylvania 18512
(412) 562-3216

OBJECTIVE: Director of Pharmacy

QUALIFICATIONS

Strong pharmacy management experience. Proven ability to introduce cost saving measures while increasing quality and productivity standards. Work effectively with all levels of hospital administration and have significantly improved relations with other departments.

EDUCATION

B.S. - Pharmaceutical Science, Northwestern University (1983)

PROFESSIONAL EXPERIENCE

Ryersly General Hospital, Ryersly, Pennsylvania 6/83 to Present

Assistant Director of Pharmacy & IV Therapy 3/93 to Present. Maintain overall responsibility for ordering medications and supervising and scheduling fifteen staff pharmacists and technicians. Implemented a mobile cart system with pharmacists making rounds and dispensing medications at nurses stations. System has increased quality control and improved relations between Nursing and Pharmacy staff.

Developed a centralized piggyback program which relieved nurses of the duty of mixing solutions and turned it over to pharmacy technicians. Program has given techs greater responsibility and has significantly reduced errors and increased quality standards.

Responsible for keeping Pharmacy, Medical and Nursing staffs current on effects and uses of new medications and developing policies regarding their use. Consult extensively with doctors on difficult cases. Currently developing a Clinical Program to provide more inservice training for doctors and nurses and completing development of a kinetic counseling program to better serve doctors. Represent the Pharmacy Department on the Pharmacy and Therapeutic Committee. Actively involved in helping the committee produce a complete formulary.

Staff Pharmacist 6/83 to 3/93. As staff pharmacist monitored and recorded patients' medications and IV therapy. Provided consultations with doctors, nurses and patients to ensure proper therapy. Ordered all medications and kept the department well supplied. Designed a diabetic program which reaches 100 diabetics annually and helps them maintain more effective therapy.

RETAILERS

In your resume do everything possible to demonstrate that you are good at what you do. Just by your job title most employers will know your basic duties, so stressing your duties is not recommended. Instead, make the most out of your results. Retailing is one of the most statistics filled industries, therefore, make use of the data available to you.

When I say don't stress duties, I do not mean that you should not list them. Listing them, however will probably be all that is required. You will rarely need to provide detailed descriptions.

If you had duties not typically associated with your job title, and you want employers to know about those duties, by all means mention them.

If your job entailed special projects, provide descriptions of the projects and emphasize the results achieved.

If you are primarily in sales, emphasize your sales success. You could indicate increases in sales, your rank among your colleagues in your department, or your rank within the region.

If you are a buyer, do everything you can to show that you have a good sense of trends and that you can sense what will become the next hot item or style.

If you are a department or store manager, you would emphasize increases in sales, your department's or store's ranking within the chain, increases in profits, or increases in market share. You might also mention such things as inventory turns, sales per square foot, or sales per employee work hours.

Make mention of any involvement in planning or coordinating an opening of a store or of a major remodel. Show that you make effective use of co-op advertising and that you work well with manufacturers for special promotions. If you introduced a special new line of products or opened a new department, you could mention the increase in sales.

As a manager you can mention such things as your ability to train staff and your ability to decrease turnover and increase productivity.

Perry Carlton
13922 Navajo Court
New Bedford, Massachusetts 02740
(617) 823-7947

QUALIFICATIONS

Strong store management background. Rapidly promoted based on exceeding sales and profit goals. Have increased sales an average of 24% per year.

EDUCATION

B.A. - English Literature, Boston College (1993)

Graduate Gemologist, Gemological Institute of America (1994)

EMPLOYMENT

Werner Jewelers, New Bedford, Massachusetts 8/88-Present

Manager - 8/00-Present
- Maintain profitable store operations and supervise nine employees.
- Control all special ordering, oversee mark-up on special orders and shop repairs, and perform all accounting functions.
- Increased sales an average of 24% per year and have taken the store from #8 to #3 in sales for this chain of 12 stores.

Assistant Manager - 7/96-8/00
- Sold jewelry to customers and assumed responsibility of sales training and scheduling.
- Promoted to store manager for improving customer service in each of three stores served.

Sales - 8/93-7/96
- Rose to the top 5 in sales among 150 salespeople.
- Became a Graduate Gemologist and was recognized as one of the most knowledgeable in gemstones within the chain.

Megan Hathaway
2401 Belle Haven Road N.W.
Roanoke, Virginia 24019
(703) 829-7913

OBJECTIVE: Retail Management

QUALIFICATIONS
* Experienced in all phases of retail marketing, merchandising, and sales.
* Quickly promoted from sales to Department Manager.
* Receive frequent compliments for creative displays and effective layout of merchandise.
* Supervise employees very effectively. Obtain excellent results from a young sales staff.

EDUCATION

AA - Merchandising, Fashion and Design Institute of Los Angeles (1993)

EMPLOYMENT

Brodericks, Roanoke, Virginia 7/93-Present

Department Manager - 3/00-Present. Manage the luggage and young men's departments with a staff of twelve. Responsible for displays, merchandising, scheduling, price changes, merchandise transfers, and twice yearly inventories. Interview, hire, and train new employees and write performance reviews.

Work closely with store buyers and manufacturer's representatives to maintain high quality merchandise. Took the luggage department from #6 in the chain to #2 in sales in the first three years. Significantly improved the look of the young men's department through creative displays and new merchandising techniques. Have increased sales in young men's an average of 15% per year.

Assistant Department Manager - 6/98-3/00. Sold handbags, accessories, and designer ready-to-wear clothing. Supervised and trained a staff of ten salespeople.

Salesperson - 7/93-6/98. Sold handbags, accessories, and young ladies' clothing. Received Salesperson of the Month in recognition for strong sales over the previous six months. Over a twelve month period, took over the duties of assistant department manager.

ACCOUNTING/FINANCE

There are four ways you can excite an employer: demonstrate you can make money for the organization, save money, solve problems, and reduce the stress and pressure the boss is under. Those in accounting and finance are typically able to demonstrate all four when they succeed in quantifying their results. In your job sketches, concentrate on recalling past projects you worked on and determine what the results of those projects were.

With so much financial and accounting information computerized these days, it should be relatively easy to review past reports and demonstrate what your successes have been.

Although you will certainly want to let employers know what your duties were, devote the greatest amount of time to determining what your results have been.

Although more and more accountants now have experience in converting from one computerized accounting system to another, make the most of your experience. If a firm anticipates a conversion in the next 2-3 years, your conversion experience could make you very valuable. Don't just indicate that you were involved in conversions, but also indicate the level of success. If the conversion was smooth, if the consultant indicated you had done a good job of preparing for the conversion, or if it was completed on schedule, say so. No conversion takes place without a hitch, so to say that it was a smooth conversion merely means that bugs were quickly fixed and that it was completed on schedule or close to schedule.

Look for various types of results. Did you produce new management reports or modify existing reports to make them more useful and timely? Many reports are extremely time sensitive, so if you reduced the time needed to produce a report from 14 days after quarter-end, to ten days after, that would make a strong statement.

Did you computerize an operation which had been done manually? Then calculate the number of man-hours saved. If it eliminated the need for a position, indicate that as well.

Perhaps you improved the accounting operation so well that your audits were much improved. Perhaps you could say that exceptions were reduced by a certain percentage or from ten the previous year to only one, or perhaps none.

If you were involved in accounts receivable perhaps you could state that 90-day and over receivables were reduced by a certain percent or that days outstanding were reduced from 40 to 30.

I've worked with several accountants who started making use of previously unutilized short-term cash. By creating a system for investing excess cash for a few days, I've seen controllers of small companies earn the equivalent of their salary just by doing so.

Other accounting people have found ways to reduce the transaction time on billings or reduce invoicing errors. Others have developed systems to avoid double paying invoices on their accounts payable.

Finance people have found ways to reduce interest expense on loans, have taken companies public and raised new monies, negotiated larger lines of credit, and found ways to reduce taxes.

PAUL HUSTED
406 Ash
Boise, Idaho 83702
(208) 361-2918

OBJECTIVE: Senior Accountant/Controller

QUALIFICATIONS

Strong accounting experience with a broad background in auditing, business and individual taxes, and cost control programs. Effectively implement computerized accounting systems.

Excellent manager. Consistently obtain high productivity from employees.

LICENSES

CPA, Idaho State Certification (1982)

EDUCATION

B.A. - Accounting, University of Idaho (1979)

EMPLOYMENT

Brandon Refrigerated Service Inc., Boise, Idaho 3/95 to Present

CONTROLLER
- For this refrigerated freight hauler, prepare financial statements and supervise 12 payroll, rate, billing, and AP/AR personnel.
- Extensively involved in customer relations, establishing credit ratings, approving credit, reviewing and approving customer claims, and making collections.
- Manage the cash flow of the company. Developed a major cost control program which has cut overhead 15%.
- Maintain the smooth functioning of a sophisticated computerized accounting system.

Bestway Freight Lines, Boise, Idaho 8/88 to 3/95

CONTROLLER
- Responsible for financial statements and tax preparation.
- Supervised ten employees handling rates, billing, payroll, claims, and AP/AR.
- Oversaw the payroll system covering six separate union agreements.
- Developed the company's first cost studies and identified areas for substantial savings.
- Cut the shop force from 21 to 14 with no reduction in work completed.
- Worked closely with vendor and contract programmer while converting to a new computerized accounting and payroll system.
- Implemented a computerized system to track commodity transactions which reduced required staff time each month from 180 to 6 hours.

Robert Perkins, CPA, Boise, Idaho 6/79 to 8/88

STAFF ACCOUNTANT
- Performed audits and developed financial statements for a wide variety of clients.
- Handled state and federal taxes for individuals, trusts, estates, partnerships, and corporations.
- Provided management services and designed cost control programs.

216

Part Four
Using Your Résumé, Cover Letter, and Marketing Letter

How To Use A Resume

WANT ADS

I recommend reading the want ads. In cities with two or more newspapers, one paper usually predominates and gets 95% of all jobs advertised. Of course, some employers will advertise in more than one paper, but typically only about 5% of the jobs will be advertised in the secondary paper and *not* in the primary one. In addition, about 95% of all jobs advertised will appear in the Sunday paper. For the sake of time, read only the primary paper, and read only the Sunday edition. Scan it from A to Z. Some very interesting jobs can be listed with job titles you would never expect.

If a want ad is vague, mail out your standard resume and hope for the best. If the ad is fairly explicit concerning the desired qualifications and experience, you must decide whether to mail your standard resume with a custom cover letter, or whether you will take the additional time to tailor your resume to the position. If you feel strongly enough about a position, and your standard resume does not adequately cover some key points, it is worth modifying the resume. It can double your chances of getting an interview.

To quickly access want ads from hundreds of newspapers in the U.S. and Canada, visit Job Factory (www.jobfactory.com).Click on Classified Ads.

Competition can be fierce when good jobs are advertised. An ad for a good position can draw up to 500 applicants (50-150 is most typical) and rarely will more than eight people be interviewed. Your results will depend on how closely the job matches your qualifications and how much time you spend tailoring your cover letter. If you emphasize accomplishments and potential, you will certainly get a better response than average. According to a Department of Labor study, about 20% of all managers, sales workers, professionals, and clerical workers who answer ads, get their jobs through a help-wanted ad.

Blind Ads

Blind ads are rarely productive, but may be worth trying. A blind ad is a help-wanted ad in which the name of the employer has been omitted, and all you are given is a box number in care of the newspaper. Most are legitimate, placed by companies that for one reason or another want to maintain anonymity. Unfortunately companies sometimes use these want ads to gather salary information and in fact have no position. No one knows how frequently it occurs. The problem is, there is no way to tell which are legitimate and which are not.

Since blind ads usually draw fewer responses than ads that include the name of the employer, you'll have an excellent shot at an interview if your background is ideal.

To respond to a blind ad follow the instructions that each paper prints in the want ad section. If you are concerned about the blind ad being placed by your own company, or merely one that you don't want to receive your resume, follow the instructions for that situation. If you were responding to an ad placed in the Seattle Times you would address your envelope to the Seattle Times and include the box number for that ad. You would also write on the envelope, **Confidential Desk.** That alerts those sorting the mail that there are certain companies which should not receive your resume. Inside the outer envelope you would enclose a second envelope which would contain your resume. That envelope would also have the box number for that ad written on the outside. Also inside the outer envelope would be a separate sheet of paper which would indicate those companies you would not want your resume to go to.

Responding to blind ads rarely gets results because the companies placing them are highly particular and may interview only three people instead of the more typical six to eight. Unless your background is almost a perfect fit for the job, blind ads are rarely worth responding to.

UNSOLICITED RESUMES

Unsolicited resumes are frequently sent to employers in hopes that a position may be available at the time the resume is received. Resume campaigns typically result in less than one interview for every hundred resumes sent out. If you use the strategy I'm about to discuss, you should get eight to ten interviews for every hundred resumes you mail.

You must start this type of campaign with an absolutely top-notch resume. Then develop a list of 50–200 employers of the right size, in the right industry, and in the right geographical area. Determine the department in which you would most likely work. Next, making about 20 calls an hour, call each organization and ask the receptionist for the name of the appropriate executive or department head. Be sure to get the correct spelling and title. Then and only then are you ready to send out resumes. Address each cover letter and resume to the specific person who has power to hire you. Addressing your letters to those with the power to hire should double your interviews compared to merely addressing it "Dear Mr. President," "Dear Marketing Manager," or "Dear Personnel Manager."

Usually you will know the typical title of the person with the power to hire you. In those cases simply ask the receptionist for the name of the person with that title. Sometimes you will be told, "We don't have anyone here with that title." Your response would then be, "Can you give me the name and title of the person who would typically hire engineers?" (or, whatever your job title is). If that does not work, ask using a different job title or ask for the personnel department.

If you simply cannot identify who your resume should go to, address it to the president *by name.* The resume may still wind up in personnel, but it is just as likely to be delivered to the most appropriate person.

Decide whether you will follow up with a phone call to each person or simply wait for interview offers. Calling and asking for an appointment will usually result in appointments 30–60% of the time, while waiting for interview offers (assuming you have a top-quality resume and sent it to a specific person) should result in an 8–12% success rate. Of course your actual percentage will be determined by the quality of your resume, the amount of experience you have in the field you are seeking, the impressiveness of your accomplishments and results, the job market, and the care with which you select potential employers.

The decision to call or wait is important because it will affect the wording in your cover letter. If you will be calling for an appointment, you simply state in the letter, "I will call you next week to set up a brief appointment." This statement will cause the reader to pay more attention to the resume, to be prepared for your call, and it likely will be kept close at hand rather than filed or discarded. With the waiting approach, you can end your letter with something like, "I look forward to hearing from you soon."

It's wise to send your chosen batch of employers a second mailing of your resume. A surprising finding, first described by Carl Boll in *Executive Jobs Unlimited*, is that resumes sent to the same organizations, six or more weeks after the first batch, will usually obtain results equal to the first mailing. In other words, if one hundred resumes netted you eight interviews, the second batch of one hundred should provide another eight. Give serious consideration to a second mailing.

FAXING

Do not fax a resume unless an employer has specifically asked you to do so. The quality at the other end looks like a poor quality dot matrix printed resume, and the paper will be typical fax paper. If you do fax a resume, also send one through the mail so the person will see its quality. If you want it there fast, but have not been asked to fax it, use an overnight express service. This approach will have more impact.

References

HAVING GOOD REFERENCES makes your job search easier. Dealing with negative references is difficult, but can be handled.

Before listing people as references, check with them to make sure they are willing to do it. Then ask them what they would feel comfortable saying about you. More than a few job seekers have been surprised to learn that an expected glowing recommendation turned out to be anything but. You can also suggest things you would like your references to say about you. Most will be happy to accommodate you.

References should virtually never be listed on a resume, even when those references are well-known people. For one thing you don't want them to be bothered by too many people calling them. You only want your references called when you are seriously being considered for a position. You want them fresh. You should notify them any time you suspect they are going to be called. You can use the brief conversation to tell the person about the position, why you would be perfect, and any points you would like the person to cover. Notifying your favorite bosses is easier but don't neglect your ex-bosses that you did not get along so well with.

Some job seekers like to write at the bottom, "Personal and Professional References Available Upon Request." All employers know you will supply references when called upon, so it's best to leave this off.

Although employers frequently do not check references, it is wise to assume they will. If you have great references, make excellent use of them. However, if you were fired from a recent job, you got poor reviews, or your boss did not like you, you have your work cut out for you.

There are personal and professional references. Personal references include friends, business associates you've gotten to know through professional associations or volunteer organizations, and former coworkers. Although it is generally assumed by employers that personal references will say only nice things about you, they are still often contacted. Therefore, choose your references carefully. John may say great things about you, but if he speaks in a monotone, gets easily flustered, and lacks tact, I would choose someone else.

Personal references should be those who know you well or have observed you for several years. It doesn't help your cause when someone says, "I don't know her well, but..." Use influential people as references only if they can speak first hand about you and know you well enough to answer questions regarding your personality and personal strengths. An influential person who knows your mother or father, but doesn't know you well, won't be of much help to your cause. An older person who knew you only as a child also will not be of much help.

Professional references include former bosses, peers in other departments, and customers. Your most important references are former bosses. Although companies are increasingly refusing to provide more than dates of employment—

due to a rash of defamation of character suits in the 1980s and '90s—those who really want information can often get former bosses to reveal something. So while company policy may require your former boss to refer such calls to HR, your boss may still supply information—good or bad. If your last three companies have strong policies of only supplying titles and dates of employment, you should think of supervisors or colleagues who have left the organization, who can attest to your capabilities. Finding former bosses who can act as references is important because it frustrates employers when they can't obtain recent information about you. It could be just enough of a frustration to cause them to hire someone with recent references.

Former bosses should be called at the start of your search and told that they may get calls from prospective employers. Explain what you've been up to since you worked together and thank the person for any positive contributions the person made to your career or personal growth. Find something positive to discuss, even if overall the job you had when that person supervised you was not a good experience.

Indicate some points you would like each person to make on your behalf. Remind each one of some of the projects you worked on and the results that were obtained. This is a way of helping your references. They can't possibly remember all of the good things you did for them. Refresh their memories. This process is relatively easy when you've had excellent relationships with each of your supervisors, harder when you haven't.

If you had a "mixed" relationship, keep the conversation positive as if the only things you remember were the good times. If you were terminated from a position, speak to that supervisor and explain how you have grown and matured since you worked for him or her. I know I'm asking you to do something difficult, but it will help your career, so go ahead and make that call. Many have been surprised to find the ex-boss very receptive.

If you are currently unemployed and you were fired from your most recent position, you face an especially difficult situation. The first thing you have to do is find out what your ex-boss will say about you if contacted as a reference. Also find out what HR will say about you. Give thought to what you would like your former boss to say as to why you were terminated and then suggest that. Most ex-bosses really do not want to destroy your career and will often back up your somewhat "softened" version of what happened.

Other people who may be appropriate as references include your peers in other departments you worked with, managers from other departments who observed your work, and customers who can attest to your problem solving ability. If you had more than one boss at a particular employer you might list the one who would have the kindest words about you, even if that person is no longer with the organization.

When listing references it is traditional to provide the title and employer of the person and an appropriate phone number. Some will not want to be called at home while others will not want to be called at work. You can also indicate how you know this person or where you worked together. Provide the e-mail address of your reference. That way if the person checking references cannot get through, the two can at least make contact through e-mail.

References are so important that if you are unsure what a reference will say, have a person who can act as a prospective employer, call to ask a few questions. That way if the person says those things that were agreed upon, you know everything is fine. When you suspect they may be saying negative things about you, this type of checking is absolutely essential. I've had clients who were criticized or damned with faint praise, and highly interested employers were scared off. If you know what is being said, there are ways to counter negative comments.

I deal with this issue in more detail in *Interview Power*. In the 2000 edition it is covered in pages 163-167.

The following reference page provides ideas on how to influence those checking your references. By indicating the areas that your references can "testify" about, you increase the likelihood that reference checkers will ask questions concerning those points. In Ken's case all three people could have spoken on any of these points, but he wisely chose to emphasize certain points with each person.

References For Ken Wong

Past Supervisor
Able to comment on my ability to organize and plan projects that achieve predetermined goals and get completed on schedule and within budget. Also able to comment on my commitment to the organization and my team members.

Rob Jensen
Senior Project Manager
Qwest
2312 Fourth Avenue
Seattle, WA 98213
(206) 281-2309 (work)

Past Supervisor
Able to comment on my ability to take on complex projects with tight deadlines and motivate a team to achieve goals. Also able to comment on my supervisory ability and the ability to develop staff that is highly regarded and gets promoted.

Cynthia Gonzalez
Acquisitions Manager
Qwest
1981 Fifth Avenue
Denver, CO 80228
(303) 760-2398 (work)

Past Supervisor
Able to comment on ability to negotiate with government entities and private organizations to acquire properties and rights of way that helped Mountain Wireless grow at a rate of 42% per year for six years.

Revokh Traczewski
Senior Vice President
Mountain Wireless
345 Mountain Drive
Boulder, CO 80303
(720) 764-0987 (work)

Letters of Recommendation

WHENEVER YOU LEAVE A JOB, get a letter of recommendation, also known as a letter of reference. You may never use it, but it has real worth for you. A strong letter of recommendation assures you that the person will say positive things about you. It also assures you that you can make positive statements about yourself, knowing that you can back up what you say with the letter.

The letter of recommendation is especially important for the person who has been terminated. In such a case you are not seeking a letter laced with superlatives, but one which at least emphasizes your positive qualities and contributions. If you can get the person to say positive things in a letter, she is almost certain to say positive things when called by prospective employers.

Feel free to suggest to the person the points or ideas you would like covered in the letter. You can begin by listing all of the points that you would like people to mention. Then ask each reference to cover some of those points. In that way your letters of recommendation are assured of covering your key points. These people are likely to appreciate your help because most people find letters of recommendation hard to write. Depending on the circumstances, you could even send a sample letter and suggest that the person adopt the portions they're comfortable with, or just use it for ideas. People will often use a sample letter as it was presented, or make only minor modifications, and have it typed on their own letterhead.

I rarely encourage people to enclose letters of recommendation with resumes. My research shows that it may be helpful for people in entry-level jobs and for those seeking office work, but most should save letters of recommendation for appropriate points during an interview. When I tested the effectiveness of letters of recommendation with engineers, the engineers were rated more highly when their resume was not accompanied by a letter of recommendation. Thus it seems that for professionals the inclusion of such letters with resumes is not appropriate. Letters of recommendation can work very well as part of a web portfolio, however.

The terminated employee can feel good about a letter of recommendation which is positive in tone. For all others, my advice is to not use a letter of recommendation unless it is glowing. Avoid using the typical letter which says, "Rosalyn worked for me for six years in such and such a capacity and she is an excellent employee. I can recommend her without reservation. Should you have any questions feel free to call me." Such a letter is simply not strong enough. It appears to have been written with little heart in it. Such a letter will have no positive impact. Don't get me wrong. Such a letter is not bad; after all, it does make some positive statements. When I say don't use a letter of recommendation that is not glowing, I mean don't go out of your way to hand it to someone. If someone asks for letters of recommendation you would not hesitate to use such a letter.

The glowing letter points out some of your specific strengths and uses terms like *excellent* and *outstanding*. The letter may even mention a project where you worked above and beyond the call of duty. That type of letter can help, but even in such a case, use it only if it seems appropriate.

Cover Letters

THE COVER LETTER is merely a letter which introduces you to an employer. All resumes sent through the mail should be accompanied by a cover letter. The cover letter personalizes your resume and gives it greater flexibility. If your resume does not contain an objective, the cover letter is the place to express it. A cover letter gives you an opportunity to share points that are not easily covered in a resume. So a resume plus a cover letter represent the ideal vehicle to get across all of the key ideas and points that you want an employer to know about you.

A resume which arrives without a cover letter gives a jolt to the receiver and makes a loud statement about the sender—the person could not even take a few minutes to make a personal statement or sign his or her name. It begs the question, "Is this the type of person we want to hire?"

When answering a want ad, specify the exact job title in the cover letter. It is not necessary, however, to specify the source of the ad or its date. The exact title will provide all the information personnel needs. When a want ad explicitly requests certain types of experience which you have, but which are not adequately covered in the resume, use your cover letter to fill in the details. The alternative would be to rewrite your resume slightly to include the necessary details. A highly targeted cover letter with a resume modified specifically for that job, will always provide better results.

If an ad does not provide a name and you are unable to obtain the name of the person with power to hire, you can address the person as Dear Hiring Manager, Dear Sales Manager (or whatever title the person likely has), Dear Human Resources Manager, Dear Sir/Madam, or even To Whom It May Concern. None of these are fully satisfactory, but when you don't have a name, you don't have many options.

View your cover letter and resume as a team. Each performs a different function, but they must work well together. Cover letters generally consist of two to four short paragraphs and seldom total more than twenty lines. The first paragraph should open with a strong statement about you that arouses interest and curiosity. Devote a middle paragraph to an accomplishment that will further arouse interest. The accomplishment can come from your resume but should be slightly reworded. When I write cover letters, I usually pick the strongest accomplishment from the resume and include it in the cover letter. Notice how this can be done:

> I can save money for your firm by utilizing my experience in cost control. At Standard Products I reduced paper usage by 24% and photocopying costs by 30%.

❖

> I can help increase the impact of your agency. While at Family Services I wrote a proposal which was funded for $22,000. This allowed us to significantly increase the quantity and quality of our services.

225

Appeal to the employer's self-interest by indicating that you are a problem solver and that hiring you will lead to increased production, greater efficiency, better planning, less waste, higher profits, and more satisfied customers.

Begin the process of responding to want ads by creating a "standard" cover letter; then modify it for each response. If you believe that "time is money," you'll save a great deal if you can modify your cover letters on your own computer. You can rent a computer by the hour at some copy shops and then print out your work on their laser printer.

To create an effective response to an ad, begin by writing down or underlining all of the key points mentioned in the ad. Check off those points which are clearly and effectively covered in your resume. If several points are not covered in your resume, determine whether you should modify your resume, or merely cover the points in your cover letter. If you decide to modify your resume you should make sure the resume covers all of the desired experience mentioned in the ad.

In using the Systematic Job Search methods (pages 250 to 278) you will want to meet the person with power to hire, even if no openings currently exist. If you intend to follow up with a phone call, indicate in your cover letter that you will be calling to arrange a meeting. Avoid using the word *interview*. Instead say, "I'll call next week to arrange a brief meeting," or "I will call next week to arrange a time when we can meet." The word *interview* is always associated with formal hiring procedures; what you want is a relaxed meeting in which both parties learn more about each other.

Cover letters should be tailored. Even if you develop a standard cover letter to be sent to 100 or more companies, you can still personalize it. Write the cover letter so you can insert the name of the company somewhere in the body of the letter. With today's word processors , you can easily do it yourself. Secretarial services can type your letters and address your envelopes for less than three dollars each, and each one will look perfect.

If you know the company by reputation or your research has revealed some interesting information, don't hesitate to include it in the cover letter. This was done quite effectively in the following excerpts from cover letters:

> One of your competitors told me Alpa has the best quality control of any winch manufacturer in the country. The quality control system I established at Braddigan Gear also became recognized as tops in the industry.

❖

> Your recent acquisition of Marley & Sons indicates to me that you could use someone with my international marketing background.

❖

> John McNamara at IBM believes you are one of the top management consulting firms in the country.

❖

> The recent article in *The Seattle Times* about your rapid expansion was of great interest to me.

Review the sample cover letters, then simply start writing.

February 20, 2003

John Travis, Director
Home Energy Department
N. W. Center for Energy Efficiency
323 Sixth Avenue
Seattle, Washington 98021

Dear Mr. Travis:

Your recent efforts to promote energy conservation are of great interest to me. My experience as Energy Consultant for Seattle City Light would make me an excellent candidate for several positions in your organization.

While at City Light, I have inspected and provided energy savings estimates on over 500 homes. Eighty percent of the homeowners have acted on one or more of my suggestions and have averaged over 17% in energy savings.

I will call you next week to arrange a brief meeting.

Sincerely,

Brad Tolliver

❖

January 11, 2003

Leslie Acosta
Regional Sales Manager
Peoples Pharmaceuticals
5825 146th Avenue S.E.
Bellevue, Washington 98006

Dear Ms. Acosta:

I was attracted to Peoples Pharmaceuticals when I read your annual report. My medical background and my customer service experience make me an excellent candidate for a sales/marketing position in your organization.

While at Danton Instruments, I was a key person involved in the writing and organization of new product manuals. My oral presentations to the sales force were always valuable and well received. District sales managers and the sales representatives themselves consistently expressed appreciation for the sales aids and information given to them. In addition, a large part of my time was spent working closely with our customers, successfully troubleshooting problems, answering questions, and informing them of new products or instrument applications that might better serve their needs.

I will look forward to hearing from you soon.

Sincerely,

Sandra Gulliver

Next is an example where the applicant has spoken to the employer by phone and is thanking the person for having given him some time. There was no opening, so the cover letter is also acting as a thank-you note. Notice that the first paragraph was written strictly for this one letter. The other paragraphs are part of the standard cover letter.

2/2/03

Paulette Meyers
National Sales Manager
San Sebastian Winery
San Sebastian, California 95476

Dear Ms. Meyers:

I very much enjoyed our conversation yesterday. As I indicated, I have always been impressed with San Sebastian Winery. At the Blue Panda in Portland, I was instrumental in taking San Sebastian wines from our sixth most popular wine to number two. I totally agree with you that a top sales rep must be highly knowledgeable about wines. I frequently invite wine reps to give wine tastings at the restaurant, both for my own benefit and for the staff. I think you would be impressed with both my knowledge and my palate.

At the Blue Panda Restaurants I have always been a producer. I run what has become one of the most profitable restaurants in the chain, and our wine sales are ranked number one. At each of the four restaurants I've managed, wine sales experienced dramatic increases. I am committed to remaining in the Northwest and am confident I can substantially increase your wine sales in this region.

I will call you in a few weeks to learn about any developments.

Sincerely

Tom Reston

❖

Dear Mr. Ronagen

Your ad for a Western Region Dealer Representative was of great interest to me. I am very impressed with the Mitsubishi Company and the cars it produces. I would very much like to be a part of Mitsubishi, particularly in the area of dealer servicing. I can help Mitsubishi establish the reputation it wants for parts and service.

I know what is required to make service and parts departments run smoothly and profitably. I have always developed close working relations with dealership owners as well as parts and service managers.

In Oregon I worked closely with 16 VW dealerships. Most were poorly managed and barely making money. The service departments were all losing money. Within a year their appearances were tremendously improved, mechanics and service managers had received additional training, and quality control and inventory control systems had been established. Parts sales jumped 85%, and sales of new cars rose 45%.

I am committed to the automotive industry. My experience in Oregon is just one example of what I have been able to do with dealerships. Please feel free to contact me so I can tell you more about my background.

Dear Mr. Swenson:

As a Project Manager and Construction Manager for Danson Construction, I have overseen both large and small projects. As an architect I can design projects or work with an architect to come up with the best and most cost effective design. I have hired contractors and have been very successful in making sure the projects were completed on time and were of high quality.

My degree in architecture, along with four years experience in designing, cost estimating, and managing construction projects, plus nearly one year of drafting, make me an ideal candidate for your Facilities Engineer position. I am a person of high energy, which has enabled me to watch the many details of a construction project and make sure everything was completed correctly. That same energy and hard work will prove most helpful as I oversee projects at your many facilities along the East Coast.

Dear Ms. Glasser:

Since age eleven I have wanted to work as a flight attendant. I've been working in restaurants the last four years because I believed it would give me the best training possible for being a flight attendant.

I moved up into restaurant management so quickly because I proved I could handle the responsibility. I mix very well with customers and make each one feel important. This has increased the number of steady customers at each restaurant I have worked.

I am also a problem solver. At Leo's I helped reduce operating costs significantly. At J. K. Jake's I reduced turnover by working more closely with the staff. At both Wooden Lake and Ashki's I helped lay the groundwork so these restaurants could be successful from the day they opened.

I am very much looking forward to interviewing for a flight attendant position.

Dear Ms. Preminger:

I have had a very exciting nine years in hotel sales, six of those years as Director of Sales. During that time I have developed highly effective techniques for attracting association and corporate business.

I would enjoy very much the opportunity to describe in more detail why those techniques have worked so well, and why I would function effectively as your next Sales Manager.

Make Your Resume And Cover Letter Work As A Team

On the next two pages you'll find Dante Jackson's resume and cover letter. Notice how Dante brings some points into the cover letter that also appear in the resume. He expands slightly on those points to give a feel for how he achieved those results.

Dante has also created a letterhead for himself that gets printed out on his laser printer with the letter. I tend not to use letterhead, which is having one's name and address printed nicely at the top of the page. Many others like it. Dante used Arial for his cover letter and resume. For his letterhead he used a slightly different font called Arial Rounded Bold. I think it adds a nice touch.

Dante Jackson
2314 Cerrito Avenue
Oakland, CA 94611
(510) 745-0980

11/5/02

Bob Hanson
Director of Operations
XYZ Corp.
2438 4th Avenue
Oakland, CA 94612

Dear Mr. Hanson,

I have a strong background in all aspects of shipping and receiving and inventory control. I am very interested in your Shipping and Receiving Manager position.

I develop strong working relations with internal and external customers and I respond quickly to their needs. I have implemented systems which have significantly reduced costs and improved customer relations.

I'm recognized as an excellent supervisor. People like working for me and I have reduced absenteeism by over 45%. I cross-train my staff and they like the variety and knowing that their market value is increased. By developing a better scheduling system and through our cross-training, we have been able to reduce late shipments from nine per month to less than two per month. Largely because of the cross-training and the improved productivity due to lower turnover, our overtime in the shipping and receiving department has been cut by 25%.

XYZ Corp is known for its customer service and its strong promotion from within policy. That is exactly the type of organization I want to be a part of. I look forward to meeting with you.

Sincerely,

Dante Jackson

Dante Jackson
2314 Cerrito Avenue
Oakland, CA   94611
(510) 745-0980

OBJECTIVE: Shipping and Receiving/Inventory Control Supervision

QUALIFICATIONS

Strong knowledge of shipping and receiving and inventory control. Develop strong working relations with internal and external customers and respond quickly to their needs. Have implemented systems that have significantly reduced costs and improved customer relations. Excellent supervisor.

EMPLOYMENT

Simplotic Corp., Oakland, CA   6/96-Present

Shipping And Receiving Supervisor -7/98 - Present. File the daily shipping and receiving log and distribute all incoming materials. Work closely with department managers to resolve discrepancies on purchase orders. Keep production manager and other supervisors apprised of products with shipment priority, and ensure products ship on schedule. Negotiate with vendors and purchase all shipping materials.

- Developed a system which has reduced late shipments from nine per month to less than two per month.

- Developed an inventory control program which has reduced stocking levels of finished printed circuit boards from $1.6 million to less than $1.0 million.

- Reduced cost of shipping materials by ordering larger quantities and receiving staggered deliveries.

- Installed a system of packaging and boxing circuit boards which has resulted in a 99% shipment completion rate and 94% accuracy rate versus 66% and 78% in the past.

Machine Operator – 6/96-7/98. Coated circuit boards with solder and inspected parts.

EDUCATION

AA—Communications, Sequoia Community College   (1997)

Tailoring Your Cover Letters To Increase Your Interviews

WHILE MANY WANT ADS provide only the barest information, some are quite explicit. Jobs posted on job bulletin boards and jobs posted on the Internet are usually fairly detailed. To create a top quality cover letter in response to a detailed description, first analyze the ad by listing all of the key requirements and then your experience, knowledge, and results that qualify you for each point.

If you have little knowledge or experience in any given area, do not let that stop you from applying. The ad has indicated the background of the ideal candidate and that person may simply not be available. The standard wisdom is that if you meet more than half the requirements, and know you could do an excellent job, take the time to create a cover letter that is tailored for that position.

The cover letters which you have just read all sell the person who sent them, but there is another type of cover letter which can be very effective. It is a cover letter which lists the key requirements from the ad and then demonstrates how the applicant more than meets the requirements.

To use this approach you should more than meet almost every point. If you completely lack background in a particular area, however, simply ignore that point in your cover letter. Rarely can you afford to skip more than one of the key points, however. If you do, it will simply be too obvious that documentation in those areas is missing.

This strategy is designed mainly to help sell you to the person who is performing the initial screening. If you can prove that you meet the qualifications in a very explicit way, that person is likely to pass you on to the hiring authority. The screener will almost assuredly not be an expert in your field. Most likely a list of points has been supplied to look for in the resume and cover letter. If those items are not obviously present in the resume and cover letter, it is "safer" for the screener to eliminate you.

The following example perfectly demonstrates why you want to do everything possible to avoid being eliminated by a screening person. Sandra, a mechanical engineer with two years' experience, applied for a position that she was excited about and felt she was perfectly suited for. Two weeks after sending her resume in response to an ad, she got a rejection letter. Rather than meekly accepting the rejection, she called the company and spoke to the hiring manager. She sold herself to him and intentionally made no mention of the rejection letter. Obviously impressed by what he was hearing, he asked her to stay on the line for a moment. While away from the phone he reviewed her resume and learned that a rejection letter had been sent out. He came back about three minutes later and told her to ignore the letter that might be arriving any day. He then set up an appointment with her. She interviewed for the position and got the job.

There are two major lessons to learn from this situation. It demonstrates how important it is for the resume and cover letter to fully sell you. Sandra's resume was good but she had not tailored it to the job and her cover letter was only adequate. The clerk who did the initial screening was unable to recognize how fully qualified she was. It also demonstrates the importance of not giving up. Many people have ultimately been hired because they did things that their competitors did not. Sandra very much wanted the job and knew she would be great at it, so she overcame her natural timidity and made that call. Although her heart was pounding as she rang the manager's office, once she got him on the phone she simply described her experience and accomplishments. He immediately recognized her potential.

Obviously there was no guarantee that Sandra's actions were going to have such a desirable outcome. It didn't matter to her, however, she simply wanted a shot at it, and she gave it her best. While Sandra is to be admired for her gumption, a better cover letter might have prevented its necessity.

Analyzing A Want Ad

Let's begin by looking at how to analyze a want ad. First you'll find an ad for an accountant. Read the ad, then notice how Jill pulled out the key points. Then she began identifying those parts of her background which met the requirements. While listing points, don't worry about producing high quality writing, just get your thoughts down on paper. You'll work on the exact wording when actually constructing the cover letter. By listing her qualifications the applicant became very confident in her ability to perform the job and then wrote a compelling cover letter.

Accountant

For manufacturing and distribution business. Accounting degree, 4 yrs experience, strong PC and spreadsheet skills. Will have GL, AP, AR, and office management responsibilities. Knowledge of Real World accounting software and human resources practices desirable. Our accountant is responsible for all aspects of our accounting, works with our outside CPA firm and reports directly to the Pres. Send resume to A&B Concrete, 1348 NW Jubilee Road, Plano, TX 75075

Accountant / Manufacturing–distribution

Requirements	Qualified By
Accounting degree	BA - accounting
4 years experience	3 years accounting plus one year office work
Strong PC skills	Excellent knowledge of Windows, NT 4.0, Word, Publisher
Strong spreadsheet skills	Heavy experience with Excel/Lotus 1-2-3 Know how to create macros

Responsibilities

General ledger Accounts payable Accounts receivable	Three years working heavily with GL, AP, AR. One year with AccPac and two with Great Plains. Converted the GL, AP, and AR to AccPac and significantly improved those areas. Reduced receivables from 12% being 90 days or over, to 4% being 90 or over
Office management	Know how to run an office — handled most responsibilities of the office and reported to the office manager for one year
All aspects of accounting	Experienced in GL, AP, AR, internal auditing, financial statements, reducing receivables, payroll, cost accounting, taxes
Works with CPA firm	Have not worked directly with CPA firm, but my boss did and I know what is required

Desirable

Knowledge of Real World Accounting software	Experienced with AccPac and Great Plains which have the same modules and similar techniques as RWA
Knowledge of human resource practices	Took a business course in human resources. Knowledgeable of benefits, wage and salary administration, 401(k) plans, and retirement plans

Tailoring Your Cover Letters To Increase Your Interviews

Jill Josephson
13289 NE Piedmont Drive
Plano, Texas 75075
(806) 764-0098

2/5/02

Accounting Manager
A&B Concrete
1348 NW Jubilee Road
Plano, TX 75075

Dear Accounting Manager:

I graduated from the University of Texas three years ago with a BA in accounting. During the past three years with a medium-size manufacturer, I have had the opportunity to work in all aspects of accounting including GL, AP, AR, internal auditing, financial statements, payroll, cost accounting, and taxes. I have had one year of experience with AccPac and two years with Great Plains. I am especially strong in accounts receivable. In the past two years I have reduced our 90 day and over receivables from 12% to less than 4%.

Last year I had to the opportunity to oversee a conversion from Great Plains to AccPac. The conversion went smoothly and we completed the process on schedule.

I have broad PC skills. I have excellent knowledge of Windows 98 as well as NT 4.0. I recently attended a three-day course in Windows 2000, which we will be converting to next month. I have heavy experience in both Excel and Lotus 1-2-3. I have created numerous timesaving macros in both programs.

A business course in human resources gave me a good overview of the field. With my accounting experience I have gained knowledge of benefits, wage and salary administration, 401(k) plans, and retirement plans. I have also had exposure to health insurance and have worked closely with our HMO in several instances.

I also have solid office experience. During college I worked part-time in an office for three years and handled virtually all of the office functions. During the office manager's vacations I functioned as the office manager and supervised a staff of four. I also trained several new employees.

I am looking for a new challenge and would welcome the opportunity to interview with you.

Sincerely,

Jill Josephson

Next study the customer service ad and the analysis that Travis performed. Then notice how he pulled out the key points and addressed them in the cover letter. Although this technique is not appropriate for everyone, when you meet virtually every point, it can be very effective.

> **Customer Service**
> NetCare, Inc., a leader in the software industry, has immediate full-time openings for Customer Service Representatives to provide order processing and quality customer service through its national call center. Mon. - Fri., various shifts available. Qualifications include excellent customer service/sales skills, professional enthusiasm to support Internet products. Previous customer service, PC/Windows experience is required, software sales experience a plus. Please mail your resume to NetCare, 534 NE Fourth, Philadelphia, PA 19108. No phone calls please.

Customer Service / Software Distributor

Duties/Responsibilities

	Qualified By
Order processing	Learn new systems quickly Excellent typist
Quality customer service	Work hard to keep customers happy Four years of customer service experience

Qualifications

Excellent customer service skills	Get to know systems and procedures well so I can get a problem fixed. Know how to satisfy customers. Work hard to resolve problems. Excellent telephone voice. Always pleasant and helpful
Excellent sales skills	Handled inside sales for two years for an electrical wholesaler. Know how to produce "add on" sales
Professional enthusiasm to support product line	Always enthusiastic and ready to help a customer
PC/Windows experience	Broad experience in Windows 95, 98, 2000, and NT 4.0
Customer service experience	Four years experience in customer service

Desirable

Software sales	Sold electrical products to electrical contractors

3428 N Wankle Drive
Philadelphia, PA 19106
(215) 527-9191

NetCare
534 NE Fourth
Philadelphia, PA 19108

Dear NetCare:

I have an excellent background in customer service and am very interested in your Customer Service Representative position. I have over four years of customer service experience and have always been highly valued by both my employers and customers. My background fits your requirements very well.

Excellent Customer Service Skills

For both of my employers I quickly got to know their systems and procedures. This enables me to quickly assess a customer's problem and then resolve it. I work hard at satisfying customers and have frequently been told that I am friendly and helpful. I know the level of service that customers expect and I know how to deliver it. I'm told I have a very pleasant phone voice. I have four years of experience in customer service and have been given progressively more responsible assignments.

Excellent Sales Skills

For two years I handled inside sales for an electrical wholesaler. I was recognized as one of the best inside sales people on staff and was particularly effective at "add on sales."

Professional Enthusiasm To Support Product Line

I have always been viewed as a person with lots of enthusiasm. When I believe in the product and service of the company I work for, I am always enthusiastic and can sell our service or product. Because I believe in my company and the quality of my work, the customer always has confidence as well.

PC/Windows Experience

I have broad experience in Windows 95, 98, and NT 4.0, and I can install software. I have also trained many people on database and word processing software.

I look forward to a personal interview. The position appears to be very challenging and I would enjoy taking on such a challenge.

Sincerely,

Travis Johanson

This cover letter will sell Travis very effectively. He also has an excellent resume to accompany the cover letter. Obviously a cover letter like this will take a little longer to compose than merely using your standard cover letter. That extra effort, however, can make a big difference in the number of interviews you obtain.

Using Your Advertisement Analysis

After analyzing an ad, as demonstrated above, you can basically do two things with the information. One, you can create a traditional cover letter as Jill did. In the cover letter you would touch on all or most of the points listed in the ad, but you would make no effort to quote those points verbatim. Or, two, you can do as Travis did, and list the points, with each point covered in detail. Either way you will create an excellent cover letter.

Marketing Letters

BEING DIFFERENT OFTEN BRINGS POSITIVE RESULTS. Marketing letters are successful for that reason—they're different. The marketing letter presents your strongest accomplishments, usually those with quantifiable results, to entice the reader. Dates and names of employers are seldom mentioned. The marketing letter acts as a substitute for a resume with cover letter. It can even be used when responding to want ads requesting resumes. In essence, the marketing letter is more like a lengthened cover letter than a resume. Compared to resumes, marketing letters are more personal in tone and more like business correspondence in appearance. Consequently, they are rarely screened out by secretaries.

Less than 5% of all job seekers use marketing letters, yet nothing I know of can lead to more appointments and job interviews. By sending only the marketing letter, your resume is held in reserve for later use. The key to success is addressing it to a specific person and informing that person that a phone call will follow. Your goal is to meet as many people with the power to hire as possible, regardless of whether any openings exist at the moment. This is accomplished by requesting just fifteen minutes of their time.

The use of marketing letters has revolutionized the way my clients find jobs. In the past I had clients cold call potential employers to ask for brief appointments. They understood the importance of the calls, knew they would work, and had practiced what they would say. However, some failed to make their calls, and those who did call, often procrastinated. Sending a marketing letter makes placing those calls easier now. Knowing that a person is expecting your call and is already convinced that you have something of quality to offer, makes a substantial difference psychologically. Using the marketing letter should get you in to see people with the power to hire, 40–80% of the time. Those needing to speak to presidents of companies should expect to make appointments 10–20% of the time. Notice the impact of the following marketing letter and you'll begin to see why these letters get results.

The following marketing letter is especially strong because each accomplishment has been quantified. Marketing letters always have more impact when results are quantified, and most people can easily come up with at least four solid accomplishments. You sense that an employer would want to meet such a person even if no position currently existed.

John Gaddly
1121 65th S.W.
Red Rock, California 92006
(916) 456-9874
jgaddly@infonet.net

January 20, 2002

John Campbell
Executive Vice President
Diversified Products Inc.
440 5th N.W.
Redding, California 96001

Dear Mr. Campbell:

When I joined my current employer two years ago as Production Superintendent, our quality control department was rejecting 6% of all printed circuit boards. Today that figure is less than 1% and continuing downward.

You may be interested in a person who has broad experience in solving production problems. Here are some other things I've done:

Reduced absenteeism 42% and turnover 31%. With less turnover we were able to invest more in training, with a corresponding increase in quality and productivity. While rejections dropped from 6% to less than 1%, productivity increased 22% per employee.

Introduced an idea program with incentives. The number of suggestions that were implemented grew from 11 in 1995 to 65 in 1999. In 1999 bonuses cost $25,000 while documented savings amounted to $197,000.

Implemented an inventory control system. We increased production 34% with only a 6% increase in inventory. Production delays due to unavailable parts dropped from 72 in 1994 to 11 in 1997.

Instituted a company-wide safety program. Lost time due to accidents was reduced 21% during the first six months. Reductions in insurance premiums saved $85,000 in 1999.

I graduated from the University of Wisconsin in 1975 with a degree in Business. Since then I have experienced rapid promotions during 24 years in manufacturing.

I'll call you next week to arrange a time when we might meet for fifteen or twenty minutes.

Sincerely,

John Gaddly

The next two examples demonstrate the flexibility of marketing letters. While they use a more narrative format and are less quantifiable, they also have a strong impact on the reader.

11918 Northeast 143rd Place
Kirkland, Washington 98034
(425) 821-3830

2/10/02

Peter Phillips
Sahalee Development Corp.
2119 Fourth Avenue
Seattle, Washington 98124

Dear Mr. Phillips:

In anticipation of the next development upsurge, you may be looking for a person with a broad background in land development and marketing. I have saved projects from failure, reduced development costs, and increased project marketability.

Recently, at the developer's request, I was retained to save a mobile home project that had been rejected during preliminary hearings. By creating a new marketing strategy, employing a more imaginative design, and representing the client throughout the remainder of the public hearings process, I was able to negotiate the project's approval.

As part of a team of consultants for a 1900-acre/$680 million dollar new town development, I prevented costly delays by reducing agency review time and ensuring project approval with appropriate planning and design concepts. This saved the developer hundreds of thousands of dollars in additional consultant fees and penalty payments for an extension of the land-purchase option.

I have nine years' combined experience in civil engineering, land planning, and urban design. I graduated from the University of Washington with a B.A. in Urban Planning.

I will call you next week to arrange a time when we might meet briefly to discuss my background and your future needs.

Sincerely,

Roger Cricky

1298 N. Rosewood Avenue
Portland, Oregon 97211
(503) 682-9874

12/1/02

Don Harris
Vice President, Sales and Marketing
MicroCad
4309 Sepulveda Blvd North
Los Angeles, California 90030

Dear Mr. Harris,

I am currently looking at sales management positions with medium-sized high tech manufacturers. During the last 15 years I have worked for Datacomp and Syngestics and am currently district sales manager for a major manufacturer of teleprocessing equipment.

I was given a mandate three years ago to strengthen the Pacific Northwest district. During that time we have increased sales an average of 35% annually, the highest rate in the region. I'm known as a motivator. I work closely with my staff to develop marketing strategies and I give them the independence they need to be effective.

I've been successful in both sales and sales management. As a senior account manager for six years with Datacomp, I took my territory from a ranking of 19th nationally to 5th and exceeded quota each year. I got my start in the industry with Syngestics. As a field marketing support rep for two years, my district exceeded its sales quota each year. Then as area supervisor for three years, I supervised six field marketing support engineers. The staff was rated number one in the region for providing technical support, two years in a row.

With a history of success behind me, I believe I can contribute to the further growth of MicroCad. I am strong in marketing, sales training, staff recruiting, and staff development. I will call you next week to learn about your future plans.

Sincerely,

Paul Sanderson

Writing an effective marketing letter requires that you first have a results-oriented resume. Once the resume is complete, the marketing letter almost writes itself. In fact, the results statements used in the marketing letter can come almost word for word from the resume.

The primary portion of any marketing letter is a description of your results and experience. To write a strong marketing letter, review your resume and think through how you want to summarize your background. If you have four to six key projects or results that can be quantified, simply describe them, as was done in the first sample marketing letter. If your background does not lend itself to that approach, the more narrative form will work best for you. Although names of companies are usually not mentioned, you can mention them if you so choose. Sometimes people will mention only well known companies. Even dates or time periods can be mentioned, but are not usually necessary.

Remember, the marketing letter is not a resume. The reader is not expecting to know everything about you. Your goal is to have impact. Your letter should cause the person to recognize your value and to remember you when you call. Write like you would in a letter. Let it flow. Take a look at your qualifications statement in your resume. Perhaps it can be included almost as is. If you are going to emphasize results, they can be lifted almost word for word from your resume, although you'll probably want to make some minor changes. Since your resume was written in telegraphic style, with incomplete sentences and certain words removed, you'll need to adapt the resume to the marketing letter. All sentences should be complete sentences.

Lead-ins for your results could be worded:

You may be interested in my labor negotiating experience. Some of my additional accomplishments are:

❖

My six years in customer relations could be valuable to you. This experience includes:

❖

If your advertising department needs a person with strong experience, you may be interested in what I've done.

If you choose to describe past jobs, as in the third marketing letter example, phrases can again be lifted from the resume. Since this is a marketing letter, you may choose to describe only the last three jobs, even if in the resume five were described. Don't be concerned if your resume and marketing letter have similar phrases in them; no one will notice.

A good closing paragraph for your marketing letter might include a summary of your background, such as the number of years in your field, and information about your degree and alma mater. The final paragraph then prepares the reader for any follow-up contact you might make. In most cases this will be a follow-up phone call.

If the person is local you would usually request a 10–15 minute meeting and indicate so in the letter. If the person is out of state, but is likely to be in your area in the next two or three months, you would request an appointment when the person is in the area. If the person is out of state and would unlikely visit your area, you'll have to sell yourself by phone.

Each marketing letter should be individually typed and addressed to the person with the power to hire. By supplying a word processing service with ten or more names at a time, you should be able to keep your costs down to about two dollars for each letter and envelope. There will be an initial inputting charge for the letter, but after that you'll be paying primarily for printing time, plus the inputting time for the additional names and addresses.

For more on how to follow up after sending a marketing letter, see pages 262–270.

OTHER USES OF THE MARKETING LETTER

The marketing letter is a very flexible tool. It can even function as a substitute for a resume when responding to a help wanted ad. Sometimes, no matter how well written your resume is, it may not work well in response to a particular job listing. Perhaps the job would make an excellent use of your talents, but requires experience you don't have. Traditionally one would write a customized cover letter and possibly even modify the resume. Using the marketing letter approach, the entire letter would be geared to the specific job. Of course you would probably keep in major sections of your standard marketing letter, but it would be customized throughout.

Perhaps your most applicable experience occurred five years ago. With the marketing letter you could mention it first and indicate how many years you did that work. The exact dates would not be mentioned.

Although I recommend that you send marketing letters to specific people, with the intention of following up by phone, they can also be used in mass mailings. Even if you do not intend to follow up with a phone call, I still recommend that you invest the time to identify the person with the power to hire. However, if you choose not to do so, address the letter to a specific title, such as Personnel Director, Chief Engineer, or Accounting Manager. Because it is a letter, and does not have the appearance of a traditional resume, it is more likely to be delivered to the most appropriate person. With this approach it is easy and fast to send out the same mailing two months later if you have not accepted another position by that time. Your success rate will be lower with this method than if you followed up by phone—quick and easy is its main selling point. Please, however, do not use this method just as an excuse to avoid the more productive and effective follow-up methods discussed.

RESUME, COVER LETTER, AND MARKETING LETTER WORKING TOGETHER

The best way to understand how a resume, marketing letter, and cover letter work together is to see a sample of each for the same person. The resume was written first, followed by the marketing letter. The greatest time was spent on the resume, making the marketing letter quite easy and quick to write. The cover letter borrowed some elements from the marketing letter, and it also was easy and quick to write.

RANDAL JOHNSON
4045 NW Abilene
Denver, Colorado 80239
(303) 765-8967

OBJECTIVE: Regional Manager

QUALIFICATIONS

Strong background in trucking with 17 years of management experience. Consistently increase market share and profitability. In a sales capacity, bring in large national accounts and significantly increase revenue from established accounts.

EDUCATION

A.A. - Business Management, Reginald Community College (1986)

EMPLOYMENT

Ryan Freight 12/93-Present

Terminal Manager - Denver, CO 7/96-Present. Responsible for the total operation and sales throughout Colorado. Planned and implemented a break bulk operation in 1998 and within two years, reduced shipment time through break bulk to 16 hours per shipment, versus the industry average of 28 hours.

Expanded the account base to include major national accounts such as Bendix, Control Data, Goodyear, and Motorola, and ultimately attained "prime general commodity status" with each of them. Through improved sales and customer service efforts, have increased revenue from $4 million to $19.5 million. Consistently ranked among the top five performers in customer service and on time deliveries within the 42 terminal system. Won award for the "best average revenue per shipment" in 1999, 2000, and 2001.

Terminal Manager - Portland, OR 12/93-7/96. Managed sales and operations for Oregon and increased revenue 74%. Significantly improved the transit service for Oregon accounts into the Rocky Mountain and Southwest regions. Took Ryan from 8th in market share to 4th in the Oregon market.

Longrider Lines 1/86-12/93

Terminal Manager - Scranton, PA 2/90-12/93. Established primary general commodity carrier status with numerous accounts including GTE, Sears, Ralston Purina, and Mattel. Terminal received annual regional awards in 1992 and 1993 for exceeding revenue and on-time delivery goals. Took the terminal from the 3rd lowest rated terminal in the 15 terminal region, to 4th highest.

Prior positions with Longrider: Operations Manager, Scranton, PA 2/89-2/90; Supervisor, Terminal Operations, Scranton, PA 1/87-2/89; Management Trainee, Pittsburgh, PA 1/86-1/87.

With the resume in place the marketing letter was easy to write.

4045 NW Abilene
Denver, Colorado 80239
(313) 765-8967

2/7/02

Ron Pitts
President
B&N Freightlines
1287 Wacker Drive
Chicago, Illinois 60626

Dear Mr. Pitts,

I have a strong background in the trucking industry gained during 17 years of management experience. With each company and at each of the four terminals managed, I significantly increased market share and quickly increased profitability. At each terminal I achieved one of the best on-time delivery records in the industry. I am now looking for a regional management position.

I have broad sales and marketing experience. At each terminal I devoted 40-50% of my time to marketing, sales, and sales management. Throughout my career I have brought in large national accounts and substantially increased the revenue from established accounts. I have achieved primary carrier status with such accounts as Bendix, Control Data, Goodyear, Motorola, GTE, Sears, Mattel, and Ralston Purina.

With my current employer, our Denver terminal won the annual award for the "best average revenue per shipment" in 1997, 1998, and 1999 in competition with the 42 terminals in the system.

I have turned problem terminals completely around and I have strengthened those already doing well. One terminal I moved from being the 3rd lowest rated terminal (out of 15) to 4th highest in a three-year period. I will call you next week to learn more about any opportunities which may come up in the next few months.

Sincerely,

Randal Johnson

With the marketing letter in place, Randal's standard cover letter was a snap.

4045 NW Abilene
Denver, Colorado 80239
(303) 765-8967

2/7/02

Jeff Smalwun
President
RoadRider Freightlines
2312 Hennepin Avenue
Minneapolis, Minnesota 55403

Dear Mr. Smalwun,

I have a strong background in all aspects of trucking line management. At each of the four terminals I've managed, I have significantly improved on-time records, revenue, market share, and profitability. I am now looking for a regional manager's position with responsibility for 4-8 terminals.

I have broad experience in both sales and operations. I have brought in large national accounts, and increased revenue with existing accounts. On the operations side I have taken over two terminals which were among the worst in the company. Within 10 months both were profitable for the first time in years. I came up through the ranks in the trucking business, so I have hands on experience in virtually all aspects of operations. I also have extensive experience with budgets and working with state and federal agencies.

I would very much like to meet with you to describe my background in more detail. I look forward to hearing from you.

Sincerely

Randal Johnson

Part Five
Finding The Job
That's Right For You

The Systematic Job Search

MANY PEOPLE ARE STARTLED to discover that only three of every ten job openings are ever advertised or listed with employment agencies. The other seven jobs have become known as "the hidden job market." This fact of life necessitates a job-finding strategy far different from those used by the average job seeker. The typical job-finding strategy consists of mailing out dozens of resumes, visiting a handful of employment agencies, and religiously reading the want ads. While 30% of all people do find jobs this way, there are many for whom this strategy simply does not work.

Finding a job that provides growth and satisfaction requires the right strategy. It takes considerable thought, time, and energy, but the payoff is tremendous.

In order to find such a job, you're going to tap into the hidden job market with the Systematic Job Search strategy. These are the requirements:

Employer Research - Develop a list of 50–200 prime organizations that match your requirements for industry, location, size, growth, and any other key factors. When an interview is arranged, learn more about the organization and go prepared.

Contacts - Send your resume to friends, relatives, and business contacts. Then talk to them about the type of position you're seeking. Your network of contacts will keep their eyes and ears open for you; when positions open up in their organizations (or in their friends' organizations), they can supply you with the names of people to contact.

Calls - In the first week, call each of your top 20 organizations and ask for the name of the person with the power to hire you. He or she will usually have a position one or two levels above the position you would fill. Send a marketing letter to that person. A marketing letter is a letter that outlines your background and acts as a substitute for your resume. (See page 239 for a complete description of the functions and purposes of a marketing letter.) State in your marketing letter that you will call to set up a brief meeting. Call those you've sent letters to and ask for a brief appointment, even if there are no openings.

Appointments - Your calls should result in appointments 40–80% of the time. Before each appointment, research the organization. During the 15-minute appointment you will learn more about the organization and what they look for in their employees. Ask intelligent questions and explain how your background could be helpful to them. Create a favorable impression of yourself so if an opening occurs, you will be given top priority.

Follow-Up - After each appointment send a thank-you note and express your interest in the organization. This causes the person to think favorably of you once again. Three weeks later, call to see if any openings have developed. If not, make a brief call every five weeks. This type of contact has at least 40 times the impact of sending a resume alone.

Interviews - All of your hard work—whether responding to want ads or getting appointments with the people with power to hire you—will result in formal interviews. Because you are ready for virtually any question, you'll shine in the interviews and get more than your share of job offers.

Finding jobs in the hidden job market will require hard work and endurance, but it can be enjoyable and rewarding. There may be frustrations and down times. But remember: your efforts will pay off. Those efforts will directly determine the success of your job search. Go to www.cmr-mvp.com to print out Focus and Speed so you can review it daily.

FOCUS AND SPEED

The key to an effective job search is focus and speed. You need focus so all of the time and energy you expend gets you closer to your goal. With the proper focus you should throw yourself into your job search and tell yourself that you are going to move quickly and make things happen quickly.

Focus Employers like people with focus and they avoid people without focus. The branch manager of a savings and loan once asked a young applicant why he was interested in the position. His response, "Because it's available." An applicant interviewing with a large manufacturer was asked what types of positions he was interested in. His response, "What have you got?" Neither of these people were offered jobs.

Having focus does not mean you have reduced your career choice down to one narrow field or job title. Employers just want to sense that you have direction, that you know where you want to go. The S&L manager was not expecting that the young man had wanted to join a savings and loan since age 12. The young man, having been invited to an interview, however, should have researched the industry.

When you're focused you make things happen. Take the time now if necessary to establish your focus.

Speed Once you achieve focus, speed is of the essence. The most successful job seekers know what they need to do and do it. They have a plan and they carry it out with dispatch. They also derive great satisfaction from checking off items in the job search that they have completed.

There are several activities that once done, they are basically done for the remainder of the job search. As an example, after posting your resume to several appropriate commercial resume databanks, your task is completed. If you get your resume into the hands of 50 key friends and relatives, that portion of your search is largely over.

Here's my list of things to get done quickly:

1. Define your job/career objective.

2. Research your desired industries and learn the jargon.

3. Create your initial resume.

4. Create your key word/plain-text resume.

5. Post your resume to 5-15 resume databanks.

6. Explore the web and identify the 4-6 websites that provide useful articles on careers, interviewing, and job finding that you will visit frequently.

7. Identify 5-15 websites that post job openings that you'll visit weekly.

8. Identify the newspaper want ads that are posted online that you will visit weekly.

9. Develop answers to at least 60 of the 101 most difficult and most commonly asked interview questions (See *Interview Power*).

10. Develop an overall strategy for your job search.

11. Develop a weekly plan and follow it, but build in flexibility.

12. Determine what days of the week and what time of the day it works best for you to carry out certain tasks such as calling employers and asking for brief appointments.

13. If it is appropriate for you to contact employment agencies, temporary agencies, or recruiters, identify who they are and complete the contact within two weeks.

14. Conduct practice interviews and hone your skills and confidence.

15. Develop a list of 50-250 prime employers.

16. Identify the 50-100 people you know who know the most people.

17. Give those people your resume, tell them what you're looking for, and show them your list of your top 100 employers. Ask if they know anyone who works for any of these employers.

18. When given names of people, call these contacts of your friends and relatives and learn more about their organizations, including whether they are growing and are good organizations to work for.

19. Develop a script for calling people with the power to hire and asking for fifteen minutes of their time.

20. Create a marketing letter to send to people with the power to hire.

21. Make calls to determine who has the power to hire you in your desired organizations.

If you're unemployed and you devote 30-35 hours per week to job hunting, you can complete these 21 steps within three weeks. Once you've laid this foundation, good things begin to happen.

Although I'm encouraging you to move with focus and speed, these things do take time. For example, even if you applied online today for a job that perfectly matched your background, it could still take two or three weeks before they call you and another week before the interview actually takes place. Build a solid foundation first, take care of all the steps, and you'll find yourself in that next job sooner than you expected.

EMPLOYER RESEARCH

Employer research is one of the most important yet most neglected aspects of a job search. Researching employers consists of two stages: 1) using directories and other resources to develop a high-priority list of 50–200 employers; 2) gathering specific information about each organization before an interview, and conducting in-depth studies of organizations that offer you a job.

Stage One: Developing Your High-Priority List of Employers

Begin with a stack of one hundred 4 x 6 cards and find a directory that will lead you to the types of organizations you're interested in. Examples of these directories include the *American Banking Directory* and the *Video Industry Directory*. As you come across appropriate organizations, write down whatever information the directory provides. They typically provide the name of the organization, its address and phone number, the number of employees, its products or services, and its sales volume. All of that information should go on the front side of the card, leaving space on the back to write information that you obtain from people or from newspaper articles.

In metropolitan Seattle there are over 60,000 employers. Since it's difficult to work effectively with an employer list over 300, a system must be devised to enable a job seeker in the Seattle area to screen out all but the 100 to 250 prime employers. By selecting 1-10 industries, limiting the search to a 30-mile radius, and by limiting the selection to organizations of 10-250 employees, a list of about 200 employers will result.

Begin this process by deciding which industries and products you'd like to be involved with. The Standard Industrial Classification (SIC) coding system was created to help you do that. Because every business functions in one or more industries, each is assigned one or more industry codes. This coding system will help you find your prospects quickly. In those directories which segregate organizations by SIC, you will find a list of the industries with their codes. If you really want to dig into the different industries, use the *Standard Industrial Classification Manual* found in most libraries.

Next, decide what size of organization you want to work for. A lot of the new jobs created in the last ten years have been in organizations of under 50 employees, so do not overlook smaller organizations. The work some people do, however, is available only in organizations of over 100 employees. These people would target companies with 100 or more employees.

Next, decide the maximum distance you are willing to commute. If the maximum commute you'd accept would be 35 minutes each way, you would use that as a guide to select organizations. For a truly outstanding company you might be willing to accept a longer commute, but there would be relatively few exceptions.

Once you've made your decisions, you will be ready to utilize the many directories available in your library.

As with any resource that lists key company officials, always call to confirm that your targeted manager still holds the title mentioned in the directory.

Resources

Info USA. Many libraries will have this CD ROM resource which lists ten million businesses—virtually every business in the US from the smallest to biggest. The information provided includes name, address, number of employees, annual sales, credit rating, name of owner or general manager, Yellow Page category, and SIC codes. You can search organizations by several criteria including geography, size, and industry. For example, you could obtain a list of every company in Milwaukee, over ten employees, that manufactures electronic equipment. You could find those same organizations in the Midwest, or even six selected cities. Searches can also be conducted by zip codes, county/counties, or city. The search is completed in seconds and you can then print out the material. Some libraries will let you download the information to your own disk. If you have database software you can then send customized letters to specific organizations. You could also do specialized searches from your home computer.

The Yellow Pages. One of the most useful directories is available in your own home—the Yellow Pages. Most organizations in your area will be listed somewhere in the Yellow Pages even if they don't advertise. The "space ads" in the Yellow Pages can be particularly useful. Those ads can give you an excellent idea of what the businesses in a particular industry do. Using the Yellow Pages will give you companies to consider that you might have easily overlooked if you relied solely on other resources.

To use the Yellow Pages, go through the listings from A to Z. Scan each page and look at each of the specific categories. Rather than assuming that you don't want to work in a particular category, start with the opposite assumption. Give each category or industry serious consideration unless you can come up with a good reason why you should not. This technique opens you to possibilities that you might otherwise have been closed to.

Librarians. Make use of the business or reference librarian at your library. Tell the librarian precisely what types of organizations you are trying to locate, and mention which directories you intend to use. Then ask the librarian if there are other directories you should use. The library will probably have several local directories that could provide exactly what you need. Don't hesitate to ask for help—that's what librarians love to do.

Industry-Specific Directories. Some industries have their own, specialized directories. To locate these directories, use the *Guide to American Directories* or *Directories In Print*. A good example of a specialized directory is the *World Aviation Directory*. It provides names, addresses, and phone numbers for every airline, airport, airplane or parts manufacturer, aviation insurance company, and dealer in the United States. For some people, a specialized directory is the only resource they need.

Associations. Determine whether there is an association that represents your field or industry. The *Encyclopedia of Associations* and the *National Trade and Professional Associations* can provide this information. You'll also find local associations listed in the Yellow Pages under "Associations." Associations are usually formed to give an industry or profession more political clout, as well as to provide a forum for new ideas. They generally publish membership lists and news magazines, hold conventions and meetings, list job openings, and distribute free literature.

The Sunday Paper. Another way to build up your employer list is to review the back issues of the Sunday newspaper in your area that has the most want ads. Read through the want ads quickly to see if certain organizations seem to be hiring. Add them to your list even if you don't know much about them.

Local Resources

People with no desire to leave their current geographical area will get better results with local, rather than national resources. It would be impossible, of course, to list all local resources, but I can help you find them. The best place to start is in the business reference section of your library. In this section you'll find *Yellow Pages* and many other directories.

After you've scouted out the reference area, talk to the reference librarian and ask about resources. You'll find reference librarians very helpful. Some libraries will have a list of useful resources and directories.

If you are looking for government, nonprofit, or social service agencies, ask the reference librarian for help. United Way generally publishes a booklet describing the agencies it funds. For state, city, or county governments there may be a telephone directory with names of departments, key staff people, and their phone numbers.

Virtually every chamber of commerce publishes information on local companies. Most of their directories cost between ten and twenty dollars but they should also be available at your library. As an example, the Seattle Chamber of Commerce produces a resource which lists the 800 local companies with over 100 employees. For those wanting to or needing to work for larger organizations, that can be the perfect resource.

National Resources

Some of the national resources listed below cost over one hundred dollars per year and are found only in libraries with a major business section. Go to your nearest library first to find out what local and national directories they have. Eventually you may need to visit a larger library.

National resources are useful primarily for those who want to work for companies over 500 employees and are willing to relocate to do so. If you want to remain in your metropolitan area, or at least in your state, there will virtually always be local directories which will be more helpful than the national directories.

Dun and Bradstreet—Million Dollar Directory. This publication lists 160,000 companies with a net worth of $1,000,000 or more. The alphabetical section includes company names, names of parent companies, addresses, telephone numbers, SIC numbers, sales figures, number of employees, principal officers, and whether companies are involved in importing and exporting. Dun and Bradstreet also has geographical and SIC sections.

Dun and Bradstreet—Middle Market Directory. Same as above except it covers companies with a net worth between $500,000 and $1,000,000.

Standard and Poor's. This directory includes 37,000 corporations, with names, addresses, telephone numbers, products made, number of employees, and sales volume. Volume 1 has an alphabetical listing, volume 2 has biographical information on 75,000 key officers listed alphabetically by last name, and volume 3 lists corporations by SIC and geographic area.

Dun's Directory of Service Companies. It lists 50,000 organizations in the following categories: management consulting, executive search, public relations, engineering and architectural services, business services, consumer services, research services, repair services, hospitality, motion pictures, amusement and recreation. All have more than 50 employees.

Industry Directories

Thousands of directories exist which are helpful to job seekers. As an example, the *Whole World Oil Directory* lists all oil and gas companies, drilling companies, oil well services, and refineries. It may be the only resource some people would need.

Several resources are available to help you locate useful directories. Most libraries will have either the *Guide to American Directories* or *Directories in Print.* Both list and describe over 5,000 directories that are divided into over 300 categories. They are quick and easy to use. They have an alphabetical section and a subject section. They will also tell you what the directories cost and where to order them. Most directories cost $15–30 but some cost in the hundreds. After you identify a useful directory, check to see if your library has it. Even if your library does not have it, an interlibrary search with the help of your reference librarian, may help you find a library which does.

A sampling has been included to give you a feel for what's available: *National Trade & Professional Associations of the U. S.; Directory of Management Consultants; American Apparel Manufacturers Association Directory; American Bank Directory; Official Directory of Data Processing; Environmental Organizations Directory; American Electronics Association Directory; Directory of Frozen Food Processors; Directory of United States Importers; National Machine Tool Builders Association Directory.*

Stage Two: Obtaining Information About The Organization

Once you've landed an appointment or an interview, it's time to shift into high gear and get prepared. Since knowledge of the organization is critical for interviews, researching an organization can enable you to go in armed with knowledge. This knowledge will give you added confidence in your appointments and interviews. Avoid overwhelming the interviewer with your knowledge about products or financial figures, though. Instead, keep your information in reserve and use it only when appropriate.

Reasons For Researching An Organization

There are four main reasons for researching employers.

1. **To determine whether the organization is right for you.** Try to discover all the pros and cons you can. Research may reveal a serious problem that might cause you to eliminate the organization, or it may reveal some outstanding opportunities that will further encourage and motivate you.

2. **To impress the interviewer.** Because so few people bother to research a company, you'll stand out in a very positive way if you've done your homework and go armed with information. Weave your information into the conversation appropriately. Some employers will ask, "What do you know about us?" Most people will hem, haw, and fail this question miserably. But you'll shine. Even when asked this question, however, don't overwhelm the interviewer with your answer. Give a thorough but concise response.

3. **To discover problems you can help solve.** Problems you have the ability to solve could come to light before or during an interview. If you discover them before the interview, you'll have time to prepare and perhaps even develop a proposal. Otherwise, listen for clues to such problems during the interview. An employer may come right out and describe problems, but will probably only allude to them. Careful listening can help you match your abilities or experience to the problem area. By all means emphasize those strengths that can help solve the organization's problems.

4. **To identify questions that must be clarified by the employer.** An annual report or a magazine article may have mentioned an exciting new product being developed by your target company. If the interviewer doesn't mention it, you may have to ask if you would have a role in developing, marketing, or selling it. If an inside source told you that a strike could cripple the company, you might ask about the effects of such a strike. If the company has lost money three years in a row, you might ask what the company is doing to reverse the losses.

Interviewing is a continuation of your research. Keep your detective cap on and discover all you can. Ask yourself if you would enjoy working for this person. Will you respect this boss? Do your management philosophies match? Will you like each other? These are some of the important questions that can be answered, in part, by the research you conduct during interviews.

Do some research before each interview, even if it's the third or fourth interview with the same company. This is particularly important if you feel really good about the job, your potential boss, and the company. Discover all you can. Answering questions effectively and asking the right questions could make the difference between being the number-one choice and the number-two choice.

The following resources will provide valuable information.

Moody's. *Moody's Industrial Manual*—Provides financial information, history, subsidiaries, products and services, sales, principal plants and properties, executives, number of employees. One to two pages are devoted to most companies. All of the *Moody's* manuals concentrate on large companies.

Moody's OTC (Over the Counter)—Same format as above but covering smaller companies.

Moody's Municipal and Government Manual
Moody's Bank and Finance Manual
Moody's Public Utilities Manual
Moody's Transportation Manual

Clipping Files. Many libraries maintain files of news articles and feature articles about local businesses clipped from local papers. While most articles are short news releases, you will also find highly informative feature articles about new developments within target companies.

House Organs. Companies publish house organs (in-house newsletters) as internal public relations vehicles and will have such things as a letter from the president describing past achievements and future goals, pictures of the bowling team and those retiring, and usually a feature article about a person, department, or a new product. House organs are especially helpful. Check with your library to see if a file of house organs is maintained.

Annual Reports. If the company is publicly owned (stock which is publicly traded), it is required by law to publish an annual financial report. Understanding the financial jargon is unnecessary. The past year's failures and achievements will be summarized along with descriptions of new products and future goals.

Recruiting Brochures. Major companies which recruit at college campuses produce recruiting brochures. The brochures describe the history and background of the company, training programs, company benefits, and desired training and characteristics of employees. College placement offices will have many on file.

Indexes. In addition to clipping files, you will want to use one or more indexes to locate articles in magazines or newspapers. First look up the company by name. If you don't find the listings you want, you could read articles about the industry that your target company falls in and possibly find a reference to your target company in that way. The indexes can also be used to research a topic, a product, a new technology, or an entire industry.

Encyclopedia of Business Information Sources. Lists trade associations, periodicals, directories, bibliographies, and an abstract index of recent articles. An outstanding resource.

Readers Guide to Periodical Literature. Lists articles found in over two hundred popular magazines, giving the periodical, date, and title of article. This is the same green-covered resource you used in high school when you did research reports.

Business Periodicals Index. The *BPI* uses business periodicals which are generally not covered in the *Readers Guide to Periodical Literature.* Examples: *Human Resource Management* and *Automotive News.*

The Magazine Index. An automated system found in many libraries which indexes articles in about 400 general interest magazines. It is published by Information Access Company which, in a similar format, also publishes: *National Newspaper Index, Business Index,* and *Legal Resource Index.*

Infotrac. A computerized database found in many libraries, it indexes 1,100 magazines, going back ten years. With the help of a librarian it takes under five minutes to learn how to use. With it you can research industries, products, new technology, and companies. The business index provides information about the companies themselves, including address, products, number of employees, etc., and articles written about them. With most articles you can also read an abstract, which is a short version of the article. Both the abstracts plus the information about the article such as the name of the periodical, date, and page number, can be printed out so you don't have to write them all down.

ABI Inform. Same concept as *Infotrac,* it abstracts 700 business journals.

F & S Index of Corporations and Industries. Lists articles on industries and companies, including mergers, acquisitions, new products, and emerging technology. Lists trade journals, addresses and their costs.

F & S Index Europe. Same format

F & S Index International. Same format. Covers Canada, Latin America, Africa, and Asia

Wall Street Journal Index. The first section is alphabetical by company; the second section is alphabetical by subject and peoples' names.

New York Times Index. Same format

Chicago Tribune Index. Same format

Los Angeles Times Index. Same format

Washington Post Index. Same format

Libraries which carry these indexes will probably also have the newspapers on microfilm.

CONTACTS

Friends, relatives, acquaintances, and business contacts can all provide useful leads if you approach them in the right way. Before they can help, people must know what you're looking for and what your qualifications are. About 26% of all jobseekers find positions through such leads. This number could be increased substantially if people made better use of this method. Include your banker, barber, broker, and butcher. Every person who has an interest in your success can be helpful.

Begin by sending your resume and a list of your top 60–80 prospects to everyone you know. Enclose a note stating that you will call in a few days. Ask your contacts to review the list carefully and to indicate if they know anyone who works for any of the organizations. Underline the word anyone. You truly want to talk to anyone whether it is a janitor, secretary, or purchasing agent. By talking to that person you can learn if it is a good organization to work for, what it's problems or strengths are, and even get inside information about the person who has power to hire you. Tell your contact what your strengths are and ask the person to call you if he or she hears of any openings. Tell the person that all you need is someone to contact and that you will take care of the rest. You are not asking for any great favors. You would certainly do the same for them.

Speaking to contacts is one of the most valuable things a person can do in a job search, yet few job hunters are willing to expend even the small amount of energy this strategy requires.

CALLS

In this phase of the process, it is crucial to meet the person who has the power to hire you. Determining who that person is and getting an appointment requires a well-planned strategy.

Determining Who Has the Power to Hire

The person with the power to hire you normally holds a position that would be one or two levels above you in the department or functional area you have focused on. Often this person will be a department head. When calling, ask for the name of the person whose job title indicates that he or she has the power to hire you.

Once you have your list of organizations, begin identifying the people who do the hiring. Getting their names is easy because nearly every business has a receptionist. Call and ask for the person's name, being sure to get the correct spelling and title. Most receptionists are so busy that they won't bother to ask you why you want to know.

Occasionally, the receptionist will not know the proper person, or will hastily connect you with personnel. Don't be startled, just ask your question again with confidence and assertiveness. If the receptionist or personnel clerk asks why you are calling, the most simple response is, "I have some material to send to your purchasing manager." Typical responses might be like these:

Receptionist:	Dearborn Insurance, may I help you?
Steve:	Hello, can you give me the name of your claims manager?
Receptionist:	Yes, that would be John Yaeger.
Steve:	Would you spell his last name, please?
Receptionist:	Sure, Y A E G E R.
Steve:	Thank you very much.

❖

Receptionist:	Medico, may I help you?
Sally:	Hello, can you give me the name of your IT manager?
Receptionist:	IT?
Sally:	Yes, Information Technology. Do you have someone in charge of computer programming?
Receptionist:	I think you probably want Bob Benson.
Sally:	What is his title?
Receptionist:	He's vice president of operations, but I think he's in charge of our three programmers and our network.
Sally:	Okay, thank you very much.

❖

Receptionist:	Continental.
Kevin:	Can you give me the name of your purchasing manager?
Receptionist:	Just a moment.
Personnel:	Personnel.
Kevin:	Can you give me the name of your purchasing manager?
Personnel:	That would be James Townsend.
Kevin:	Thank you.

❖

Receptionist:	Malco, may I help you?
Holly:	Could you please give me the name of your advertising manager?

Receptionist:	Just a moment.
Personnel:	Personnel.
Holly:	Could you please give me the name of your advertising manager?
Personnel:	What is this concerning?
Holly:	I have some material to send and I want to make sure it gets to the right person. Could you give me the name of your advertising manager?
Personnel:	That would be Janet Lynn.
Holly:	What is her title?
Personnel:	She's director of marketing.
Holly:	Thank you.

Whether you list 70 or 250 organizations, I would recommend going through the entire list in two or three days to get the names of all the hiring authorities. You can then check off that activity as being completed.

Calling the Person With the Power To Hire

Once you know the names of the people with the power to hire in your organizations, start setting up appointments. This part is more challenging than just getting the names. Your first task will be getting past the person's secretary. One of the secretary's duties is to protect the boss from unnecessary calls, and some exercise this duty with a vengeance. Don't be afraid, though; you can get past even the toughest secretary. Once you get to your potential boss, you must present yourself quickly and ask for an appointment. With a polished opening, you should be able to get appointments 40–80% of the time.

Getting Past Secretaries

When talking to a secretary, present yourself as a confident businessperson with legitimate business reasons for calling. Give your name immediately since the secretary will invariably ask for it. You'll also sound more authoritative. If, after trying all the styles given below, you just can't get past the secretary, try calling very early in the morning or after 5:30 p.m. A busy executive will often answer the phone when the secretary is not there. One of the techniques below will usually work:

Receptionist:	Glasgow and Associates.
Polly:	I'd like to speak to Marilyn Shelton.
Receptionist:	Just a moment, please.
Secretary:	Marilyn Shelton's office.
Polly:	This is Polly Preston. I'd like to speak with Marilyn Shelton.
Secretary:	What is this concerning?
Polly:	Don Drummer of Polycorp suggested I speak with her.
	or
	I have some advertising concepts I would like to discuss with her.
	or
	I have some personal matters to discuss with her.
	or
	I have some business matters to discuss with her.
Secretary:	Just a moment, I'll ring her office.

Avoid Return Calls

If the person is out when you call (or so the secretary says), avoid leaving your phone number. Say that you will be in and out yourself and ask for the best time to call back. It is much better for you to initiate contact. If the employer returns your call, you may be caught unprepared. If you have been calling several people, you may not even recognize the person's name at first. This can be very embarrassing. Furthermore, by leaving your name and number you lose control of the situation. Once you leave your name and number, you are basically obligated to give the person two or three days to return your call. If the person never calls, you've lost three days. When you finally do get through, more days will have passed since the person read your marketing letter. The dialogue below illustrates how to handle this situation.

Secretary:	Janet Spurrier's office.
John:	This is John Bradley. I'd like to speak with Janet Spurrier.
Secretary:	I'm sorry, she's in a meeting now. Can I have her return your call?
John:	No, I'll be out most of the day. What do you think would be a good time to reach her?
Secretary:	That's hard to say, but probably about 3:30.
John:	Thank you.

What Do You Say After Hello?

After your future boss answers, you have 20–30 seconds to sell yourself. A prepared script can give you added confidence and just the right words to make a great first impression. Since it is so easy to say "no," make it easy for the employer to say "yes" when you ask for a brief appointment.

To sell yourself, you must quickly summarize your background and present evidence that you are a highly desirable person. Upon concluding your pitch, ask for an appointment. Ask to "get together" or have a "brief meeting," but never call it an interview. You are *not* seeking a traditional job interview.

Practice by first making a few of these calls to low-priority firms. Your voice should convey self-confidence and enthusiasm. Your words should convey potential. Naturally, if you are reading from a script, you won't want the employer to sense this. Practice until you speak in a normal conversational tone. After a few calls you should keep the script by you for reference, but you should begin varying your words slightly each time to provide a sense of spontaneity. You might even record your first few calls to check your enthusiasm level. Record your portion of the call on a portable recorder. Be sure to project enough enthusiasm so that it is conveyed to the person at the other end of the line.

In the first sample script below, a recent college grad is making a cold call. It takes only about ten seconds to complete the call. Notice that the introduction is brief but sufficient for the purpose.

Mr. Crenshaw, this is Brian Dawlar. I just graduated from the University of Washington with a degree in business, emphasizing marketing. I realize you may not have any openings at this time, but I would appreciate setting up a time when we could meet for 10 or 15 minutes.

In the next example, Sandra is reminding Mrs. Garner that a marketing letter was sent. Sandra is hoping Mrs. Garner remembers, but even if she does not, Sandra will still provide only a brief summary of her background and then ask for an appointment. If the person has not received the letter, there is no need to tell the person that you will send another copy of the letter—once you have the person on the line, go for the appointment.

The example below demonstrates how a marketing letter works. It is followed by the script from Sandra's phone call.

Roberta Garner
District Sales Manager
Salvo Corp.
1878 116th N.E.
Bellevue, Washington 98004

Dear Ms. Garner:

I have a strong sales personality. During six years as an educator teaching French and history, I have sold programs and ideas to school administrators, teachers, parents, and community leaders. Selling comes naturally to me. Because of this ability, and a desire to achieve a high income, I am now looking at sales opportunities.

I am a high-energy person with real initiative. I make things happen. I am quick to take on responsibility and I succeed at whatever I put my heart into. The people I know in sales all say I will be successful. I believe them.

I will call you next week to set up a time when we might meet briefly.

Sincerely,

Sandra Bennett

Having read the marketing letter you can see why Sandra is confident as she calls Garner and seeks a brief appointment.

Mrs. Garner? Hi, this is Sandra Bennett. I wanted to confirm that you received the letter I sent a few days ago describing my teaching background in French and history...Good...I've been teaching for the last six years, but all my sales friends tell me I'd be a natural in sales. I realize you may not have any openings at this time, but I would appreciate arranging, oh, a 10- or 15-minute get-together. I'd like to tell you a little more about me and at the same time learn about some of the directions Salvo is headed. Would early next week work for you?

Read Sandra's spiel again and notice what she did. As she introduced herself she mentioned her letter which had described her background in teaching French and history. We all know that teaching French and history are not prerequisites for a career in sales. Nevertheless, she mentioned her teaching because it would act as a "cue" for Garner. Providing a cue is an important part of making the marketing letter and the phone call result in an appointment.

Your marketing letters that are sent to local people should go out on a Friday. You can be quite certain that a letter you mail on a Friday will arrive on Monday.

To allow for a delay in the postal system, or in case the person was out of the office on Monday, you should begin calling people Tuesday afternoon. If you send out 10–20 marketing letters each week, that means Tuesday and Wednesday will be your heavy telephone days. By waiting until Tuesday to call, you can be quite sure that the person will have received it, but not so much time will have elapsed that the person is likely to have forgotten it. If you send your marketing letter any other day of the week, you will not be so certain about its arrival time. Also, by beginning your calls on Tuesday, you have the rest of the week to call the people that you were not able to reach on Tuesday and Wednesday. Even those you reach on Friday should not have forgotten you.

There are some cases in which a marketing letter may not be necessary. In the example below, Jim Thomas decided not to use a marketing letter. He has a strong background in sales and is accustomed to setting up sales appointments over the phone. By dispensing with the marketing letter he saves time and money, and he'll end up with just as high a success rate as he would if he sent a marketing letter. Anyone who feels confident in their phone skills should give consideration to skipping the marketing letter and simply making direct contact with the hiring authority.

> Hi Mr. Bradley, this is Jim Thomas. I've been selling radio advertising for the last six years and I'm seriously considering changing stations. I've been in the top 15% in sales for the last three years. I'm not in a rush to leave, but I would like to set a time when we could get together for 15 minutes or so.

Each of the scripts presented here as examples can be said in 10-20 seconds. When you've just reached a stranger on the phone, and the most the person has said is "Hello" or "This is Crenshaw," twenty seconds is quite a long time.

Below is an example of a more complete script where the applicant is going to ask for a 15-minute appointment. The employer will respond by saying he doesn't have any openings. That will be the most common response, even though you will have just said something like, "I realize you may have no openings at this time, but I would like to meet briefly with you for perhaps 15 minutes." Either employers don't hear that statement, or they choose to ignore it. Those who ignore it do so, I believe, because they know that by stating that there are no openings, 90% of all job seekers will lose interest in coming in. By asking for a meeting you'll demonstrate that you're not like all the rest.

The key to the success of this technique is that you are making such a reasonable request. Initially, you ask for 15 minutes. If that does not succeed, you make a second request, but drop the time down to ten minutes. When asking a third time you would ask either for just five minutes or for two minutes just to introduce yourself. Notice how skillfully this is done in the following example.

Jay: This is John Jay.

Sur: Mr. Jay, this is Bob Sur. I was calling to confirm that you received my letter which describes my 15 years in purchasing, including purchasing all the steel, glass, and concrete for the Columbia Center in Seattle.

Give the listener a cue so he can recall you from among the 10–30 letters received in the last few days. In this case, the Columbia Center project mentioned in the marketing letter served as the cue.

Jay: Yes, I believe I saw that yesterday.

Sur: I'm glad you had a chance to review it. I do have a strong purchasing background. For Maynard and Wyatt Construction I implemented a very effective just-in-time program. I realize you may not have any openings at this moment, but I did want to set up a time when we might meet for 15 minutes or so. I'd like to tell you a little more about my background, and at the same time learn more about some of the directions you're moving in. Would early next week work for you?

Make it easy for the person to say yes.

Tell the person exactly what you want him to do for you.

Ask for a time in the next few days but do not try the worn out sales technique by saying something like, "Would Wednesday at four or Thursday at one work for you?" Let the employer select a time.

Jay: Bob, I'm sure you have a very good background, but I simply don't have any opening at this time and don't anticipate any for at least six months.

Sur: I can certainly understand that. I really didn't expect that you'd have any openings. What I did want to do is to just set up a time, even ten minutes, when we might meet briefly. Would late next week work for you?

Show that you are not like other people. As soon as most people discover there are no openings, they are no longer interested in an appointment.

If necessary, make it even easier to meet: reduce the requested time from 15 minutes to 10.

Jay: Bob, I just don't have any openings. I'm in the middle of developing my budget and it just wouldn't be worth my time or your time.

Sur: While I have you on the line Mr. Jay, perhaps I could just take a couple minutes to tell you more about my background.

(Gives a two minute summary)

As you can see Mr. Jay, I do have a strong purchasing background. And I really do understand your situation. It's always helpful to me, however, when I can meet a person face-to-face. It enables them to remember me better in case something would unexpectedly develop. Or you may hear of something elsewhere and be able to refer me. Could I stop by next week to introduce myself. I promise I wouldn't take up more than two minutes of your time.

Be tactful but be persistent. Asking for just an additional two minutes of time on the phone allows the person to relax; he or she realizes that the conversation is coming to a close.

Provide a two minute summary which sells you. This summary must be concise and have impact, so work on it carefully.

This is such a reasonable request. Everyone understands the value of face-to-face contact. And you're only asking for a couple minutes.

Jay: Well, I suppose we could do that. Stop over at my office at 11:55 on Friday.

Ideally the person with the power to hire will immediately arrange a time. This happens surprisingly often. You must also be prepared, however, for any objections the person might raise. The example below illustrates my point. Objections are often raised, so you must be prepared.

Employer: We won't be hiring for at least six months.

(How does she know? An employee may quit tomorrow.)

You: I can understand that. Actually I'm not in a hurry to leave my present job. It would certainly be beneficial to me if we could meet for just ten minutes.

Employer: I'm really tied up for the next three weeks.

You: That's fine. Would the Monday following that week work for you?

Employer: Probably you should go through personnel and fill out an application.

You: I'd be glad to at the appropriate time. But really my goal is just to meet you and introduce myself.

Employer: Right now we're laying off people in your field.

You: I can appreciate your concern. I know the economy is rough right now. I think that makes it even more important that we get together. My company went through a similar situation a year ago. My money-saving ideas helped turn the company around.

Employer: I really don't think you have the right experience.

You: It is a bit unusual, but really, the problems I've dealt with are not much different than the ones you are undoubtedly facing. My new procedures at Silco created a 7% increase in productivity.

It's unlikely you will face all of these objections from one person, but be prepared for them. Make it easy for the person to say "yes." Asking for only ten minutes is a very reasonable request. Most people can spare at least that much time. And because you have much to offer, the interview will prove mutually beneficial. At the very least, such a meeting can give the employer a pleasant and relaxing ten minutes.

Below is an outline of the procedure you should follow when making your phone calls.

1. Speak to the person with power to hire and ask for a 15-minute meeting. Indicate that you realize there may be no openings.

2. If the person responds by saying there are no openings and therefore doesn't want to meet with you, explain again that you understand there are no openings, but that you want only ten minutes to talk about the field and your background.

3. If the person counters by saying there is a freeze on hiring, or gives some other reason why he thinks a visit would be a waste of time for both of you, say something like this: "I can sure appreciate the tough economic climate in this area. Since I have you on the phone, let me just take a minute to tell you a little more about myself." Then give a one- to two-minute summary of your strengths and experience.

4. When you finish your summary, ask once more for an appointment. Ask for a five-minute appointment, or just two minutes for an introduction. You might approach it in one of the following ways:

Mr. Belquez, I can certainly understand your situation. I'm working at this time, and what I'd really like to do is meet you and tell you a little more about myself so when openings do develop you'll be able to keep me in mind. I promise I won't take more than five minutes of your time.

Ms. Baum, that gives you just a sketch of my experience and abilities. It's certainly not uncommon these days for a company to have a hiring freeze, and I can understand your reluctance to take time out of your busy schedule. But it would be very helpful to me if we could meet for just five minutes.

❖

Mr. Baker, as you can see, I have a strong background in purchasing. It would really help me if I could merely introduce myself to you. It wouldn't take more than two minutes.

At that point you will have asked three times for an appointment. Don't give up with just two tries; many people relent on the third request. The first two requests were based on your merit. You're a very capable person and you requested an appointment because most people in management continually have their eyes open for new talent. Make the third request on the basis of a favor. When you appeal to their desire to help others, many people will consent. You should also reduce your request for time by asking for two to five minutes.

5. If you still don't get an appointment, you may yet get some valuable information if you hold the person on the phone another two to three minutes. Remember, you worked hard to get this hiring person on the phone, so don't give up too easily. Consider these: "Mr. Bledsoe, when you *do* have a position open, what can I do to make sure I'll be considered?" "Mr. Bledsoe, when you have openings in your marketing department, what do you look for in candidates?" "Mr. Bledsoe, I've briefly described my background. Is it the type of background you'd be looking for?" "If someone quit, would they be replaced?" As you are getting responses to your questions, jot notes down on the back of your 4 x 6 card. Asking whether a replacement would be hired if someone quit is particularly important. If a replacement would not be hired, that organization should go to the bottom of your priority list.

6. In addition, you could ask about the size of the department, particularly the number of people who do your type of work. Ask about turnover. If no one has left in the last four years, that certainly tells you something. You may want to assign that company a lower priority because of the unlikelihood of an opening. Or you may give it a higher priority because low turnover often indicates employee satisfaction. You're the best judge of priority.

7. By this time you've probably convinced the person that you are a highly desirable employee. The person may know of something happening in other companies. Do not ask the person if she knows of any openings. Instead, try this: "Mrs. Kelsoe, I think you have a pretty good feel for my background. What other companies do you think I should be contacting?" The reason for not asking about specific openings is that referrals are more important to you than knowledge of specific openings. And besides, the phrasing of the question will surely cause her to tell you about any openings she knows of. If the person says "Nothing comes to mind right now," she may need some help to jog her memory. Your response might be, "Basically, I'm looking for a progressive firm like yours in the electronics industry. I realize you may not know of specific openings, but your advice on good companies would sure be helpful." If she names some companies, ask for the name of a person to contact in each. Then ask, "Do you mind if I say you suggested I call?" Nearly always you will be given permission. You would simply say, "Beverly Kelsoe at Utalco suggested I call you. During the

last five years, I've been purchasing microcircuits. I realize you may not have any openings, but I would like to set up a time when I could meet with you for about 15 minutes."

8. Thank the person for his or her time. If no appointment was made, indicate that you'll be sending your resume, and that you'll be staying in touch. If the person asks you to simply talk to his or her secretary, respond with a thank you. This employer is implying that the secretary will know in advance if any positions become available. Send a brief thank-you note with your resume to confirm your appreciation.

Your goal is still to get in and see as many hiring authorities as possible. A personal meeting always creates a much stronger and more lasting impression than just talking by phone. But think of it this way: if *you've* been unable to make an appointment, virtually *no one else* is going to, either. When you got the person on the phone, you made the most of it and sold yourself. The employer was impressed. Once the person receives your thank-you note, resume, and a follow-up phone call, you'll undoubtedly be one of the first to be informed when a position becomes available.

Your primary goal in using this strategy is to locate job openings in the hidden job market. While personal meetings with employers increase your chances of finding such positions, your telephone conversation, resume, thank-you note and follow-up are the next best things.

Let's look at an additional benefit of this telephone strategy. During a period of high unemployment, you may get appointments only 25–40% of the time, compared to the 40–80% rate most experience during better economic times. When you don't get an appointment, chances are great that it will be because there really are no openings, and when vacancies occur, they are not filled. So an appointment really would have been a waste of your time. While the employer is saving only ten minutes, you'll be saving the two to three hours it would take to research the organization, drive there, meet the person, and return home. When you get a turndown, be thankful that you just saved yourself three hours, and then go ahead and call the next person on your list.

In your phone calls, use humor whenever possible. My clients report that making the employer laugh has significantly increased their ability to get valuable information, even when they do not get in to see the person.

Produce 40 Times The Impact

Meeting a hiring authority in person has many times the impact of merely sending a resume. A resume, no matter how good it is, is just a piece of paper. You will virtually always be more impressive in person than on paper.

Your goal is to meet hiring authorities in person, even if it is for only ten minutes. Lasting impressions are made from person-to-person contact, not from resumes or even telephone conversations. The person meeting you will associate your name with a face, a voice, a personality.

In each meeting, create a lasting, positive impression so that when a job opening occurs, you'll be the first person considered. Suppose five weeks ago you spent 15 minutes with Mrs. Johnson, a key hiring authority in one of your most desired companies. No opening existed at the time, but you had a pleasant conversation. You learned more about her organization and you shared some of your accomplishments. Mrs. Johnson told you she was impressed with your background, and even mentioned three companies she felt you should look at. Two days later Mrs. Johnson received a nice thank-you note, and she once again remembered you and recalled your potential. She also felt good about herself because she knew she had been helpful. Three weeks later you called her and had a one-minute conversation asking if there had been any job developments. Not surprisingly, there had been none.

Two weeks after your call, however, someone informed Mrs. Johnson that he was leaving the company for a better position. What could Mrs. Johnson do? She could have informed personnel immediately and asked them to place an ad. She could also delve into her file cabinet and review the hundred or so resumes she has accumulated over the last six months. Instead, she thought of you. She picked up the telephone and called you for an interview.

Consider for a moment why the strategy of meeting hiring authorities works so well. During the first twelve weeks after mailing your marketing letter, you will have eight high-quality contacts. The average job seeker has one low-quality contact—a mediocre resume. These eight high-quality contacts produce at least 40 times the impact of mailing a typical resume. The eight contacts include: 1) mailing a marketing letter; 2) following up with a phone call and obtaining an appointment; 3) meeting the person face-to-face; 4) leaving a copy of your resume; 5) sending a thank-you note that evening; 6) following up with a one-minute call three weeks later; 7) a second short call five weeks later; and 8) mailing an interesting article five weeks after that. From that point on, a call would be made or an article sent about every five weeks.

Going through the strategy step by step will show you how this combined approach has at least 40 times the impact of a resume.

An excellent first impression is created when the person reads your marketing letter. The marketing letter is a nice touch because it is different from what employers are used to receiving. While your background may not be so powerful that the employer calls you on the phone immediately, a favorable impression has been created, nonetheless. The person will notice that you've indicated that you will call in a few days. While not necessarily excited about taking your call, particularly if there are no suitable openings, the person will probably speak with you. You may have to call several times because such people are often in meetings, out of the office, or out of town. But when you speak to the person you are going to come across as very confident and capable. Most people will agree to meet with you.

When you meet the person, you will have prepared a monologue. You'll use it if the first thing the person says is, "How can I help you?" Frequently the person will not even remember why you are there. The person may only know that your name is on his schedule for a fifteen-minute appointment. The "How can I help you?" question, or any one of its derivatives, are cordial ways of getting down to business right away. By having a five- to seven-minute summary of your background and strengths prepared, you'll be ready to sell yourself. When you leave the meeting, this person should be thinking, "If I had an opening, this is the type of person who could really help us."

As you leave, you will give the person your resume unless the person had already asked for it. Some people prefer not to bring a resume with them. Instead they tailor the resume to the situation after they get home. If you really do intend to tailor each resume, then this is a good strategy.

That evening you would compose a personal thank-you note. Although many notes are no more than four lines, they can be considerably longer if you want to supply additional information about your background or strengths. The person who met with you will receive the thank-you note a day or two later and think favorably of you once more.

Three weeks later you will call and reintroduce yourself so that the person will remember the conversation, if not your name. Then you will ask if there have been any developments (which there probably have not) and then state once more your interest in the organization. There is no need to feel that you are impinging on this person's time because you will take only a minute. Then five weeks later you will make yet another one-minute call. While you are only taking up one minute of the employer's time, it has probably taken you at least ten minutes to prepare and make several calls before getting through. That's okay, though. You are making an impression.

For your next follow-up, I recommend finding an article that your hiring authorities would enjoy reading but are fairly unlikely to have already seen. You would simply write, "Thought you might be interested," and then sign your name. Once again this person will think of you and realize that you are really serious about working there.

When you add up the impact of those eight contacts, I believe it has to be at least 40 times the impact of a resume alone. Let's face it, most resumes are not well written, and they have little impact. Rarely does a person read a resume and say, "We've got to have that person." When an employer speaks to a potential employee, however, and the person is self-confident and enthusiastic, and follows-up by contacting the employer again and again—that has impact.

Tips For Appointments

Your preparation for appointments will be key. Developing a five- to seven-minute summary of yourself is especially important. Some appointments consist of genuine conversation, but if the employer has no openings and wants to keep the meeting short, he or she is likely to say, "How can I help you?" When you get such a questions, respond with something like, "Mrs. Klevinger, I really do appreciate your taking time to meet with me. And I understand that you don't have any openings at this time. Perhaps the best thing I can do is simply share my background and describe some of my strengths. Basically I . . ." Then you'll give your summary.

Seven minutes may seem like a long time to talk nonstop, but it really isn't. It gives you just enough time to summarize your work history and education and then have a couple minutes left to share some strengths. Of course, while you are describing your work history you should briefly mention some of your accomplishments. This will give the employer an excellent overview of your background. It will also allow the employer to ask some questions if he or she is so inclined.

Often the employers you meet with will have no questions for you. Assuming a fifteen-minute appointment, half of your time will be gone when you've completed your monologue. If the person does not ask you to clarify or expand on anything, you should ask some questions. For instance, you might ask questions like: "Do you see any expansion in the next six months?" "Do you think there will be any openings in the next few months?" "When you have openings, what skills, qualities, and experience are you looking for?"

After the person has finished answering your questions, your time will be almost up. You should indicate the appointment is drawing to a close by saying, "Mr. Klucewski, I don't want to take up any more of your time. Maybe I should just summarize what I think my strengths are." You would then share some of your key strengths. This would all be part of a two-minute summary you should have practiced numerous times. In addition to recapping your prepared summary, you would also cover some of the points the employer mentioned just minutes earlier in response to your question about desired qualities and skills. Some of the words you use might be identical to the ones the employer used, some you would paraphrase. All the while, however, you'd be showing that you possess those skills and qualities. After sharing your points, you would then thank the person for the meeting, stand up, and say goodbye. Whenever possible, you should be the one to terminate the conversation to show that you are a person of your word: you asked for fifteen minutes and you got your fifteen minutes, so it's time for you to leave.

Unless the employer is truly keeping the conversation going, you should terminate it at the set time. This is a crucial point. Sometimes conversations go on for an hour, and I'm sure that, in most cases, the employer gladly gives the additional time. I also know that sometimes a person walks out the door and the employer is saying, "She asked for fifteen minutes and she stayed almost 45 minutes. Now I'm really behind in my work." No matter how impressive the person was, no matter how well she sold herself, and no matter how good some of her stories were, this person will be remembered primarily as the one who did not keep her word.

The way to avoid this potential problem is to be aware of time. If you sense time is drawing to a close, you should very deliberately look at your watch. Do it in an obvious way. By doing so you are demonstrating that you are concerned about taking too much of this person's time.

If you really are hoping for some additional time, and it appears that the employer is enjoying the conversation, and perhaps even keeping it alive, you might say, "Mr. Barratt, I appreciate the time you've given me. I did ask for just fifteen minutes. Do you have an upcoming appointment?" If he wants to terminate the conversation you have provided a perfect out, with the person probably saying, "Well, I do need to get back to my project in about five minutes." Or, the person may say, "No, that's fine, I've got another fifteen minutes."

If the person is clearly directing and continuing the conversation, then you may continue past the allotted time. After the appointed time has passed, however, be very alert for signals that the meeting has gone on long enough. If you notice the person looking at a clock or watch, looking away as if bored, or fidgeting, quickly draw your comments to a close and thank the person for the time.

If the person begins asking you specific questions about your experience, the appointment has probably turned from an appointment into an interview. A person who has no openings and knows there will be no openings in the next few months will rarely ask those types of questions. One of the few exceptions would be if the person were considering referring you to someone who has or may have an opening. In any case, being asked questions is a very positive sign.

The reasons why an employer would ask you questions include: 1) The person has no openings but will remember you and probably offer you an interview if something opens up; 2) the person will refer you to someone else if he learns of an opening; 3) the person is thinking of creating a position in a few months and may move that date up if a really capable person comes along; 4) the person thinks someone is about to quit; 5) the person is considering firing someone, but may do so only if the replacement is ready to be hired; 6) the person is always looking for people who can make money or solve problems for him.

During your appointment, do your best to get the employer involved in a true conversation. The more involved the person is, the more likely the person will want to talk beyond the requested ten or fifteen minutes.

FOLLOW-UP

Following up begins the same day as the appointment. Between appointments or when you get home, write a brief, typed or handwritten thank-you note. The five minutes it takes to write a thank-you note could be the most valuable time you spend. It will cause an important person to think favorably of you once more. A successful job search includes doing all the little things right.

The note can be anywhere from three sentences to two pages in length. The note might read like this:

Dear Mr. Mathews,

I really appreciated the time you gave me yesterday. After talking to you, I'm even more sure that personnel is the right field for me. I'll keep you informed of my progress.

Sincerely,

John Stevens

❖

Dear Mrs. Kelser:

Thank you so much for seeing me yesterday. Our conversation confirmed what others have told me--that Dalco is an exciting company to work for. Of course, when I first called you, I did not expect you to have any openings. Since our conversation, however, I am convinced that I could be a real asset in the accounting department. Through my auditing and computer programming background I think I could really contribute to Dalco.

I will stay in touch to check on any developments.

Sincerely,

Ron Sakulski

❖

Dear Mrs. Madison:

I really enjoyed today's interview and I appreciate the fact that I was invited from among so many candidates. I just wanted to say again that I am quite excited about the prospect of working for Sentry, and especially within your department.

Sincerely,

Roberta Marsh

The first note was in response to an informational interview, the second an appointment in which no opening existed, and the third, a formal job interview. Any of these letters could have been longer, but that is usually unnecessary. Write a longer note only if you have a definite purpose in doing so. For instance, you may want to write a proposal describing a problem you discovered during the interview, along with your proposed solution. Or, if you did not have an opportunity to make an important point during an interview, a letter provides you with an excellent opportunity to cover it, even if it extends the letter's length to more than a page. If an objection was raised during the interview, and you missed it, didn't handle it adequately, or simply want to attack it from another angle, you can do so in a letter. Unlike shorter thank-you notes which may be handwritten, proposals or lengthy letters should be typed.

Everyone you interview with should get a thank-you note, so whenever you have multiple interviews or a panel interview, ask for people's business cards or write their names down when you meet them. For multiple interviews where you will meet three or more people in separate interviews, ask the person who is coordinating the interviews to supply you with the names and titles of the people you'll be meeting.

Most of your appointments will be with employers who do not have current openings. Your process of following up with them can last weeks or even months. Three weeks after your first appointment, call to ask if there have been any developments. Don't worry about bothering the person; you'll only talk for a minute. When you get the person on the phone, introduce yourself, indicate when you met, and briefly describe what you talked about. Do not assume the employer will remember you. He or she may have met 40 people in the last three weeks and will probably need a reminder.

Odds are there is still no opening. In closing, emphasize your interest in the company, and perhaps bring the person up to date on your efforts, particularly if you have contacted any of the people you were referred to. If you had not received referrals before, this would be a good time to ask for the names of organizations that this person thinks you should contact. If you think the person may have a position fairly soon, however, avoid asking for referrals. By not asking for referrals in this type of situation, you will be indicating that the organization is one of your top choices.

A follow-up call might go like this:

Bob: Hi, Mr. Benson, this is Bob Phillips. We met about three weeks ago when I came in to talk about microprocessors and the directions Microdata is taking. I just wanted to find out if there have been any new developments in your marketing department.

Benson: Bob, I remember you and I still have your resume, but there haven't been any openings.

Bob: I really appreciated your taking time to see me. The more I hear about Microdata, the more excited I get. I did call Mr. Jensen at Datasoft. He was very helpful. I'll probably talk to you again in four or five weeks. Thanks again.

When making your follow-up calls, you will frequently talk to a secretary if the person with power to hire is out or unavailable. You will generally be asked to leave a message and your number so the call can be returned. Instead, ask when a good time to call would be. After three or four unsuccessful calls, you might explain that you saw the person three weeks earlier and that you just need to talk to him or her for a minute to ask a couple questions. If the secretary has been brushing you off, that may help. *Always stay on good terms with the secretary.* On the second or third call, ask the secretary's name. You may talk to the secretary six or seven times, so you'll want to maintain your composure and sense of humor. Try to get to know this person. Make him or her want to help you.

After your first follow-up call, call every four to five weeks. Try to create and maintain enough interest so that if any openings occur, you'll be notified. Even if they don't call you, you're never more than five weeks away from discovering the opening through one of your calls. In the hidden job market, jobs frequently stay open for six to ten weeks.

If the person asks you to speak to the secretary in the future, that's okay as long as the secretary will know of openings as they occur. One advantage to you is that the secretary will be readily available. Seek to get to know this person and exchange pleasantries each time you call.

Another method of follow-up is to send a note accompanying an article the person may find interesting. This would usually occur after you have made two follow-up calls.

You should also follow up with your contacts. Every six weeks you'll need to call them to let them know about your experiences and your progress. If they referred you to someone, tell them what happened. Make them an integral part of your search and make them feel valued. This kind of follow-up will counter a psychological fact—with every passing week their ears become duller. In the beginning, you'll be notified if they hear of a job that remotely resembles the one you want. But by seven weeks, your contacts may assume you've found another job. By nine weeks they may hear about your perfect job but fail to even think of you.

OPTIONAL STRATEGIES

In addition to the main strategy I've described of meeting hiring authorities face-to-face, there are other options which deserve consideration. When using these next two options you will still eventually contact the people with the power to hire. The advantage of these two strategies is speed. In a few days, you can contact 100–200 organizations to learn if they have any immediate openings in your field. If they do, you may get some interviews that you might otherwise have missed.

Try A Large Mailing

Because I believe it is more effective for you to meet as many hiring authorities as possible face-to-face, I rarely recommend that people rely on the mass mailing of resumes. There is, however, a place for large mailings. On the chance that there may be an immediate opening with one of their 150 target organizations, some people send out resumes or marketing letters to their prospects during the first week of their job search. The attitude these people have is that they do not want to miss any immediate opportunities as they begin the long-term process of sending out 10–25 marketing letters each week.

A marketing letter, or a resume with a cover letter, have impact in and of themselves only if they arrive two weeks before or after a job has officially opened up. If your material arrives sooner, it usually ends up in a file cabinet somewhere. If it arrives later, it receives no consideration because the candidates for interviews have probably already been selected.

So, with all of this in mind, give consideration to a large mailing. This strategy still requires that you develop your list of 75–200 employers, and that you determine who the person is with the power to hire you.

Either a marketing letter or a resume with a cover letter can be quite effective. Be sure to invite the employer to call you if an opening exists.

Once you have the names of the hiring authorities, decide how the letters will be produced. If you have your own computer and "mail merge" software with your word processing software, you may want to key in the names and addresses yourself. Mail merge software enables you to merely type in the names and addresses of your prospects all at one time, then the software joins, or merges, those names and addresses with your letter. It can save hours of typing.

If you don't have your own computer with mail merge software, you should take your letter and your names and addresses to a secretarial service. It will cost you under two dollars per letter for them to type the letter and the accompanying envelope. All you will need to do is sign each letter and mail your material.

Once your materials go out, you would begin concentrating on sending marketing letters to your top-twenty group of employers. You would continue sending out about 20 each week. If you get some invitations for interviews based on your resume or marketing letter, great. If not, you'll soon be getting appointments as a result of following up on your marketing letters.

Call Your Prospects

Calling your prospects is another strategy that has the advantage of speed. This strategy works most effectively when the companies you're interested in are large and have personnel departments. Once you have your list of prospects, call their personnel departments and simply ask if they are currently looking for people with your background. If the personnel manager is unavailable, a personnel clerk will usually know what positions are open. When speaking to someone in personnel, briefly describe your background, and suggest one or more job titles that might be suitable for you. Using this strategy you will learn only of those openings that have been made known to personnel. With whatever information you have garnered, thank the person and move on to the next one.

This strategy has several advantages over just sending a resume. Two negative things can happen when you mail a resume—a rejection or no response at all. In either case, you still don't know what the real situation is. A quick call, on the other hand, can give you a great deal of information. Whether you get a clerk or the personnel manager, ask questions. If you learn that there are no suitable openings, you could confirm that the company does in fact have the types of positions you're interested in. You can also discover whether the organization is growing, and if so, whether there are any plans to expand in your specialty.

At a rate of eight calls per hour, you can get through your entire prospect list in three to five days. With this strategy, do not expect lots of interviews. Think of it instead as a way to gain some additional information about the firm. It is another way to ensure that you are not missing out on any opportunities as you begin the longer process of meeting hiring authorities.

AN IMPORTANT JOB FINDING OPTION

I typically recommend that job seekers develop a list of at least 70 potential employers and seek face-to-face meetings with the hiring authorities. There are exceptions, however. In some types of positions, particularly office and clerical jobs, you are actually better off calling the personnel department of larger companies or the office manager of smaller companies. The reason for this is that clerical people work in almost any department of an organization, so there may be many people who hire clerical staff. If you use this strategy you could still identify 10–20 organizations that you are especially interested in and meet the personnel manager or office manager. Simply walking in and meeting someone in personnel can also be effective.

When using the calling strategy, you would begin by introducing yourself, briefly explaining your background, and asking if any openings currently exist. You should be able to average 12 calls an hour. If you have 120 organizations on your list and call once a week to learn of openings, your total time expended is only ten hours weekly. The strategy should yield two to three interviews each week. Although 120 may seem like a lot of organizations, when using this strategy you need large numbers. Even 150 is not too many. If you are looking for office positions and you live in an urban area, there will probably be over 150 potential organizations within 15 minutes of your home.

If personnel informs you that no openings are currently available, carry on a conversation similar to this:

Personnel: Personnel, may I help you?

Carol: This is Carol Prescott, I have a diploma from Harrington Business College and two years of clerical experience. Do you have any clerical positions available at this time?

Personnel: No we don't.

Carol: Do you anticipate adding any office staff in the next month or two?

Personnel: It's highly doubtful that we'll be adding any positions in the next four months.

Carol: If someone quit, would the person be replaced?

Personnel: I'm sure they would.

Carol: Approximately how many clerical positions do you have?

Personnel: Counting bookkeepers, probably around 30.

Carol: What kind of turnover do you have?

Personnel: It's nothing unusual, I'm sure it's about average.

Carol: Thanks a lot for your help, who am I speaking to?

Personnel: I'm Betty.

Carol: Betty, you've been really helpful. I plan to call once a week and if it's all right, I'll probably just ask for you. Is there anything else I can do to learn of any openings?

In less than two minutes, Carol learned so much more than if she had hung up after hearing that no openings existed. She also has a person to talk to in personnel. In a short time, Betty may actually recognize Carol's voice, and because Carol is friendly and courteous, Betty may actually go out of her way to help her. Of course, don't feel you can only talk to one person. If your regular person is unavailable, ask questions of whomever happens to be on the line. Also, notice what Carol did at the end of her call. Although she stated her intention to call periodically, she specifically asked if there was anything else she could do to ensure that she would learn about all potential openings. Although she plans to call weekly, she is prepared to do anything else that will help her.

This strategy is fast and gets excellent results—but don't use it as a shortcut if you are one of those who should be talking with the person with the power to hire.

MAKING THE SYSTEMATIC JOB SEARCH WORK

The people who succeed with the Systematic Job Search strategies become detectives. Successful detectives never get discouraged. They follow up on each lead until the case is solved. Dozens of leads may dead end, but eventually one pays off. Remember, it only takes one good job offer, and you'll never be able to predict where the lead will come from.

The number-one cause of failure in job hunting is inaction, and the number-one cause of inaction is fear of rejection. Many people are not technically inactive; in fact they may be very busy. But they're inefficient, spinning their wheels, and making no headway. Such ineffective tactics can lead to a vicious cycle. It usually starts like this: when people lose their jobs, they start looking at the want ads. They throw their slightly revised resume around with very little success, but finally an invitation for an interview is offered. Since most people "wing it" in interviews with no research, practice, or forethought, the first few interviews go very poorly, leading to a string of rejections. Eventually, many people reach what Richard Bolles calls "Desperation Gulch," that feeling of hopelessness and depression that can lead to giving up.

By all means, avoid the vicious cycle. You will do that by: 1) following the strategy as it has been described; 2) keeping busy and using good time management; and 3) enjoying several low-stress appointments each week.

A New Definition Of Success

I have one more thought to offer you. I'd like to give you a new definition of success. For most job seekers the only success is getting the right job offer. That's *all* wrong. You can experience success each day and should reward yourself for it by feeling good about yourself. I believe success is having one or more pleasant experiences every day. Success is talking to someone who opens up to you and tells you everything about a field you're interested in. Success is completing your employer list. Success is getting in to see an employer and having an interesting conversation. Success is getting a good lead from a friend. Success is being a finalist among 50 applicants.

If you have at least one success each day, that ultimate success—a job—will come about as a matter of course. Start your day as if you had a full-time job. If you're used to getting up at 6:30 a.m., continue that habit. Put in a solid six-hour work day. You're different from the rest of your competition. While they're complaining about their rotten luck, you're doing your employer research. While they're sitting next to the telephone waiting for interviews to be arranged for them, you're on the telephone setting up your own appointments. While they're watching soap operas and game shows, you're meeting hiring authorities and getting job leads. While they're hoping for a lucky break, you're creating your own breaks.

Relaxing is one of the most difficult things for an unemployed job seeker to do. Turning your job search into a full-time job is the best medicine. If you're busy with research and appointments, you won't have time for negative thoughts. If you spend six full hours each day on your job search, you've done your job for the day. When you were employed, you didn't try to finish big projects in a single day. You knew you would get part of it done each day. In a job search you can't do it all in one day. That's what tomorrow is for. Monday through Friday stay busy between 8:30 a.m. and 4:30 p.m., then call it a day. You've done all you can do. Relax. Enjoy your family. Read a book. Go for a long walk.

REAL EXPERIENCES

The following examples demonstrate some of the many ways people find out about their new jobs. These weren't just lucky breaks, the people created these situations. These examples demonstrate how the hidden job market works.

> I had spoken to someone in each of my top-ten companies, but there were no openings. I then developed a new list and was starting to talk to key people. One of the firms had no openings but suggested that I talk to someone in a very young but growing firm that I had never heard of. Sure enough, this firm was expanding and I got there at just the right time. The training I'm getting is excellent, and the income potential is excellent, too.

❖

> I was just calling people to get information. I spoke to one person who thought his company was looking for a person with my background. The next day I went in for an interview and got the job.

❖

> After I clarified what I really wanted to do, I contacted a former co-worker who had moved into the field I was interested in. We talked by phone and later had several meetings. He needed someone to assist him and he knew I had the ability and the background. We're now working together.

❖

> A former supervisor went to work for a new company, and when an opening occurred he recommended me to his boss. I was hired after several interviews.

Job Hunting On The Internet

THE INTERNET CAN BE A GREAT RESOURCE for a job search, but it must be used systematically or you can spend hours and have little to show for it. Initially, just allow time to surf the web to identify your most useful sites. When you find a good site mark it as a "favorite" or "bookmark." Once you've done that you can return to the site by simply clicking on it.

The Net is most useful for discovering posted job openings, submitting resumes to resume databanks, and for obtaining information about organizations of interest.

Information about organizations can be obtained in two primary ways. By using the various search engines you can type in the name of an organization you have an interest in. When your "hits" come on screen you simply click on those articles that have titles indicating they may be useful. You can also utilize the websites described in Excellent Resources on page 282.

To use the Net effectively you need the attitude of an explorer. Once you arrive at one of the key sites simply follow links to other sites that look interesting. If you don't find what you expected, you simply use the back button to return to where you just came from. You cannot get lost on the Internet.

The best way to get started is to select one of the recommended sites. Visit the site and click on any item or subject that interests you. Figure you'll spend eight to twelve hours on the Internet before you feel you've identified the sites that you want to return to on a consistent basis, particularly to search for open positions. While twelve hours might sound like a lot, most people enjoy their time on the Internet and time goes by quickly.

Plan to enjoy yourself. If you find an interesting article, read it on the screen or print it out so you can read it later. Once you click to print you can go on to another page at your current site or even move on to another website.

If you're going to post your resume, simply start with one site and then go to another. Once you've created your plain-text electronic resume, it is a quick and straight forward process.

Before starting your Internet search, keep in mind that most jobs never get advertised anywhere, not in your local newspaper, not on a website. You must be aware that the hidden job market is alive and well even in cyberspace. Use the Internet as a tool, get everything out of it you can, and determine to carry out the most effective job search possible.

The Key Internet Trio

The following three websites are great because they provide excellent advice on how to use the Internet for a job search and give great links to other valuable sites.

The Job Hunter's Bible (www.jobhuntersbible.com). This site is produced by Richard Bolles, author of *What Color Is Your Parachute?* I like the site because he not only provides links to some of the best sites on the web, but he provides a description of what you'll find and what makes each one useful. In his unique way, he also provides his view on how to best use the Internet. You can also access many of Bolles' articles on various aspects of job finding. Start with this site.

The Riley Guide (www.rileyguide.com/jobguide). This is Bolles' top pick for a must visit site. Margaret Riley Dikel has been showing job seekers for years how to use the Internet for job hunting. She also has great links to key sites with explanations of their value. There are also great links to highly useful articles on job finding.

Career Resource Center (www.careers.org). Another key pick by Bolles. CRC has the most links to job, career, and educational sites of any resource on the Net.

The Big Eight

These are the key sites that are devoted entirely to job hunting. Visit these and explore them.

America's Job Bank	www.ajb.dni.us/
Career Builder.com	www.careerbuilder.com
Monster Board	www.monster.com
JobBank USA	www.jobbankusa.com
NationJob Network	www.nationjob.com
Flip Dog	www.flipdog.com
Wet Feet	www.wetfeet.com
Career Journal	www.careerjournal.com

Search Engines

Google	www.google.com
MSN	www.msn.com
Alta Vista	www.altavista.com
Lycos	www.lycos.com
Excite	www.excite.com
Snap	www.snap.com

To research a company or industry, start with any of the search engines. If you choose Yahoo you would type in www.yahoo.com and you would find yourself at the Yahoo site. Click on Business and Economy then type in aerospace (in the search box if you wanted it to search the Internet to find articles on aerospace). If you wanted to find information on a specific company, you might type in Paccar in the search box to find articles on the truck manufacturer. When the findings come on screen, click on any that seem that they will provide you with what you want. You will be taken immediately to that article.

In addition to their career and job finding content and resources, they are search engines. By typing in the name of a company, or an industry, or a subject, the search engines will find it for you. Each search engine uses different methodologies for coming up with "hits" or titles of articles that would be of interest to you. Because of that, you may want to try more than one search engine for a particular search. Often they will try to prioritize for you so that the first articles are the ones the search engine has determined are most related to your request.

Web Sites Where You Can Post Your Resume

There are dozens of sites where you can post your resume. The following are merely the biggest. Follow each site's instruction as to how to post your resume. If privacy is a concern of yours, look for their link to their privacy policy and read it. All of the search engines (except Google) and all of the Big Eight mentioned above also offer resume posting.

The MonsterBoard	www.monster.com
NationJob Network	www.nationjob.com
JobTrak	www.jobtrak.com
CareerSite	www.careersite.com
PassportAccess	www.passportaccess.com
Net-Temps	www.net-temps.com
Career.Com	www.career.com
E.span	www.espan.com
HotJobs	www.hotjobs.com
US Resume	www.usresume.com
America's Employers	www.americasemployers.com
America's Talent Bank	http://atb.mesc.state.mi.us
Headhunter.net	www.HeadHunter.net
Career City	www.careercity.com
Career Mart	www.careermart.com
Job Bank USA	www.jobbankusa.com
The Online Career Center	www.occ.com
The Internet Job Locator	www.joblocator.com/jobs/
BrassRing	www.brassring.com
Flip Dog	www.flipdog.com

Salary Information

Most sites provide salary information. Yahoo is one of the best. Go to Yahoo and click on Business & Economy, then click on Jobs. Then click on Salary Information to find appropriate sites for your type of salary search.

Employer Web Sites

Flip Dog (www.flipdog.com) has a somewhat unique way of gather job openings—it goes directly to company web sites and pulls them all together, enabling you to find them by location (state, city, or metro area) and by occupational field. When you find an interesting job you can learn more about it and then go directly to the company web site.

Excellent Resources

Electric Library (www.elibrary.com) provides full articles from many different magazines and wire services. It is great for information on companies and industries as well as other topics. You will frequently access press releases which give you a good sense of the hottest things the company is doing. You can subscribe for 30 days for free, afterward it is $9.95 per month. It is well worth the subscription rate. When you want information about an organization, this is one of the best resources.

Business Journal (www.bizjournals.com). I'm most familiar with the *Puget Sound Business Journal*, but there are approximately 30 from around the US. Find the one you want and then search for companies or industry information. Excellent search engine to quickly find articles about your target organizations.

American Journalism Review NewsLink (www.newslink.org.news.html). This site takes you to thousands of newspapers and magazines where you can review help wanted ads and articles about companies and industries.

Books To Help You Navigate The Internet

Books on Internet job finding offer little value if they are more than two years old. The older books will list sites that no longer exist and will miss sites that are less than two years old. The following books all provide excellent information and tips.

Guide to Internet Job Searching 2002–2003, Margaret Riley Dikel, Frances Roehm, McGraw-Hill/Contemporary Book, 2002. Richard Bolles feels it is the best Internet book on the market.

Job Hunting on the Internet, Richard Bolles, Ten Speed Press, 2002. This is the book form of his website at www.jobhuntersbible.com. A very clear description of what the Internet can and cannot do for you.

Job Searching Online For Dummies, Pam Dixon, IDG Books, 2000. This book is really complete and is a great book despite its age. It's clear that Pam spends a lot of time online, checking out these sites. She provides excellent advice and excellent reviews of websites.

Cyberspace Job Search Kit 2001–2002: The Complete Guide to Online Job Seeking and Career Information, Mary Nemnich, Fred Jandt, Jist Works, 2001. Very complete and thorough.

Weddle's 2002 Job seekers's Guide To Employhment Web Sites, Peter Weddle, 2002. Weddle has been studying the web for years and has produced this very thorough and well-written guide.

Part Six
Appendix

Bibliography

Career Planning

The Three Boxes of Life, Richard Bolles, Ten Speed Press, 1981

Finding A Job You Can Love, Ralph Mattson and Arthur F. Miller, P&R Publishing, 1999

Job Finding

Career Satisfaction And Success: A Guide To Job And Personal Freedom, Bernard Haldane, JIST Works, 1996.

The Complete Job Search Handbook, Howard Figler, Henry Holt & Co., 1999

How To Get a Better Job In This Crazy World, Robert Half, NAL/Dutton, 1994

Interviewing

Interview Power: Selling Yourself Face To Face, Tom Washington, Mount Vernon Press, 2000

Negotiating Your Salary: How To Make $1000 a Minute, Jack Chapman, Ten Speed Press, 2001

Sweaty Palms: The Neglected Art Of Being Interviewed, Anthony Medley, Ten Speed Press, 1992

Internet Job Search

See page 282 for a complete list of high quality and current books on using the Internet for job hunting.

Index

About The Author

Career Management Resources — (425) 454-6982

Tom Washington holds a master's degree in counseling from Northeastern Illinois University and is the founder of Career Management Resources (1979), a career exploration and outplacement counseling firm in Bellevue, Washington. He has personally written over 800 resumes and edited hundreds more, with most clients receiving 10-15 times more interviews than the national average.

He has shared his resume writing and job finding strategies on radio and television talk shows across the country. Mr. Washington is also the author of *Interview Power: Selling Yourself Face To Face* (2000).

Mr. Washington speaks to college audiences, career and job finding professionals, associations, job fairs, schools, and professional groups. He covers a wide range of topics and always instills a motivation to conduct an effective job search. If you would like him to speak to your group, call him at (425) 454-6982.

Career Management Resources provides outplacement assistance to people throughout the Puget Sound Region who are terminated or laid off. Organizations desiring to provide job finding assistance to their employees can reach Mr. Washington at CMR.

Career Management Resources
1750 112th NE C-224
Bellevue, WA 98004

tomw@cmr-mvp.com
www.cmr-mvp.com

What Satisfied Users Are Saying About *Resume Power*

Congratulations on your outstanding book, *Resume Power: Selling Yourself On Paper*. Among the many resume books I have seen, yours is the most practical one I have encountered.
    P.R. Chico, California

Resume Power has been easy to read, easy to follow, and filled with practical and workable information which can benefit readers of all ages who work in many wide-ranging occupational industries.
    T.R. Arlington Heights, Illinois

This spring I will be teaching a course in career planning. *Resume Power: Selling yourself On Paper* is an excellent resource for practical resume information.
    N.G. Fargo, North Dakota

I found your book *Resume Power* both enjoyable and extremely informative. It is, by far, the best book that I have read on the subject of resumes and job search. I will recommend your book to everyone.
    N.B. Auburn, Indiana

Resume Power is a must for job seekers . . . I have recommended your book to my friends, relatives, students, and business contacts.
    R.S. Auckland, New Zealand

Thank you for your wonderful book, *Resume Power*. From it I have gained valuable insights into job searching and resume construction.
    A.W., Employment Coordinator Anchorage, Alaska

Your book *Resume Power* is the best thing that has ever happened to me. Wow! Thanks a million for writing it. It has given me so much more confidence!
    R.A. Rough and Ready, California

I wanted to write and thank you for coming out with the book *Resume Power*. I responded to ads in the *Chicago Tribune* if I had at least 50% of the credentials requested. I received the most interviews of any similar period in my working life, approximately 12 interviews. There is no question the format of the resume was critical. I learned from each interview and built on the experience. After accepting my last offer, I feel almost as giddy as my first major success in a serious job search.
    D.W. Chicago, Illinois

I operate a small typing service from my home. More and more my business is specializing in resume writing. Your book, *Resume Power*, has become my bible. From it I have learned many techniques that have improved my resume writing, thereby bringing me more referrals and increasing my business.
    K.L St. Clair, Michigan

Since I and several of my direct reports will be searching for new jobs, due to the relocation of our present operation, we need effective resumes. I reviewed over twenty books on writing resumes and purchased four. After reading all four it was very clear to me that *Resume Power* was by far the best.

A.H. Atlanta, Georgia

Please count me as one of your satisfied customers. I have thoroughly read your book and I have made all of the corrections you suggested. After years of applying for jobs with a poorly written resume, miracles started to happen when I used your methods.

V.R. Friendswood, Texas

In November we ordered three copies of *Resume Power*. We have found this book to be very valuable and useful to the department and would like to order eight additional copies.

S.J., Duke University Durham, North Carolina

I purchased *Resume Power* to help me get my thoughts together on resumes. I will be conducting workshops for those who ask assistance in their job search and intend to have them use your book as a guide in writing. The format of your book is easy to follow and moves along.

M.K., Personnel Director Milwaukee, Wisconsin

I have just finished using your book to revise my five year old resume. I was delighted with my results. *Resume Power* is a treasure of practical gems. Hints and ideas flow freely to inspire and encourage.

C.P. Miami, Florida

I just want to let you know how fantastically successful your book was to me in my search for employment. A total of fifteen resumes were sent out in a two week period and I got four interviews. I accepted a position where I can better my career. Thank you for the tremendous insights into "handling" a very uncertain time in my life.

J.Y. Fullerton, California

Thank you for writing such an excellent book. *Resume Power* is the best book I have read on resumes and I have read at least six others from the library.

S.J. Kent, Washington

RESOURCES BY TOM WASHINGTON

Interview Power: Selling Yourself Face To Face

Interview Power is a complete and comprehensive interviewing guide. Filled with hundreds of practical ideas, strategies, and tips, *Interview Power* enables you to obtain more job offers and negotiate higher salaries. It provides you with the most up-to-date interviewing techniques—enabling you to have real impact on today's tough interviewers. (2000, 274 pg.)

Interview Power...

Opens up the secret to effective interviewing—the art of selling your strengths by describing past accomplishments.

Provides the principles for answering 101 tough questions.

Shows you how to overcome objections and get the offer.

Prepares you for behavior-based interviewing—the fastest growing type of interview.

Reveals techniques that enable you to truly sell yourself.

Demonstrates how to deal with illegal questions.

Shows you how to quickly build rapport with your interviewer.

Gives you ways to prove you have the "right stuff."

Ensures that nothing will take you by surprise.

Interview Power (The Video)

Written by Tom Washington (1995), this video takes key concepts from *Interview Power: Selling Yourself Face To Face* and uses video to *show* the viewer how to interview effectively. *Interview Power* demonstrates how to impact the interviewer with stories and anecdotes. You have the opportunity to see and hear how to best perform in an interview. This 70-minute video will enable you to get job offers that previously might have gone to your competitors. Purchase *Interview Power* and get a 30-day, money-back guarantee. This video continues to have the same impact as when first released.

What others are saying about Interview Power:

This video will give viewers the skills, practice and confidence to interview well and get the job they want. Information is presented using dramatizations and graphics, interlaced with cogent on-screen comments by employment officers from Microsoft, Boeing, and US West. The pace moves along at a rapid rate with summary graphics at the end of each topic.

Video Librarian, *November-December 1995 issue*

Interview Power is a state-of-the-art presentation and guide for today's job seeker. This video is packed with useful information. The wealth of teaching examples are guaranteed to improve the presentation of even the most confident and prepared interviewee.

Larry Gaffin, President, Center For Life Decisions

Anyone using these techniques will increase their self-confidence and effectiveness in selling themselves at an interview. The systematic approach given in this video provides the best method I've seen for fully preparing for successful interviewing.

John Knapp, Human Resources Consultant

Every question you're likely to get about "Why should we hire you?" is covered with practical examples. It sets you up for no-surprise interviews.

Jack Chapman, author of Negotiating Your Salary: How To Make $1000 a Minute

The Psych Yourself Up Audio Tape

The Psych Yourself Up Audio Tape is designed to be listened to just prior to leaving for an interview, or on your way to an interview while driving or riding a bus. It reminds you of all the positive things you will do in your interview and does so in a motivating and calming way. It can give you just the edge you need to fully sell yourself. Author/Reader: Tom Washington.

Interview Power: Selling Yourself Face To Face @ $14.95   _____

Interview Power (VHS video, 70 minutes) @ $29.95   _____

The Psych Yourself Up Audio Tape @ $9.95   _____

Resume Power: Selling Yourself On Paper @ $14.95   _____

    Shipping and handling add $3.95 for first item,
        $1.50 for each additional item   _____

    Subtract $3.00 if you buy 3 or more items   _____

    Washington residents add 8.8% sales tax   _____

    Grand total (U.S. dollars only)   _____

Payment   ❏ Check or Money Order   ❏ Visa   ❏ MasterCard

Account #_____ Expiration Date _____

Signature _____

Name (print) _____

Street Address _____

City _____ State _____ Zip _____

Phone (_____) _____

Mail your order to:

Career Management Resources
1750 112th N.E. #C-224
Bellevue, WA 98004

All products have a 30-day money-back guarantee. Items will be shipped within 48 hours of receipt of your order.
